A New Star-Rating System
& Other Exciting News
from Frommer's!

In our continuing effort to publish the savviest, most up-to-date, and most appealing travel guides available, we've added some great new features.

Frommer's guides now include a new **star-rating system.** Every hotel, restaurant, and attraction is rated from 0 to 3 stars to help you set priorities and organize your time.

We've also added **seven brand-new features** that point you to the great deals, in-the-know advice, and unique experiences that separate travelers from tourists. Throughout the guide look for:

Finds	Special finds—those places only insiders know about
Fun Fact	Fun facts—details that make travelers more informed and their trips more fun
Kids	Best bets for kids—advice for the whole family
Moments	Special moments—those experiences that memories are made of
Overrated	Places or experiences not worth your time or money
Tips	Insider tips—some great ways to save time and money
Value	Great values—where to get the best deals

Frommer's®

PORTABLE

Puerto Vallarta, Manzanillo & Guadalajara

3rd Edition

by David Baird & Lynne Bairstow

Hungry Minds™

Best-Selling Books • Digital Downloads • e-Books •
Answer Networks • e-Newsletters • Branded Web Sites • e-Learning
New York, NY • Cleveland, OH • Indianapolis, IN

ABOUT THE AUTHORS

David Baird (chapters 6 and 7) is a writer, editor, and translator based in Austin, Texas. He spent part of his childhood in Morelia, Mexico, and later lived for 2 years among the Mazatec Indians in Oaxaca while he was doing graduate fieldwork.

Lynne Bairstow (chapters 1, 2, 3, 4, and 5) is a writer specializing in travel and the Internet who has lived in Puerto Vallarta, Mexico, at least part time for the past 10 years. She now lives there year-round and was assisted in her research for this book by Claudia Velo. In a previous professional life, Lynne was a vice president for Merrill Lynch in Chicago and New York.

David and Lynne are also the authors of *Frommer's Mexico* and *Frommer's Cancún, Cozumel & the Yucatán*.

Published by:

HUNGRY MINDS, INC.   JAN 2 1 2002
909 Third Avenue
New York, NY 10022

ISBN: 0-7645-6436-6
ISSN: 1093-6998

3 9082 08595 0437

Editor: Kelly Regan
Production Editor: M. Faunette Johnston
Photo Editor: Richard Fox
Cartographer: Roberta Stockwell
Production by Hungry Minds Indianapolis Production Services

SPECIAL SALES

For general information on Hungry Minds' products and services please contact our Customer Care department; within the U.S. at 800-762-2974, outside the U.S. at 317-572-3993 or fax 317-572-4002. For sales inquiries and reseller information, including discounts, bulk sales, customized editions, and premium sales, please contact our Customer Care department at 800-434-3422.

Manufactured in the United States of America

5   4   3   2   1

Contents

List of Maps

AN INVITATION TO THE READER

In researching this book, we discovered many wonderful places—hotels, restaurants, shops, and more. We're sure you'll find others. Please tell us about them, so we can share the information with your fellow travelers in upcoming editions. If you were disappointed with a recommendation, we'd love to know that, too. Please write to:

Frommer's Portable Puerto Vallarta, Manzanillo & Guadalajara
Hungry Minds, Inc. • 909 Third Avenue • New York, NY 10022

AN ADDITIONAL NOTE

Please be advised that travel information is subject to change at any time—and this is especially true of prices. We therefore suggest that you write or call ahead for confirmation when making your travel plans. The authors, editors, and publisher cannot be held responsible for the experiences of readers while traveling. Your safety is important to us, however, so we encourage you to stay alert and be aware of your surroundings. Keep a close eye on cameras, purses, and wallets, all favorite targets of thieves and pickpockets.

WHAT THE SYMBOLS MEAN

The following abbreviations are used for credit cards:

| AE | American Express | DISC | Discover | V | Visa |
| DC | Diners Club | MC | MasterCard | | |

FROMMERS.COM

Now that you have the guidebook to a great trip, visit our website at www.frommers.com for travel information on nearly 2,000 destinations. With features updated regularly, we give you instant access to the most current trip-planning information available. At Frommers.com, you'll also find the best prices on air fares, accommodations, and car rentals—and you can even book travel online through our travel booking partners. At Frommers.com you'll also find the following:

* Daily Newsletter highlighting the best travel deals
* Hot Spot of the Month/Vacation Sweepstakes & Travel Photo Contest
* More than 200 Travel Message Boards
* Outspoken Newsletters and Feature Articles on travel bargains, vacation ideas, tips & resources, and more!

Here's what critics say about Frommer's:

"Amazingly easy to use. Very portable, very complete."

—*Booklist*

"The only mainstream guide to list specific prices. The Walter Cronkite of guidebooks—with all that implies."

—*Travel & Leisure*

"Complete, concise, and filled with useful information."

—*New York Daily News*

"Hotel information is close to encyclopedic."

—*Des Moines Sunday Register*

"Detailed, accurate, and easy-to-read information for all price ranges."

—*Glamour Magazine*

Planning Your Trip to Mid-Pacific Mexico

Along the Pacific coast of Mexico, palm-studded jungles sweep down to meet the deep blue of the Pacific Ocean, providing spectacular backdrops for three modern resort cities and smaller coastal villages. This lovely stretch of coastline extending from Puerto Vallarta down to Manzanillo is known as the Mexican Riviera. Modern hotels, easy air access, and a growing array of activities and adventure tourism attractions have transformed this region of Mexico into one of the country's premier resort areas.

A little advance planning can make the difference between a good trip and a great trip. When should you go? What's the best way to get there? How much should you plan on spending? What festivals or special events will be taking place during your visit? What safety or health precautions are advised? We'll answer these and other questions for you in this chapter.

In addition to these basics, I highly recommend taking a little time to learn a little about the culture and traditions of Mexico. It can make the difference between simply "getting away" and truly adding understanding to the experience.

1 The Region in Brief

Puerto Vallarta, with its traditional Mexican architecture and gold-sand beaches bordered by jungle-covered mountains, is currently the second most visited resort in Mexico (trailing only Cancún). Vallarta maintains a small-town charm despite sophisticated hotels, great restaurants, a thriving arts community, an active nightlife, and a growing variety of ecotourism attractions. **Mazatlán** may be the greatest resort value in Mexico, luring visitors with its exceptional fishing, historic downtown, and new championship golf facilities. **Manzanillo** is surprisingly relaxed; even though it's one of Mexico's most active commercial ports, it also offers great fishing and golf. And along the **Costa Alegre,** between Puerto Vallarta and

Manzanillo, pristine coves are home to unique luxury and value-priced resorts that cater to travelers seeking seclusion and privacy. Just north of Puerto Vallarta is **Punta Mita,** home of the first Four Seasons resort in Latin America and a Jack Nicklaus golf course. With four more luxury resorts and two more golf courses on tap, it is emerging as Mexico's most exclusive luxury address.

If you're looking for a more "authentic" Mexican experience, head inland over the mountains to **Guadalajara,** Mexico's second-largest city and the birthplace of many of the country's traditions.

International airports at all three cities make getting to each easier; Guadalajara and Puerto Vallarta have the most frequent connections. Distances in the region are easily managed by car; most drives between major points take from 45 minutes to 6 hours on roads that are generally good.

If you decide to visit this region, you have several choices about how to allot your time. Most people pick one coastal resort and stay there for the duration of their vacations, but you can easily enjoy more than one resort during your time in Mexico.

Barra de Navidad, for example, is so close to Manzanillo that it's easy to combine several days there with a stay in Manzanillo. From Puerto Vallarta, Bucerías, Yelapa, San Sebastian, and San Blas all offer a change of pace and scenery. Hotelito Desconocido and Las Alamandas are both closer to Puerto Vallarta, with the remainder of the luxury coastal resorts between Manzanillo and Puerto Vallarta nearer to Manzanillo. There are more frequent flights, however, to and from Puerto Vallarta, and many people find Puerto Vallarta provides the best access to the coastal area.

2 Visitor Information, Entry Requirements & Money

SOURCES OF INFORMATION   The **Mexico Hot Line** (© 800/44-MEXICO) is an excellent source for general information, requesting brochures on the country, and for answers to the most commonly asked questions. More information (15,000 pages worth, they say) about Mexico is available on the Mexico Ministry of Tourism's website: http://mexico-travel.com.

The **U.S. State Department** (© 202/647-5225 for travel information and Overseas Citizens Services) offers a Consular Information Sheet on Mexico, with a compilation of safety, medical, driving, and general travel information gleaned from reports by official U.S. State Department offices in Mexico. You can also request

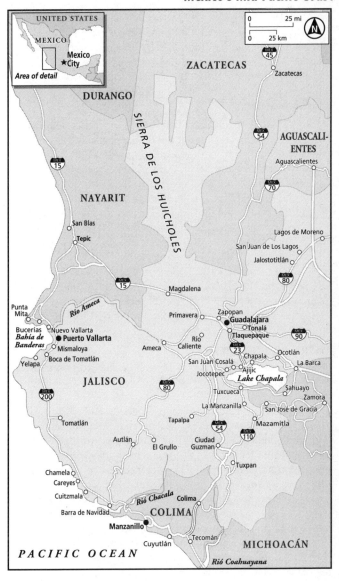

the Consular Information Sheet by fax (© 202/647-3000). The State Department is also on the Internet; check out http://travel. state.gov/mexico.html for the Consular Information Sheet on Mexico; http://travel.state.gov/travel_warnings.html for other Consular Information sheets and travel warnings; and http:// travel.state.gov/tipsmexico.html for the State Department's Tips for Travelers to Mexico.

MEXICO TOURISM BOARD OFFICES   The Mexico Tourism Board has several offices in major North American cities, in addition to their main office in Mexico City (© **5/203-1103**).

United States: Chicago, IL (© **312/606-9252**); Houston, TX (© **713/772-2581,** ext. 105); Los Angeles, CA (© **213/351-2069;** fax 213/351-2074); Miami, FL (© **305/718-4095**); New York, NY (© **212/821-0304**); and the Mexican Embassy Tourism Delegate, 1911 Pennsylvania Ave., Washington, D.C. 20005 (© **202/ 728-1750**).

Canada: 1 Place Ville-Marie, Suite 1931, Montréal, QUEB, H3B 2C3 (© **514/871-1052**); 2 Bloor St. W., Suite 1502, Toronto, ON, M4W 3E2 (© **416/925-0704**); 999 W. Hastings, Suite 1110, Vancouver, BC, V6C 2W2 (© **604/669-2845**). Embassy office: 1500-45 O'Connor St., Ottawa, ON, K1P 1A4 (© **613/233-8988;** fax 613/235-9123).

ENTRY REQUIREMENTS

DOCUMENTS   All travelers to Mexico are required to present **proof of citizenship,** such as an original birth certificate with a raised seal, a valid passport, or naturalization papers. Those using a birth certificate should also have current photo identification such as a driver's license or official ID. Those whose last name on the birth certificate is different from their current name (women using a married name, for example) should also bring a photo identification card *and* legal proof of the name change, such as the *original* marriage license or certificate. This proof of citizenship may also be requested when you want to reenter either the U.S. or Mexico. Note that photocopies are *not* acceptable. When reentering the U.S., you must prove both your citizenship and your identification, so always take a picture ID, such as a driver's license or, better yet, a valid passport. Birth certificates alone will enable you to enter Mexico but will not enable you to reenter the U.S.

Note: Although the U.S. State Department endorses these entry requirements outlined, some readers have reported problems trying to enter Mexico using only a birth certificate. To ensure against any needless delay at immigration, make sure you follow the requirements to the letter—the birth certificate must be the *original* version with the raised seal. Or, avoid any potential problem by carrying your U.S. passport.

You must also carry a **Mexican Tourist Permit (FMT),** which is issued free of charge by Mexican border officials after proof of citizenship is accepted. (These forms are also provided by the airlines.) The FMT is more important than a passport in Mexico, so guard it carefully. If you lose it, you may not be permitted to leave the country until you can replace it—a bureaucratic hassle that can take anywhere from a few hours to a week. (If you do lose your tourist permit, get a police report from local authorities indicating that your documents were stolen; having one *might* lessen the hassle of exiting the country without all your identification.) You should also contact the nearest consular office to report the stolen papers so that they can issue a reentry document.

A tourist permit can be issued for up to 180 days, although your stay south of the border may be shorter than that. Sometimes officials don't ask—they just stamp a time limit, so be sure to say "6 months" (or at least twice as long as you intend to stay). If you decide to extend your stay, you may request that additional time be added to your FMT from an official immigration office in Mexico.

Note that children under age 18 traveling without parents or with only one parent must have a notarized letter from the absent parent or parents authorizing the travel.

LOST DOCUMENTS To replace a lost passport, contact your embassy or nearest consular agent (see "Fast Facts: Mexico," later in this chapter). You must establish a record of your citizenship and also fill out a form requesting another Mexican Tourist Permit (assuming it, too, was lost). Without the tourist permit you can't leave the country, and without an affidavit affirming your passport request and citizenship, you may have problems at Customs when you get home. So it's important to clear everything up before trying to leave. Mexican Customs may, however, accept the police report of the loss of the tourist permit and allow you to leave.

CUSTOMS ALLOWANCES When you enter Mexico, Customs officials will be tolerant as long as you have no illegal drugs or firearms. You're allowed to bring in two cartons of cigarettes, or 50 cigars, plus a kilogram (2.2 lb.) of smoking tobacco; the liquor allowance is two 1-liter bottles of anything, wine or hard liquor; you are also allowed 12 rolls of film. A laptop computer, camera equipment, and sporting equipment (golf clubs, scuba gear, a bicycle) that could feasibly be used during your stay are also allowed. The underlying guideline is that they will disallow anything that they feel you will be attempting to resell in Mexico.

When you reenter the United States, federal law allows you to bring in up to $400 in purchases duty-free every 30 days. The first $1,000 over the $400 allowance is taxed at 10%. You may bring in a carton (200) of cigarettes or 100 cigars or 2 kilograms (4.4 lb.) of smoking tobacco, plus 1 liter of wine, beer, or spirits.

Canadian citizens are allowed $50 in purchases after a 24-hour absence from the country, $300 after a stay of 48 hours or $750 after a stay of 7 days or more. In addition, Canadian citizens may bring 200 cigarettes or 50 cigars plus 1 kilogram (2.2 lbs.) of chewing tobacco, plus 1.5 liters of hard liquor or wine.

British travelers returning from outside the European Union are allowed to bring in £145 worth of goods, in addition to the following: up to 200 cigarettes, 50 cigars or 250 grams of tobacco; 2 liters of wine; 1 liter of liquor greater than 22% alcohol by volume, and 60cc/milliliters of perfume. If any item worth more than the limit of £145 is brought in, payment must be made on the full value, not just on the amount above £145.

Citizens of New Zealand are allowed to return with a combined value of up to NZ$1,000 in goods, duty-free.

GOING THROUGH CUSTOMS   Mexican Customs inspection has been streamlined. At most points of entry, tourists are requested to press a button in front of what looks like a traffic signal, which alternates on touch between red and green signals. Green light and you go through without inspection; red light and your luggage or car may be inspected briefly or thoroughly. If you have an unusual amount of luggage or an oversized piece, you may be subject to inspection despite the traffic signal routine.

MONEY

CASH/CURRENCY   The currency in Mexico is the Mexican **peso.** Paper currency comes in denominations of 20, 50, 100, 200, and 500 pesos. Coins come in denominations of 1, 2, 5, 10, and 20 pesos and 50 centavos (100 centavos equal 1 peso). The current exchange rate for the U.S. dollar is around 9 pesos; at that rate, an item that costs 9 pesos would be equivalent to US$1.

Getting change continues to be a problem in Mexico. Small-denomination bills and coins are hard to come by, so start collecting

Tips A Few Words About Prices

The peso's value continues to fluctuate—at press time, it was roughly 9 pesos to the dollar. Prices in this book (which are always given in U.S. dollars) have been converted to U.S. dollars at 9 pesos to the dollar. Most hotels in Mexico—with the exception of places that receive little foreign tourism—quote prices in U.S. dollars. Thus, currency fluctuations are unlikely to affect the prices charged by most hotels.

Mexico has a **value-added tax** of 15% (*Impuesto al Valor Agregado*, or IVA, pronounced "ee-bah") on most everything, including restaurant meals, bus tickets, and souvenirs. Hotels charge the usual 15% IVA, plus a locally administered bed tax of 2% (in many but not all areas), for a total of 17%. IVA will not necessarily be included in the prices quoted by hotels and restaurants. You may find that upper-end properties (three stars and above) quote prices without IVA included, while lesser-price hotels include IVA in their quotes. Always ask to see a printed price sheet, and always ask if the tax is included.

them early in your trip and continue as you travel. Shopkeepers everywhere seem always to be out of change and small bills; that's doubly true in a market.

EXCHANGING MONEY   The rate of exchange fluctuates a tiny bit daily, so you probably are better off not exchanging too much of your currency at once. Don't forget, however, to have enough pesos to carry you over a weekend or Mexican holiday, when banks are closed. In general, avoid carrying the U.S. $100 bill. It is the most commonly counterfeited bill in Mexico, and therefore, the most difficult to exchange, especially in smaller towns. Since small bills and coins in pesos are hard to come by in Mexico, the U.S. $1 bill is very useful for tipping.

The bottom line on exchanging money of all kinds: It pays to ask first and shop around. Banks pay the top rates.

Exchange houses (*casas de cambio*) are generally more convenient than banks since they have more locations and longer hours; the rate of exchange may be the same as a bank or only slightly lower. *Note:* Before leaving a bank or exchange-house window, always count your change in front of the teller before the next client steps up.

Large airports have currency-exchange counters that often stay open whenever flights are arriving or departing. Though convenient, these generally do not offer the most favorable rates.

A hotel's exchange desk commonly pays less favorable rates than banks; however, when the currency is in a state of flux, higher-priced hotels are known to pay higher than bank rates, in their effort to attract dollars. The bottom line: It pays to shop around, but in almost all cases you receive a better exchange by changing money first, then paying for goods or services, rather than by paying with dollars directly to an establishment.

BANKS & ATMS   Banks in Mexico are rapidly expanding and improving services. New hours tend to be from 9am until 5 or 6pm, with many open for at least a half day on Saturday, and some even offering limited hours on Sunday. The exchange of dollars, which used to be limited until noon, can now be accommodated anytime during business hours in the larger resorts and cities. Some, but not all, banks charge a service fee of about 1% to exchange traveler's checks. However, most purchases can be paid for directly with traveler's checks at the stated exchange rate of the establishment. Don't even bother with personal checks drawn on a U.S. bank—although theoretically they may be cashed, it's not without weeks of delay, and the bank will wait for your check to clear before giving you your money.

Travelers to Mexico can also access money from automated teller machines (ATMs), now available in most major cities and resort areas in Mexico. Universal bank cards (such as the Cirrus and PLUS systems) can be used, and this is a convenient way to withdraw money from your bank and avoid carrying too much with you at any time. There is often a service fee charged by your bank for each transaction, but the exchange rate is generally more favorable than one found at a currency house. Most machines offer Spanish/English menus and dispense pesos, but some offer the option of withdrawing dollars. Be sure to check the daily withdrawal limit before you depart (generally about $900 US). For Cirrus locations abroad, call ✆ **800/424-7787** or check out MasterCard's website (www.mastercard.com/atm/). For PLUS usage abroad, call ✆ **800/843-7587** or visit Visa's website (www.visa.com/atms).

TRAVELER'S CHECKS   Traveler's checks are readily accepted nearly everywhere, but they can be difficult to cash on a weekend or holiday or in an out-of-the-way place. Their best value is their easy

Money Matters

Note: The universal currency sign ($) is used to indicate pesos in Mexico. The use of this symbol in this book, however, denotes U.S. currency. Many establishments dealing with tourists, especially in coastal resort areas, quote prices in dollars. To avoid confusion, they use the abbreviations "Dlls." for dollars and "M.N." (moneda nacional, or national currency) for pesos. All dollar equivalencies in this book were based on an exchange rate of 10 pesos per dollar.

replacement in case of theft. Frequently in Mexico, a bank or establishment will provide a better rate for traveler's checks than for cash dollars.

CREDIT CARDS   You'll be able to charge most hotel, restaurant, and store purchases, as well as almost all airline tickets, on your credit card. You can get cash advances of several hundred dollars on your card, but there may be a wait of 20 minutes to 2 hours. You generally can't charge gasoline purchases in Mexico; however, with the new franchise system of Pemex stations taking hold, this may change as well. Visa ("Bancomer" in Mexico), MasterCard ("Carnet" in Mexico), and American Express are the most accepted cards.

Credit-card charges will be billed in pesos, then later converted into dollars by the bank issuing the credit card. Generally you receive the favorable bank rate when paying by credit card.

THEFT   Almost every credit-card company has an emergency 800-number that you can call if your wallet or purse is stolen. They may be able to wire you a cash advance off your credit card immediately, and in many places, they can deliver an emergency credit card in a day or two. The issuing bank's 800-number is usually on the back of the credit card—though of course that doesn't help you much if the card was stolen. The toll-free information directory will provide the number if you dial © **800/555-1212.** From within Mexico, dial **001-880-555-1212**—this will not be a toll-free call, but it does provide you with access to this toll-free number. Citicorp Visa's U.S. emergency number is © **800/336-8472.** American Express cardholders and traveler's check holders should call © **800/221-7282** for all money emergencies. MasterCard holders should call © **800/307-7309.**

If you opt to carry traveler's checks, be sure to keep a record of their serial numbers, separately from the checks of course, so you're ensured a refund in just such an emergency.

Odds are that if your wallet is gone, the police won't be able to recover it for you. However, after you realize that it's gone and you cancel your credit cards, it is still worth informing them. Your credit-card company or insurer may require a police report number. If you do lose your wallet, before panicking, retrace your steps—you'll be surprised at how many honest people are in Mexico and it is likely that you'll find someone trying to find you to return your wallet.

CRIME, BRIBES & SCAMS
CRIME

Crime in Mexico received much attention in the North American press a few years ago, but either the reality has improved or the coverage has diminished. The most severe crime problems were concentrated in Mexico City, located far away from the Mexican Riviera; however, the city of Guadalajara has experienced an increase in street crime.

Precautions are necessary, but travelers should be realistic. When traveling anyplace in the world, common sense is essential. The crime rate is on the whole much lower in Mexico than in most parts of the United States, and the nature of crimes in general is less violent—most crime is motivated by robbery, or by jealousy. Random, violent crime or serial crime is essentially unheard of in Mexico. You are much more likely to meet kind and helpful Mexicans than you are to encounter those set on thievery and deceit. A good rule of thumb is that you can generally trust people whom you approach for help, assistance, or directions—but be wary of anyone who approaches you offering the same. The more insistent they are, the more cautious you should be.

BRIBES & SCAMS

As is the case around the world, there are the occasional bribes and scams, targeted at people believed to be naive in the ways of the place—for example, obvious tourists. For years Mexico was known as a place where bribes—called *propinas* (tips) or *mordidas* ("bites")—were expected; however, the country is rapidly changing. Offering a bribe today, especially to a police officer, is frequently considered an insult, and it can land you in deeper trouble.

If you believe a bribe is being requested, here are a few tips on dealing with the situation. Even if you speak Spanish, don't utter a word of it to Mexican officials. That way you'll appear innocent, all the while understanding every word.

When you are crossing the border, should the man who inspects your car ask for a tip, you can ignore this request—but understand that the official may suddenly decide that a complete search of your belongings is in order. If faced with a situation where you feel you're being asked for a propina, how much should you offer? Usually $3 to $5 or the equivalent in pesos will do the trick. To report irregularities with Customs officials, call © **01/800-0-014800** in Mexico. Your call will go to the office of the Comptroller and Administrative Development Secretariat (SECODAM); however, be forewarned that most personnel do not speak English. Be sure you have some basic information—such as the name of the person who requested a bribe or acted in a rude manner, as well as the place, time, and day of the event.

Whatever you do, avoid impoliteness; under no circumstances should you insult a Latin American official. Mexico is ruled by extreme politeness, even in the face of adversity. In Mexico, gringos have a reputation for being loud and demanding. By adopting the local custom of excessive courtesy, you'll have greater success in negotiations of any kind. Stand your ground, but do it politely.

As you travel in Mexico, you may encounter several types of scams, which are typical throughout the world. One involves some sort of a distraction or feigned commotion. While your attention is diverted, a pickpocket makes a grab for your wallet. In another common scam, an unaccompanied child pretends to be lost and frightened and takes your hand for safety. Meanwhile the child, or an accomplice, manages to plunder your pockets. A third involves confusing currency. A shoeshine boy, street musician, guide, or other individual might offer you a service for a price that seems reasonable—in pesos. When it comes time to pay, they tell you the price is in dollars, not pesos, and become very hostile if payment is not made. Be very clear on the price and currency when services are involved.

3 When to Go

SEASONS

Mexico has two principal travel seasons: high and low. High season begins around December 20 and continues to Easter, although in some places high season can begin as early as mid-November. Low season begins the day after Easter and continues to mid-December; during low season, prices may drop 20% to 50%. In beach destinations, the prices may also increase during the months of July and August, the traditional national summer vacation period. Prices in inland cities, such as Guadalajara, seldom fluctuate from high to low season, but may rise dramatically during Easter and Christmas weeks.

THE CLIMATE

From Puerto Vallarta south to Huatulco, Mexico offers one of the world's most perfect winter climates—dry, balmy, and with temperatures ranging from the 80s during the day to the 60s at night. From Puerto Vallarta south, you can swim year-round.

High mountains shield Pacific beaches from *nortes* (northers—freezing blasts out of Canada via the Texas Panhandle). The states of Jalisco and Colima, like most of Mexico, have the most rain May through September; the rainiest month is September. Tropical showers generally begin around 4 or 5pm and last a few hours. Though these rains can come on suddenly and be quite strong, they usually end just as fast and cool off the air for the evening.

For more on climate, see the "Fast Facts" sections in the destination chapters.

HOLIDAYS & SPECIAL EVENTS

On national holidays, banks, stores, and businesses are closed; hotels fill up quickly; and transportation is crowded. Also note that Mexican governmental offices—including immigration—are all closed.

January

New Year's Day (Año Nuevo). National holiday. Parades, religious observances, parties, and fireworks welcome in the New Year everywhere. In traditional indigenous communities, new tribal leaders are inaugurated with colorful ceremonies rooted in the pre-Hispanic past. January 1.

Three Kings Day. Commemorates the Three Kings' bringing of gifts to the Christ Child. On this day, children receive gifts, much like the traditional gift-giving that accompanies Christmas in the United States. Friends and families gather to share the *Rosca de Reyes,* a special cake. Inside the cake there is a small doll representing the Christ Child; whoever receives the doll in his or her piece must host a tamales-and-atole party the next month. January 6.

February

Candlemas. Music, dances, processions, food, and other festivities lead up to a blessing of seed and candles, a ritual that mixes pre-Hispanic and European traditions marking the end of winter. All those who attended the Three Kings Celebration reunite to share atole and tamales at a party hosted by the recipient of the doll found in the Rosca. February 2.

Carnaval. Carnaval takes place the 3 days preceding Ash Wednesday and the beginning of Lent. It is celebrated with special gusto in Mazatlán. Here, the celebration resembles New Orleans's Mardi Gras, with a festive atmosphere and parades. Transportation and hotels are packed, so it's best to make reservations 6 months in advance and arrive a couple of days ahead of the beginning of celebrations. In 2002, the dates are from February 10 to 12.

Ash Wednesday. The start of Lent and time of abstinence. It's a day of reverence nationwide, but some towns honor it with folk dancing and fairs. In 2002, the date is February 13.

March

Benito Juárez's Birthday. National holiday. March 21.

Holy Week. Celebrates the last week in the life of Christ, from Palm Sunday to Easter Sunday, with somber religious processions almost nightly, spoofings of Judas, and reenactments of specific biblical events, plus food and craft fairs. Businesses close during this week of Mexican national vacations.

If you plan on traveling to or around Mexico during Holy Week, make your reservations early. Airline seats on flights into and out of the country will be reserved months in advance. Buses to almost anywhere in Mexico will be full, so try arriving on the Wednesday or Thursday before Good Friday. Easter Sunday is quiet. In 2002, March 24 through 29 is Holy Week, Easter Sunday is March 31, and the week following is a traditional vacation period.

May

Labor Day. Workers' parades countrywide and everything closes. May 1.

Holy Cross Day (Día de la Santa Cruz). Workers place a cross on top of unfinished buildings and celebrate with food, bands, folk dancing, and fireworks around the work site. May 3.

Cinco de Mayo. A national holiday that celebrates the defeat of the French at the Battle of Puebla. May 5.

June

National Ceramics Fair and Fiesta, Tlaquepaque, Jalisco. This pottery center on the outskirts of Guadalajara offers craft demonstrations and competitions as well as mariachis, dancers, and colorful parades. June 14.

Día de San Pedro (St. Peter and St. Paul's Day). Celebrated wherever St. Peter is the patron saint, and honors anyone named Pedro or Peter. It's especially festive at San Pedro Tlaquepaque, near Guadalajara, with numerous mariachi bands, folk dancers, and parades with floats. In Mexcatitlan, Nayarit, shrimpers hold a regatta to celebrate the season opening. June 29.

September

Mariachi Festival, Guadalajara, Jalisco. Public mariachi concerts, including visiting mariachi groups from around the world (even Japan!). Workshops and lectures are given on the history, culture, and music of the mariachi in Mexico. Plans for an extension of this festival in Puerto Vallarta were being worked out— call ✆ **800-44-MEXICO** to confirm dates and schedule of performances. September 1 to 15.

Independence Day. Celebrates Mexico's independence from Spain. A day of parades, picnics, and family reunions throughout the country. At 11pm on September 15, the president of Mexico gives the famous independence grito (shout) from the National Palace in Mexico City, which is duplicated by every presidente municipal (mayor) in every town plaza in Mexico. Both Guadalajara and Puerto Vallarta have great parties in the town plaza on the nights of September 15 and 16.

October

Fiestas de Octubre (October Festivals), Guadalajara. This "most Mexican of cities" celebrates for a whole month with its mariachi music trademark. A bountiful display of popular culture and fine arts, and a spectacular spread of traditional foods, Mexican beers, and wines adds to the celebration. All month.

November

Day of the Dead. What's commonly called the Day of the Dead is actually 2 days, All Saints' Day-honoring saints and deceased children—and All Souls' Day, honoring deceased adults. Relatives gather at cemeteries countrywide, carrying candles and food, and often spend the night beside the graves of loved ones. Weeks before, bakers begin producing bread shaped like mummies or round loaves decorated with bread "bones." Decorated sugar skulls emblazoned with glittery names are sold everywhere. Many days ahead, homes and churches erect special altars laden with Day of the Dead bread, fruit, flowers, candles, and favorite foods and photographs of saints and of the deceased. On the

2 nights, children, dressed in costumes and masks, carry mock coffins and pumpkin lanterns through the streets, expecting people to drop money in them. November 1 to 2.

Fiesta del Mar, Puerto Vallarta. A month-long calendar of activities including art festivals, sports competitions, the Governor's Cup golf tournament, and an outstanding Gourmet Dining festival, with featured guest chefs from around the world working with local chefs in select restaurants. Among the sporting events are sailing regattas, windsurfing exhibitions, and beach volleyball competitions. November 10 to 30.

Revolution Day. Commemorates the start of the Mexican Revolution in 1910 with parades, speeches, rodeos, and patriotic events. November 20.

December

Feast of the Virgin of Guadalupe. Throughout the country the patroness of Mexico is honored with religious processions, street fairs, dancing, fireworks, and masses. It is one of Mexico's most moving and beautiful displays of traditional culture. The Virgin of Guadalupe appeared to a young man, Juan Diego, in December 1531, on a hill near Mexico City. He convinced the bishop that he had seen the apparition by revealing his cloak, upon which the Virgin was emblazoned. It's customary for children to dress up as Juan Diego, wearing mustaches and red bandannas. December 12.

In Puerto Vallarta, the celebration begins on December 1 and extends through December 12, with traditional processions to the church for a brief misa (mass) and blessing. In the final days, the processions and festivities take place around the clock, with many of the processions featuring floats, mariachis, Aztec dancers, and fireworks. The central plaza is filled with street vendors and a festive atmosphere, and a major fireworks exhibition takes place on December 12 at 11pm.

Christmas Posadas. On each of the 9 nights before Christmas, it's customary to reenact the Holy Family's search for an inn, with door-to-door candlelit processions in cities and villages nationwide. Most business and community organizations host them in place of the northern tradition of a Christmas party. December 15 to 24.

Christmas. Mexicans extend this celebration, often beginning 2 weeks before Christmas, all the way through New Year's. Many businesses close, and resorts and hotels fill up. December 24 and 25.

New Year's Eve. As in the rest of the world, New Year's Eve in Mexico is celebrated with parties, fireworks, and plenty of noise. December 31.

4 Active Vacations

The diverse geography of the area has made it a natural favorite of travelers looking for more active vacations, offering a wealth of eco- and adventure-tour options.

Excellent golf courses are located in Guadalajara, Puerto Vallarta, Punta Mita, and along the coastline down to Manzanillo. Tennis, water-skiing, surfing, biking, and horseback riding are all sports vis- itors can enjoy in this region. Scuba diving is excellent along the Pacific Coast at Puerto Vallarta and Manzanillo, where a wide array of sea life can be observed, including dolphins, sea turtles, and giant mantas.

ORGANIZATIONS & TOUR OPERATORS

There's an active association in Mexico of eco- and adventure-tour operators called **AMTAVE** (Asociación Mexicana de Turismo de Aventura y Ecoturismo, A.C.). They publish an annual catalog of participating firms and their offerings, all of which must meet cer- tain criteria for security, and for quality and training of the guides, as well as for sustainability of natural and cultural environments. For more information, contact them (in Cancún) at ✆/fax: **9/884-9580,** www.amtave.com.mx).

Bike Mex Adventures, calle Guerrero s/n, 48300 Puerto Vallarta, Jalisco (✆ **3/223-1680;** www.bikemex.com), offers day or over- night mountain-biking excursions in the Sierra Madre foothills near Puerto Vallarta. One overnight trip travels to the old mountain mining towns of Mascota, Talpa de Allende, and San Sebastian. This excellent trip is a combination of van transport and biking between towns, with stays in old haciendas.

Culinary Adventures, 6023 Reid Dr. NW, Gig Harbor, WA 98335 (✆ **253/851-7676;** fax 253/851-9532), offers a short but special list of cooking tours of particular regions of Mexico known for excellent cuisine, and featuring well-known cooks. The owner, Marilyn Tausend, is the co-author of *Mexico the Beautiful Cookbook,* and *Cocinas de la Familia (Family Kitchens).*

One World Workforce, P.O. Box 3188, La Mesa, CA 91944 (✆ **800/451-9564**), has weeklong "hands-on conservation trips" that offer working volunteers a chance to help with sea-turtle conservation along the Majahuas beach 60 miles south of Puerto Vallarta during the summer and fall.

Open Air Expeditions, calle Guerrero 339, Col. Centro, Apdo. Postal 105-B, Puerto Vallarta, Jal. C.P. 48300 (© **3/222-3310;** fax 3/223-2407; www.vivamexico.com), offers true eco-adventures guided by experts trained as marine biologists, oceanographers, or geologists. Their specialty is whale-watching tours (December through May); they have documented the returning whale population in an annual photo-ID study for the past 5 years. Other offerings include tours to sea turtle preservation camps, hiking, sea kayaking, and bird watching. All are in small groups, with minimal environmental impact and great sensitivity to the natural surroundings.

Trek America, P.O. Box 189, Rockaway, NJ 07866 (© **800/ 221-0596** or 973/983-1144; fax 973/983-8551) organizes lengthy, active trips that combine trekking, hiking, van transportation, and camping in the Yucatán, Chiapas, Oaxaca, the Copper Canyon, and Mexico's Pacific coast, and touching on Mexico City and Guadalajara.

Vallarta Adventures, Edif. Marina Golf Local 13c, Marina Vallarta, Puerto Vallarta, Jal., C.P. 48354 (© **3/297-1212,** or 3/ 221-0657; www.vallarta-adventures.com), Puerto Vallarta's premier adventure tour company, offers expeditions by boat to the Marietas Islands nature preserve, by land to the foothills of the Sierra Madre, and by air to the remote mining village of San Sebastian and the town of Tequila. They also have two adjacent dolphin-swim facilities, with an emphasis on education and interactive communication, and a day spa at the private cove of Caletas, the former home of film great John Huston. All adventures are top quality, led by enthusiastic guides who mix adventure with spirited fun.

5 Health, Safety & Insurance

STAYING HEALTHY

BUG OFF   Mosquitoes and gnats are prevalent along the coast. Insect repellent (*repelente contra insectos*) is a must, and it's not always available in Mexico. If you'll be in these areas and are prone to bites, bring a repellent along that contains the active ingredient DEET. Avon's "Skin So Soft" also works extremely well. If you're sensitive to bites, pick up some antihistamine cream from a drugstore at home.

Most readers won't ever see a scorpion (*alacrán*). But if you're stung, go immediately to a doctor.

MORE SERIOUS DISEASES   You shouldn't be overly concerned about tropical diseases if you stay on the normal tourist routes and don't eat street food. However, both dengue fever and cholera have appeared in Mexico in recent years. Talk to your doctor, or a medical specialist in tropical diseases, about any precautions you should take. You can also get medical bulletins from the U.S. State Department and the Centers for Disease Control (see "Sources of Information," earlier in this chapter). You can protect yourself by taking some simple precautions. Watch what you eat and drink; don't swim in stagnant water (ponds, slow-moving rivers, or wells); and avoid mosquito bites by covering up, using repellent, and sleeping under mosquito netting. The most dangerous areas seem to be on Mexico's west coast, away from the big resorts (which are relatively safe).

EMERGENCY CARE   Puerto Vallarta has a modern, U.S.-standards health care facility that offers insured care while in Mexico. **Ameri-Med,** Plaza Neptuno, in Marina Vallarta (© **800/ 815-1921** or 3/221-0023; fax 3/221-0026; www.amerimed-hospitals.com), provides complete, 24-hour, emergency health care adhering to U.S. medical standards. Facilities include CAT scan, radiology, ultrasound, and emergency air-evacuation services. Prices are in line with the standard of care, meaning that it's more costly than other medical facilities in Mexico.

For extreme medical emergencies, there's a service from the United States that will fly people to American hospitals: **Air-Evac,** a 24-hour air ambulance (© **888/554-9729,** or call collect 510/293-5968). You can also contact the service in Guadalajara (© **01-800/305-9400,** 3/616-9616, or 3/615-2471). There are several companies that offer air evac service; for a list refer to the U.S. State Department website at http://travel.state.gov/medical.html.

SAFETY

I have lived and traveled in Mexico for over 9 years, have never had any serious trouble, and rarely feel suspicious of anyone or any situation. You will probably feel physically safer in most Mexican cities and villages than in any comparable place at home. See "Crime, Bribes & Scams," and "Sources of Information," both earlier in this chapter, for more information and how to access the latest U.S. State Department advisories.

INSURANCE

There are three kinds of travel insurance: trip cancellation, medical, and lost luggage coverage. Trip cancellation insurance is a good idea

Over-the-Counter Drugs

Antibiotics and other drugs that you'd need a prescription to buy in the States are sold over-the-counter in Mexican pharmacies. Mexican pharmacies also have common over-the-counter cold, sinus, and allergy remedies, although not the broad selection we're accustomed to finding easily in the States.

if you have paid a large portion of your vacation expenses up front. The other two types of insurance, however, don't make sense for most travelers. Rule number one: Check your existing policies before you buy any additional coverage.

Your existing health insurance should cover you if you get sick while on vacation (though if you belong to an HMO, you should check to see whether you are fully covered when away from home). If you need hospital treatment, most health insurance plans and HMOs will cover out-of-country hospital visits and procedures, at least to some extent. However, most make you pay the bills up front at the time of care, and you'll get a refund after you've returned and filed all the paperwork. Members of Blue Cross/Blue Shield can now use their cards at select hospitals in most major cities worldwide (℄ 800/810-BLUE or www.bluecares.com/blue/bluecard/wwn for a list of hospitals).

Your homeowner's insurance should cover stolen luggage. The airlines are responsible for $2,500 on domestic flights if they lose your luggage; if you plan to carry anything more valuable than that, keep it in your carry-on bag.

The differences between travel assistance and insurance are often blurred, but in general the former offers on-the-spot assistance and 24-hour hot lines (mostly oriented toward medical problems), while the latter reimburses you for travel problems (medical, travel, or otherwise) after you have filed the paperwork. The coverage you should consider will depend on how much protection is already contained in your existing health insurance or other policies. Some credit- and charge-card companies may insure you against travel accidents if you buy plane, train, or bus tickets with their cards. Before purchasing additional insurance, read your policies and agreements over carefully. Call your insurers or credit/charge-card companies if you have any questions.

⸤Tips⸥ What to Do If You Get Sick

It's called "travelers' diarrhea" or *turista*, the Spanish word for "tourist": the persistent diarrhea, often accompanied by fever, nausea, and vomiting, that used to attack many travelers to Mexico. Some in the United States call this "Montezuma's revenge," but you won't hear it referred to this way in Mexico. Widespread improvements in infrastructure, sanitation, and education have practically eliminated this ailment, especially in well-developed resort areas. In resort areas, and generally throughout Mexico, only purified ice is used.

Doctors say it's not caused by just one thing, but by a combination of consuming different foods and water, upsetting your schedule, lack of sleep, and the stresses of travel. A good high-potency (or "therapeutic") vitamin supplement, and even extra vitamin C is a help; yogurt is good for healthy digestion. If you do happen to come down with this ailment, nothing beats Pepto Bismol, readily available in Mexico.

Since dehydration can quickly become life threatening, the Public Health Service emphasizes the importance of **replacing fluids and electrolytes** (potassium, sodium, and the like) during a bout of diarrhea. Do this by drinking Pedialyte, a rehydration solution available at most Mexican pharmacies, glasses of natural fruit juice (high in potassium) with a pinch of salt added, or a glass of boiled pure water with a quarter teaspoon of sodium bicarbonate (baking soda) added.

Some credit cards (American Express and certain gold and platinum Visa and MasterCards, for example) offer automatic flight insurance against death or dismemberment in case of an airplane crash.

If you'll be driving in Mexico, see "By Car," under "Getting There," and "Getting Around," below for information on collision and damage and personal accident insurance.

Even the most careful of us can still experience a traveler's nightmare: You discover you've lost your wallet, your passport, your airline ticket, or your tourist permit. Always keep a photocopy of these documents in your luggage—it makes replacing them easier. To be reimbursed for insured items once you return, you'll need to report the loss to the Mexican police and get a written report. If you don't speak Spanish, take along someone who does. If you lose official documents, you'll need to contact both Mexican and U.S. officials in Mexico before you leave the country.

6 Tips for Travelers with Special Needs

FOR FAMILIES   I can't think of a better place today to introduce children to the exciting adventure of exploring a different culture. Hotels can often arrange for a baby-sitter. Some hotels in the moderate-to-luxury range have small playgrounds and pools for children and hire caretakers with special activity programs during the day. Few budget hotels offer these amenities.

Before leaving, you should check with your doctor to get advice on medications to take along. Disposable diapers cost about the same in Mexico but are of poorer quality. You can get Huggies Supreme and Pampers identical to the ones sold in the United States, but at a higher price. Gerber's baby foods are sold in many stores. Dry cereals, powdered formulas, baby bottles, and purified water are all easily available in midsize and large cities and resorts.

Cribs, however, may present a problem. Only the largest and most luxurious hotels provide cribs. However, rollaway beds to accommodate children staying in the room with parents are often available. Child seats or high chairs at restaurants are common, and most restaurants will go out of their way to accommodate your child.

FOR GAY & LESBIAN TRAVELERS   Mexico is a conservative country, with deeply rooted Catholic religious traditions. As such, public displays of same-sex affection are rare and still considered shocking for men, especially outside of urban or resort areas. Women in Mexico frequently walk hand in hand, but anything more would cross the boundary of acceptability. However, gay and lesbian travelers are generally treated with respect and should not experience any harassment, assuming the appropriate regard is given to local culture and customs.

Puerto Vallarta is perhaps the most welcoming and accepting destination in Mexico, with a selection of accommodations and nightlife oriented especially toward gay and lesbian travelers. **Vicki Skinner's Doin' It Right in Puerto Vallarta** is a special travel service that rents gay-friendly condos and villas for individuals and groups up to 75. She also has a newsletter, "The PV Purple Pages," that offers travel specials and features tips, special events, and activities. It's free to Doin' It Right clients, or $10 plus a SASE with $1.01 postage to nonclients. To subscribe, write to 1010 University Ave. #C113-741, San Diego, CA 92103 (✆ **800/936-3646** or 619/297-3642). The newsletter is also available online by sending an email to GayPVR@aol.com.

Arco Iris is a gay-owned, full-service travel agency and tour operator specializing in Mexico packages and special group travel, including to Puerto Vallarta. Contact them by phone (✆ **800/795-5549**), or through their website (www.freeyellow.com/members/arco/index.html). The **International Gay & Lesbian Travel Association** (IGLTA) (✆ **800/448-8550** or 954/776-2626; fax 954/776-3303; www.iglta.org), can provide helpful information and additional tips. The **Travel Alternative Group** (TAG) maintains a database and Gay-Friendly Accommodations Guide. For details, call ✆ **415/437-3800** or e-mail info@mark8ing.com.

FOR TRAVELERS WITH DISABILITIES   Mexico may seem like one giant obstacle course to travelers in wheelchairs or on crutches. At airports, you may encounter steep stairs before finding a well-hidden elevator or escalator—if one exists. Airlines will often arrange wheelchair assistance for passengers to the baggage area. Porters are generally available to help with luggage at airports and large bus stations, once you've cleared baggage claim. Few airports offer the luxury of boarding an airplane from the waiting room. You either descend stairs to a bus that ferries you to the waiting plane that's boarded by climbing stairs, or you walk across the airport tarmac to your plane and ascend the stairs. Deplaning presents the same problem in reverse.

Few rest rooms are equipped for travelers with disabilities, or when one is available, access to it may be via a narrow passage that won't accommodate a wheelchair or someone on crutches. Many deluxe hotels (the most expensive) now have rooms with baths for people with disabilities. Those traveling on a budget should stick with one-story hotels or those with elevators. Even so, there will probably still be obstacles somewhere. Stairs without handrails abound in Mexico, and escalators (there aren't many in the country) are often out of operation. Generally speaking, no matter where you are, someone will lend a hand, although you may have to ask for it.

FOR SENIORS   Mexico is a popular country for retirees. For decades, North Americans have been living indefinitely in Mexico by returning to the border and recrossing with a new tourist permit every 6 months. Mexican immigration officials have caught on, and now limit the maximum time in the country to 6 months within any year. This is to encourage even partial residents to comply with the proper documentation.

Some of the most popular places for long-term stays are Guadalajara, Lake Chapala, Ajijic, and Puerto Vallarta—all in the state of Jalisco; and to a lesser extent Manzanillo, in Colima.

AIM, Apdo. Postal 31–70, 45050 Guadalajara, Jalisco, Mexico, is a well-written, candid, and very informative newsletter on retirement in Mexico. Subscriptions cost $18 to the United States and $21 to Canada. Back issues are three for $5.

Sanborn Tours, 2015 S. 10th St., Post Office Drawer 519, McAllen, TX 78505-0519 (© **800/395-8482**), offers a "Retire in Mexico" Guadalajara orientation tour. American Express, Discover, MasterCard, and Visa are accepted.

One of the most enjoyable ways to take a sneak peak at retired life in Mexico is to read *Tales of Retirement in Paradise,* by Polly Vicars, an entertaining account of the pleasures of "retired" (but amazingly active) life in Puerto Vallarta. Proceeds of the book benefit the America-Mexico Foundation (**www.puerto-vallarta.com/amf/**), which provides scholarships to needy and deserving Mexican students. Buy the $20 book online through Amazon (www.amazon. com), or e-mail the author directly at phvicars@pvnet.com.mx.

FOR WOMEN   As a female traveling alone, I can tell you firsthand that I feel safer traveling in Mexico than in the United States. But I use the same commonsense precautions I use traveling anywhere else in the world, and I am alert to what's going on around me.

Mexicans in general, and men in particular, are nosy about single travelers, especially women. If a taxi driver or anyone else with whom you don't want to become friendly asks about your marital status, family, etc., my advice is to make up a set of answers (regardless of the truth): "I'm married, traveling with friends, and I have three children."

Saying you are single and traveling alone may send out the wrong message about availability. Movies and television shows exported from the United States have created an image of sexually aggressive North American women. If bothered by someone, don't try to be polite—just leave or head into a public place.

7 Getting There

BY PLANE

The airline situation in Mexico is changing rapidly, with many new regional carriers offering scheduled service to areas previously not served. In addition to regularly scheduled service, charter service direct from U.S. cities to resorts is making Mexico more accessible. It has become much easier to fly to destinations without having to go through Mexico City than in the past.

THE MAJOR INTERNATIONAL AIRLINES   The main airlines operating direct or nonstop flights from the United States to points in Mexico include **Aero California** (© 800/237-6225), **Aeromexico** (© 800/237-6639), **Alaska Airlines** (© 800/426-0333), **America West** (© 800/235-9292), **American** (© 800/433-7300), **Continental** (© 800/231-0856), **Lacsa** (© 800/225-2272), **Mexicana** (© 800/531-7921), **Northwest** (© 800/225-2525), **United** (© 800/241-6522), and **US Airways** (© 800/428-4322).

BY CAR

Driving is not the cheapest way to get to Mexico, but it is the best way to see the country. Even so, you may think twice about taking your own car south of the border once you've pondered the bureaucratic requirements that affect foreign drivers here. One option would be to rent a car, for touring around a specific region, once you arrive in Mexico. Rental cars in Mexico are now generally new, clean, and very well maintained. Although pricier than in the United States, discounts are often available for rentals of a week or longer, especially when arrangements are made in advance from the United States. (See "Car Rentals," under "Getting Around," later in this chapter, for more details.)

If, after reading the section that follows, you have any additional questions or you want to confirm the current rules, call your nearest Mexican consulate, or the Mexican Government Tourist Office. Although travel insurance companies are generally helpful, they may not have the most accurate information available. To check on road conditions or to get help with any travel emergency while in Mexico, call © **01-800/903-9200,** or 5/250-0151 in Mexico City. Both numbers are staffed by English-speaking operators.

In addition, check with the U.S. State Department (see "Sources of Information," earlier in this chapter) for their warnings about dangerous driving areas.

CAR DOCUMENTS

You must carry your temporary car-importation permit, tourist permit (see "Entry Requirements," earlier in this chapter), and, if you purchased it, your proof of Mexican car insurance (see "Mexican Auto Insurance," below) in the car at all times. The temporary car-importation permit papers will be issued for 6 months to a year, while the tourist permit is usually issued for 30 days. It's a good idea to overestimate the time you'll spend in Mexico, so that if something unforeseen happens and you have to (or want to) stay longer, you'll avoid the hassle of getting your papers extended. Whatever you do, don't overstay either permit. Doing so invites heavy fines and/or confiscation of your vehicle, which will not be returned. Remember also that 6 months does not necessarily work out to be 180 days—be sure to return before the expiration date

To drive your car into Mexico, you'll need a **temporary car-importation permit,** which is granted after you provide a strictly required list of documents (see below). The permit can be obtained either through Banco del Ejército (Banjercito) officials, who have a desk, booth, or office at the Mexican Customs (Aduana) building after you cross the border into Mexico. Insurance companies such as AAA and Sanborn's used to be able to issue this permit, however no longer are.

The following requirements for border crossing were accurate at press time:

- A **valid driver's license,** issued outside of Mexico.
- **Current, original car registration and a copy of the original car title.** If the registration or title is in more than one name and not all the named people are traveling with you, a notarized letter from the absent person(s) authorizing use of the vehicle for the trip is required; have it ready just in case. The car registration and your credit card (see below) must be in the same name.
- A **valid international major credit card.** With a credit card, you are only required to pay a $16 car-importation fee. The credit card must be in the same name as the car registration. If you do not have a major credit card (Visa, MasterCard, American Express, or Diners Club) you will have to post a bond or make a deposit equal to the value of the vehicle. Check cards are not accepted.
- **Original immigration documentation.** This will either be your tourist permit (FMT), or the original immigration booklet, FM2 or FM3, if you hold this more permanent status.

- A **signed declaration promising to return to your country of origin** with the vehicle. This form (Carta Promesa de Retorno) is provided by AAA or Sanborn's before you go or by Banjercito officials at the border. There's no charge. The form does not stipulate that you must return through the same border entry you came through on your way south.
- **Temporary Importation Application.** Upon signing this form, you are stating that you are only temporarily importing the car for your personal use, and will not be selling the vehicle. This is to help regulate the entry and restrict the resale of unauthorized cars and trucks. Vehicles in the U.S. are much less expensive, and for years were brought into Mexico for resale.

If you receive your documentation at the border, Mexican officials will make two copies of everything and charge you for the copies. For up-to-the-minute information, a great source is the Customs office in Nuevo Leon (Módulo de Importación Temporal de Automóviles, Aduana Nuevo León), © **52-8/712-2071.**

Important reminder: Someone else may drive the car, but the person (or relative of the person) whose name appears on the car-importation permit must always be in the car at the same time. (If stopped by police, a nonregistered family member driving without the registered driver must be prepared to prove familial relationship to the registered driver—no joke.) Violation of this rule makes the car subject to impoundment and the driver subject to imprisonment and/or a fine. You can only drive a car with foreign license plates if you have an international (non-Mexican) driver's license.

MEXICAN AUTO INSURANCE

Liability auto insurance is legally required in Mexico. U.S. insurance is invalid in Mexico; to be insured in Mexico, you must purchase Mexican insurance. Any party involved in an accident who has no insurance may be sent to jail and his or her car impounded until all claims are settled. This is true even if you just drive across the border to spend the day. U.S. companies that broker Mexican insurance are commonly found at the border crossing, and several will quote daily rates.

Car insurance can also be purchased through **Sanborn's Mexico Insurance,** P.O. Box 52840, 2009 S. 10th, McAllen, TX 78505-2840 (© **956/686-3601;** fax 956/686-0732 800/222-0158, www.sanbornsinsurance.com). The company has offices at all of the border crossings in the United States. Its policies cost the same as the competition's do, but you get legal coverage (attorney and bail bonds if needed) and a detailed mile-by-mile guide for your proposed route. Most of Sanborn's border offices are open Monday through Friday, and a few are staffed on Saturday and Sunday. AAA auto club also sells insurance.

RETURNING TO THE U.S. WITH YOUR CAR

The car papers you obtained when you entered Mexico must be returned when you cross back with your car or at some point within 180 days. (You can cross as many times as you wish within the 180 days.) If the documents aren't returned, heavy fines are imposed ($250 for each 15 days late), and your car may be impounded and confiscated or you may be jailed if you return to Mexico. You can only return the car documents to a Banjercito official on duty at the Mexican Customs (Aduana) building before you cross back into the United States. Some border cities have Banjercito officials on duty 24 hours a day, but others do not; some also do not have Sunday hours. On the U.S. side, customs agents may or may not inspect your car from stem to stern.

BY SHIP

Numerous cruise lines serve Mexico's Central Pacific coast, known as the Mexican Riviera. Ships from California cruise down to the Baja Peninsula (including specialized whale-watching trips) and ports of call along the Pacific Coast.

If you don't mind taking off at the last minute, several cruise-tour specialists arrange substantial discounts on unsold cabins. One such company is **The Cruise Line,** 150 NW 168 St., North Miami Beach, Miami, FL 33169 (© **800/777-0707** or 305/521-2200).

8 Planning Your Trip Online

With a mouse, a modem, and a certain do-it-yourself determination, Internet users can tap into the same travel-planning databases that were once accessible only to travel agents. Sites such as **Travelocity, Expedia,** and **Orbitz** allow consumers to comparison shop for airfares, book flights, learn of last-minute bargains, and reserve hotel rooms and rental cars.

But don't fire your travel agent just yet. Although online booking sites offer tips and hard data to help you bargain shop, they cannot endow you with the hard-earned experience that makes a seasoned, reliable travel agent an invaluable resource, even in the Internet age. And for consumers with a complex itinerary, a trusty travel agent is still the best way to arrange the most direct flights to and from the best airports.

The benefits of researching your trip online can be well worth the effort:

- **Last-minute specials,** known as "E-savers," such as weekend deals or Internet-only fares, are offered by airlines to fill empty seats. Most of these are announced on Tuesday or Wednesday and must be purchased online. They are only valid for travel that weekend, but some can be booked weeks or months in advance. Sign up for weekly e-mail alerts at airline websites (see below) or check megasites that compile comprehensive lists of E-savers, such as Smarter Living (smarterliving.com) or WebFlyer (www.webflyer.com).
- Some sites will send you **e-mail notification** when a cheap fare becomes available to your favorite destination. Some will also tell you when fares to a particular destination are lowest.
- The best of the travel planning sites are now **highly personalized;** they track your frequent-flier miles, and store your seating and meal preferences, tentative itineraries, and credit-card information, letting you plan trips or check agendas quickly.
- All major airlines offer **incentives**—bonus frequent-flier miles, Internet-only discounts, sometimes even free cell phone rentals—when you purchase online or buy an E-ticket.
- Advances in mobile technology provide business travelers and other frequent travelers with **the ability to check flight status, change plans, or get specific directions** from handheld computing devices, mobile phones, and pagers. Some sites will e-mail or page a passenger if a flight is delayed.

TRAVEL PLANNING & BOOKING SITES

The best travel planning and booking sites cast a wide net, offering domestic and international flights, hotel and rental-car bookings, plus news, destination information, and deals on cruises and vacation packages. Keep in mind that free (one-time) registration is often required for booking. Because several airlines are no longer willing to pay commissions on tickets sold by online travel agencies, be aware that these online agencies will either charge a $10 surcharge if you book a ticket on that carrier—or neglect to offer those air carriers' offerings.

The sites in this section are not intended to be a comprehensive list, but rather a discriminating selection to get you started. Recognition is given to sites based on their content value and ease

> ⌒Tips **Frommers.com: The Complete Travel Resource**
>
> For an excellent travel planning resource, we highly recommend **Arthur Frommer's Budget Travel Online** (www.frommers.com). Among the special features are: **"Ask the Expert"** bulletin boards, where Frommer's authors answer your questions via online postings; **Arthur Frommer's Daily Newsletter,** for the latest travel bargains and inside travel secrets; and Frommer's **Destinations archive,** where you'll get expert travel tips, hotel and dining recommendations, and advice on the sights to see for more than 200 destinations around the globe. Once your research is done, the **Online Reservation System** (www.frommers.com/book travelnow) takes you to Frommer's favorite sites for booking your vacation at affordable prices.

of use and is not paid for—unlike some website rankings, which are based on payment. Remember: This is a press-time snapshot of leading websites—some undoubtedly will have evolved or moved by the time you read this.

- **Travelocity** (www.travelocity.com or www.frommers.travelocity.com) and **Expedia** (www.expedia.com) are the most longstanding and reputable sites, each offering excellent selections and searches for complete vacation packages. Travelers search by destination and dates coupled with how much they are willing to spend.
- The latest buzz in the online travel world is about **Orbitz** (www.orbitz.com), a site launched by United, Delta, Northwest, American, and Continental airlines. It shows all possible fares for your desired trip, offering fares lower than those available through travel agents. (Stay tuned: At press time, travel-agency associations were waging an antitrust battle against this site—but it appeared that Orbitz would emerge victorious.)
- **Qixo** (www.qixo.com) is another powerful search engine that allows you to search for flights and hotel rooms on 20 other travel-planning sites (such as Travelocity) at once. Qixo sorts results by price, after which you can book your travel directly through the site.

Tips **Sleeping in Style**

Mexico lends itself beautifully to the concept of small, private hotels set in idyllic settings. These may vary in style from grandiose to a return to the basics of palm-thatched bunga- lows. **Mexico Boutique Hotels** (www.MexicoBoutiqueHotels. com) is a new company that specializes in smaller places to stay with a high level of personal attention and service. Most options have fewer than 50 rooms, and the type of accom- modations can consist of entire villas, casitas, bungalows, or a combination of these. The Yucatán is especially noted for the luxury haciendas found throughout the peninsula.

AIRLINE WEBSITES

Below are the websites for the major airlines that service Mexico. These sites offer schedules and booking, and most of the airlines have E-saver alerts for weekend deals and late-breaking bargains.

- **Aeromexico.** www.aeromexico.com
- **Alaska Airlines.** www.alaskaair.com
- **American Airlines.** www.aa.com
- **America West.** www.americawest.com
- **Continental Airlines.** www.continental.com
- **Delta.** www.delta.com
- **Mexicana.** www.mexicana.com
- **Northwest Airlines.** www.nwa.com
- **United Airlines.** www.ual.com
- **US Airways.** www.usairways.com

9 The Pros & Cons of Package Tours

Say the word "package tour" and many people automatically feel as though they're being forced to choose: money or lifestyle. This isn't necessarily the case. Most Mexican packages let you have both your independence and your in-the-black bank-account balance. Package tours are not the same thing as escorted tours. They are simply a way of buying your airfare, accommodations, and other pieces of your trip (usually airport transfers, and sometimes meals and activities) at the same time.

For popular destinations like Mexico's beach resorts they're often the smart way to go, because they can save you a ton of money. In many cases, a package that includes airfare, hotel, and transportation to and from the airport will cost you less than just the hotel alone if you booked it yourself. That's because packages are sold in bulk to tour operators, who resell them to the public.

You can buy a package at any time of the year, but the best deals usually coincide with low season—from May to early December—when room rates and airfares plunge. But packages vary widely. Some offer a better class of hotels than others. Some offer the same hotels for lower prices. Some offer flights on scheduled airlines while others book charters. In some packages, your choices of accommodations and travel days may be limited. Each destination usually has some packagers that are better than the rest because they buy in even bigger bulk. Not only can that mean better prices, but it can also mean more choices—a packager that just dabbles in Mexico may have only a half-dozen or so hotels for you to choose from.

WARNINGS

- **Read the fine print.** Make sure you know exactly what's included in the price you're being quoted, and what's not.
- **Don't compare Mayas and Aztecs.** When you're looking over different packagers, compare the deals that they're offering on similar properties. Most packagers can offer bigger savings on some hotels than others.
- **Know what you're getting yourself into**—and if you can get yourself out of it. Before you commit to a package, make sure you know how much flexibility you have.
- **Use your best judgment.** Stay away from fly-by-nights and shady packagers. Go with a reputable firm with a proven track record. This is where your travel agent can come in handy.

WHERE TO BROWSE

- For one-stop shopping on the Web, go to **www.vacation packager. com**, an extensive search engine that'll link you up with more than 30 packagers offering Mexican beach vacations— and even let you custom design your own package.
- At **www.2travel.com** you'll find a page with links to a number of the big-name Mexico packagers, including several of the ones listed here.
- For last minute air-only or package bargains, check out Vacation Hotline, **www.vacationhotline.net**. Once you find your "deal" you'll need to call them to make final booking arrangements, but they offer packages from both the popular Apple and Funjet vacation wholesalers.

RECOMMENDED PACKAGERS

- **Aeromexico Vacations** (© 800/245-8585; www.aeromexico. com): Year-round packages for Puerto Vallarta, including connections to Guadalajara, with a large selection of hotels in these destinations in a variety of price ranges.
- **Alaska Airlines Vacations** (© 800/468-2248; www.alaskair. com) sells packages to Puerto Vallarta from Los Angeles, San Diego, San Jose, San Francisco, Seattle, Vancouver, Anchorage, and Fairbanks.
- **American Airlines Vacations** (© 800/321-2121; www. americanair.com): American has year-round deals for Puerto Vallarta. You don't have to fly with American if you can get a better deal on another airline; land-only packages include hotel, airport transfers, and hotel room tax. American's hubs to Mexico are Dallas/Fort Worth, Chicago, and Miami, so you're likely to get the best prices—and the most direct flights—if you live near those cities.
- **America West Vacations** (© 800/356-6611; www.america west.com) has deals to Manzanillo and Puerto Vallarta, mostly from its Phoenix gateway.
- **Apple Vacations** (© 800/365-2775): Apple offers inclusive packages with the largest choice of hotels: 6 in Manzanillo and 31 in Puerto Vallarta. Apple perks include baggage handling and the services of an Apple representative at the major hotels.
- **Classic Custom Vacations** (© 800/221-3949 and 800/344-5687; www.classiccustomvacations.com) is a newer company that specializes in package vacations to Mexico's finest luxury resorts. They combine discounted first class and economy airfares on American, Continental, Mexicana, Alaska, America West, and Delta Airlines with stays at the most exclusive hotels in Guadalajara, Puerto Vallarta, Mazatlán, Costa Alegre, and Manzanillo. In many cases, these packages also include meals, private airport transfers, and upgrades.
- **Continental Vacations** (© 800/634-5555; and 888/989-9255; www.continental.com): With Continental, you've got to buy air from the carrier if you want to book a room. The airline has year-round packages available to Puerto Vallarta, and the best deals are from Houston; Newark, New Jersey; and Cleveland.
- **Funjet Vacations** (bookable through travel agents or online at **www.funjet.com**): One of the largest vacation packagers in the

United States, Funjet has packages to Mexico's resorts, including Puerto Vallarta. You can choose a charter or fly on American, Continental, Aeromexico, Alaska Airlines, or TWA.

- **Mexicana Vacations** (or MexSeaSun Vacations) (© **800/531-9321;** www.mexicana.com) offers getaways to Puerto Vallarta from Los Angeles, Chicago, and Denver.
- **Pleasant Mexico Holidays** (© **800/448-3333;** www.pleasantholidays.com) is another of the largest vacation packagers in the United States, with hotels in the most popular destinations including Mazatlán and Puerto Vallarta.

10 Getting Around

An important note: If your travel schedule depends on an important connection, say a plane trip between points or a ferry or bus connection, use the telephone numbers in this book or other information resources mentioned here to find out if the connection you are depending on is still available. Although we've done our best to provide accurate information, transportation schedules can and do change.

BY PLANE

To fly from point to point within Mexico, you'll rely on Mexican airlines. Mexico has two privately owned large national carriers: **Mexicana** (© **800/366-5400**) and **Aeromexico** (© **800/021-4000**), in addition to several up-and-coming regional carriers. Mexicana and Aeromexico both offer extensive connections to the United States as well as within Mexico.

Several of the new regional carriers are operated by or can be booked through Mexicana or Aeromexico. Regional carriers are **Aerocaribe** (see Mexicana); **Aerolitoral** (see Aeromexico); and **Aero Mar** (see Mexicana). The regional carriers are expensive, but they go to difficult-to-reach places. In each applicable section of this book, we've mentioned regional carriers with all pertinent telephone numbers.

Because major airlines can book some regional carriers, read your ticket carefully to see if your connecting flight is on one of these smaller carriers—they may leave from a different airport or check in at a different counter, especially true in the Guadalajara airport.

AIRPORT TAXES   Mexico charges an airport tax on all departures. Passengers leaving the country on an international departure pay $18.00—in dollars or the peso equivalent. It has become a common practice to include this departure tax in your ticket price, but double-check to make sure. Taxes on each domestic departure you make within Mexico cost around $12.50, unless you're on a connecting flight and have already paid at the start of the flight; you shouldn't be charged again if you have to change planes for a connecting flight. These taxes are usually included in the price of your ticket.

Starting in May 1999, Mexico began charging an additional $18 "tourism tax," the proceeds of which go into a tourism promotional fund. This may or may not be included in your ticket price, so be sure to set aside this amount in either dollars or pesos to pay at the airport upon departure.

RECONFIRMING FLIGHTS   Although airlines in Mexico say it's not necessary to reconfirm a flight, it's still a good practice. To avoid getting bumped on popular, possibly overbooked flights, check in for an international flight an hour and a half in advance of travel.

BY CAR

Most Mexican roads are not up to U.S. standards of smoothness, hardness, width of curve, grade of hill, or safety marking. Driving at night is dangerous—the roads aren't good enough and are rarely lit; the trucks, carts, pedestrians, and bicycles usually have no lights; and you can hit potholes, animals, rocks, dead ends, or bridges out with no warning.

The "spirited" style of Mexican driving sometimes requires super vision and reflexes. Be prepared for different behavior, as when a truck driver flips on his left-turn signal when there's not a crossroad for miles. He's probably telling you the road's clear ahead for you to pass—after all, he's in a better position to see than you are. Another custom that's very important to respect is how to make a left turn. Never turn left by stopping in the middle of a highway with your left signal on. Instead, pull off the highway onto the right shoulder, wait for traffic to clear, then proceed across the road.

GASOLINE   There's one government-owned brand of gas and one gasoline station name throughout the country—Pemex (Petroleras Mexicanas). There are two types of gas in Mexico: magna, an 87-octane unleaded gas; and the newer premium 93-octane. In Mexico, fuel and oil are sold by the liter, which is slightly more than a quart (40 liters equals about 10½ gal.). *Important note:* No credit cards are accepted for gas purchases. There is a new trend toward franchise Pemex stations, many of which have bathroom facilities and convenience stores—a great improvement over the old Pemex stations.

TOLL ROADS   Mexico charges among the highest tolls in the world for its network of new toll roads. As a result, they are little used. Generally speaking, using the toll roads will cut your travel time between destinations. Older toll-free roads are generally in good condition but travel times are usually longer, since they tend to be mountainous and clotted with slow-moving trucks.

BREAKDOWNS   Your best guide to repair shops is the Yellow Pages. For specific makes and shops that repair cars, look under "Automoviles y Camiones: Talleres de Reparación y Servicio"; auto-parts stores are listed under "Refacciones y Accesorios para Automoviles." To find a mechanic on the road, look for a sign that says TALLER MECÁNICO.

If your car breaks down on the road, help might already be on the way. Radio-equipped, green repair trucks operated by uniformed English-speaking officers patrol the major highways during daylight hours to aid motorists in trouble. These "Green Angels" will per-form minor repairs and adjustments for free, but you pay for parts and materials.

MINOR ACCIDENTS   When possible, many Mexicans drive away from minor accidents to avoid hassles with police, or try to make an immediate settlement to avoid involving the police. If the police arrive while the involved persons are still at the scene, every-one may be locked in jail until blame is assessed. In any case, you have to settle up immediately, which may take days of red tape. Foreigners who don't speak fluent Spanish are at a distinct disad-vantage when trying to explain their side of the event. Three steps may help the foreigner who doesn't wish to do as the Mexicans do: If you're in your own car, notify your Mexican insurance company, whose job it is to intervene on your behalf. If you're in a rental car, notify the rental company immediately and ask how to contact the nearest adjuster. (You did buy insurance with the rental, right?) Finally, if all else fails, ask to contact the nearest Green Angel, who may be able to explain to officials that you are covered by insurance.

See also "Mexican Auto Insurance" under "Getting There," ear-lier in this chapter.

CAR RENTALS
You'll get the best price if you reserve a car a week in advance in the United States. U.S. car-rental firms include **Avis** (© **800/331-1212** in the U.S.; 800/TRY-AVIS in Canada), **Budget** (© **800/527-0700** in the U.S. and Canada), **Hertz** (© **800/654-3131** in the U.S. and Canada), and **National** (© **800/CAR-RENT** in the U.S. and

Canada). For European travelers, **Kemwel Holiday Auto** (© **800/ 678-0678**) and **Auto Europe** (© **800/223-5555**) can arrange Mexican rentals, sometimes through other agencies. These and some local firms have offices in Mexico City and most other large Mexican cities. You'll find rental desks at airports, all major hotels, and many travel agencies.

Cars are easy to rent if you have a major credit card, are 25 or over, and have a valid driver's license and passport with you. Without a credit card you must leave a cash deposit, usually a big one. Rent-here/leave-there arrangements are usually simple to make but more costly.

Car-rental costs are high in Mexico, because cars are more expensive here. The condition of rental cars has improved greatly over the years, however, and clean, comfortable, new cars are the norm. At press time, the basic cost of a 1-day rental of a Volkswagen Beetle, with unlimited mileage (but before 17% tax and $15 daily insurance) was $40 in Puerto Vallarta. Renting by the week gives you a lower daily rate. Avis was offering a basic 7-day weekly rate for a VW Beetle (before tax or insurance) of $220 in Puerto Vallarta. Prices may be considerably higher if you rent around a major holiday.

Car-rental companies usually write up a credit-card charge in U.S. dollars.

DEDUCTIBLES   Be careful—these vary greatly in Mexico; some are as high as $2,500, which comes out of your pocket immediately in case of car damage. Hertz's deductible is $1,000 on a VW Beetle; Avis's is $500 for the same car.

INSURANCE   Insurance is offered in two parts: Collision and damage insurance covers your car and others if the accident is your fault, and personal accident insurance covers you and anyone in your car. Read the fine print on the back of your rental agreement and note that insurance may be invalid if you have an accident while driving on an unpaved road.

DAMAGE   Always inspect your car carefully and note every damaged or missing item, no matter how minute, on your rental agreement, or you may be charged.

Tips **Bus-riding**

There's little English spoken at bus stations, so come prepared with your destination written down, then double-check the departure.

Changes to Mexico's Phone Numbers Announced

As this book went to press, Mexico had announced a sweeping change in the country's long-distance dialing codes, to take effect at the end of 2001. The new plan, in most cases, will replace the current one-digit area code with a three-digit area code. For example, in Puerto Vallarta the area code is presently 3, and all seven-digit local phone numbers begin with 22 (as in, ✆ 3/22X-XXXX). The new area code will incorporate the first two digits of the local phone number, making Puerto Vallarta's new area code **322**; however, the seven-digit local phone number will not change. So the new complete number, including area code, will be ✆ **322/22X-XXXX**. The exceptions to this three-digit area code change are three of the country's largest cities; Mexico City, Guadalajara, and Monterrey will get a two-digit area code, followed by an eight-digit local number. Mexico City's new area code is **55,** Guadalajara's is **33,** and Monterrey's is **81.**

The following table supplies new area codes for some of the major destinations in this book. If you are trying to dial a town that is not listed in this table, try adding the first two digits of the local phone number to the area code, and then dialing the local number as it appears in the book. For further information regarding phones in Mexico, please see "Telephone/Fax" in "Fast Facts," below

City	Present Area Code	New Area Code
Barra de Navidad	3	315
Guadalajara	3	33 + 8-digit local #
Manzanillo	3	314
México City	5	55 + 8-digit local #
Puerto Vallarta	3	322
Punta de Mita	3	329
Tequila	3	374

TROUBLE NUMBER   It's advisable to carefully note the rental company's trouble number, as well as the direct number of the agency where you rented the car.

BY TAXI

Taxis are the preferred way to get around almost all of the resort areas of Mexico, and also within Guadalajara. Short trips within towns are generally charged by preset zones, and are quite reasonable compared with U.S. rates. For longer trips or excursions to nearby cities, taxis can generally be hired for around $10 to $15 per hour, or for a negotiated daily rate. Even drops to different destinations, say between Puerto Vallarta and Barra de Navidad, can be arranged. A negotiated one-way price is usually much less than the cost of a rental car for a day, and service is much faster than traveling by bus. For anyone who is uncomfortable driving in Mexico, this is a convenient, comfortable route. An added bonus is that you have a Spanish-speaking person with you in case you run into any car or road trouble. Many taxi drivers speak at least some English. Your hotel can assist you with the arrangements.

BY BUS

Mexican buses are frequent, readily accessible, and can get you to almost anywhere you want to go. They're often the only way to get from large cities to other nearby cities and small villages. Don't hesitate to ask questions if you're confused about anything.

Dozens of Mexican companies operate large, air-conditioned, Greyhound-type buses between most cities. Travel class is generally labeled first (primera), second (segunda), and deluxe, which is referred to by a variety of names. The deluxe buses often have fewer seats than regular buses, show video movies en route, are air-conditioned, and have few stops; some have complimentary refreshments. Many run express from the origin to the final destination, and they are well worth the few dollars more that you'll pay. In rural areas, buses are often of the school-bus variety, with lots of local color.

Whenever possible, it's best to buy your reserved-seat ticket, often via a computerized system, a day in advance on many long-distance routes and especially before holidays. Schedules are fairly dependable, so be at the terminal on time for departure. Current information must be obtained from local bus stations.

 Fast Facts: Mexico

Abbreviations Dept. (apartments); Apdo. (post office box); av. (avenida; avenue); c/ (calle; street); calz. (calzada; boulevard).

"C" on faucets stands for caliente (hot), and "F" stands for fría (cold). PB (planta baja) means ground floor, and most buildings count the next floor up as the first floor (1).

Business Hours In general, businesses in larger cities are open between 9am and 7pm; in smaller towns many close between 2 and 4pm. Most are closed on Sunday. Bank hours are Monday through Friday from 9 or 9:30am to 5 or 6pm. Increasingly, banks are offering Saturday hours for at least a half-day.

Cameras/Film Film costs about the same as in the United States.

Customs See "Visitor Information, Entry Requirements & Money," earlier in this chapter.

Doctors/Dentists Every embassy and consulate can recommend local doctors and dentists with good training and modern equipment; some of the doctors and dentists even speak English. Hotels with a large foreign clientele can often recommend English-speaking doctors. Almost all first-class hotels in Mexico have a doctor on call.

Drug Laws To be blunt, don't use or possess illegal drugs in Mexico. Mexican officials have no tolerance for drug users, and jail is their solution, with very little hope of getting out until the sentence (usually a long one) is completed or heavy fines or bribes are paid. Remember—in Mexico the legal system assumes you are guilty until proven innocent. (*Important note:* It isn't uncommon to be befriended by a fellow user, only to be turned in by that "friend"—he's collected a bounty for turning you in.) Bring prescription drugs in their original containers. If possible, pack a copy of the original prescription with the generic name of the drug.

U.S. Customs officials are also on the lookout for diet drugs that are sold in Mexico but are illegal in the U.S. If you buy antibiotics over the counter (which you can do in Mexico)—say, for a sinus infection—and still have some left, you probably won't be hassled by U.S. Customs.

Drugstores Drugstores (farmacias) will sell you just about anything you want, with a prescription or without one. Most drugstores are open Monday through Saturday from 8am to 8pm. There are generally one or two 24-hour pharmacies in each major resort area. If you are in a smaller town and need to buy medicines after normal hours, ask for the *farmacia de turno*; pharmacies take turns staying open during off-hours.

Electricity The electrical system in Mexico is 110 volts A/C (60 cycles), as in the United States and Canada. However, in reality it may cycle more slowly and overheat your appliances. To compensate, select a medium or low speed for hair dryers. Many older hotels still have electrical outlets for flat two-prong plugs; you'll need an adapter for any modern electrical apparatus that has an enlarged end on one prong or that has three prongs. Many first-class and deluxe hotels have the three-holed outlets (*trifásicos* in Spanish). Those that don't may have loan adapters, but to be sure, it's always better to carry your own.

Embassies/Consulates They provide valuable lists of doctors and lawyers, as well as regulations concerning marriages in Mexico. Contrary to popular belief, your embassy cannot get you out of a Mexican jail, provide postal or banking services, or fly you home when you run out of money. Consular officers can provide you with advice on most matters and problems, however. Most countries have a representative embassy in Mexico City, and many have consular offices or representatives in the provinces.

The Embassy of the United States in Mexico City is next to the Hotel María Isabel Sheraton at Paseo de la Reforma 305, at the corner of Río Danubio (© 5/209-9100). There is a U.S. Consulate General in Guadalajara, Progreso 175 (© 3/825-2998); and a consular agency in Puerto Vallarta (© 3/222-0069).

The Embassy of Canada in Mexico City is at Schiller 529, in Polanco (© 5/724-7900); it's open Monday through Friday from 9am to 1pm and 2 to 5pm (at other times the name of a duty officer is posted on the embassy door). Additionally, Canada has consular services in Guadalajara (© 3/615-6215) and in Puerto Vallarta at Zaragoza 160, 1st floor (© 3/222-5398).

The Embassy of the United Kingdom in Mexico City is in Río Lerma 71, Col. Cuahutemoc (© 5/207-2089 or 5/207-7672; www.embajadabritanica.com.mx); it's open Monday through Friday from 8:30am to 3:30pm. There's also a UK consular office in Guadalajara (© 3/761-6405).

Irish and South African citizens must go to the British Consulate.

The Embassy of New Zealand in Mexico City is at José Luis Lagrange 103, 10th floor, Col. Los Morales Polanco (© 5/281-5486; kiwimexico@compuserve.com.mx); it's open Monday through Thursday from 9am to 2pm and 3 to 5pm, and Friday from 9am to 2pm.

Emergencies The 24-hour Tourist Help Line in Mexico City is © 800/903-9200 or 5/250-0151. A tourist legal assistance office (Procuraduría del Turista) is located in Mexico City (© 5/625-8153 or 5/625-8154). Though the phones are frequently busy, they do offer 24-hour service, and there is always an English-speaking person available.

Internet Access In large cities and resort areas a growing number of hotels offer Internet access. You'll also find at least one cybercafe. Note that many ISPs will automatically cut off your Internet connection after a specified period of time (say, 10 min.), because telephone lines are at a premium. Some Telmex offices also have free access Internet kiosks in their reception areas.

Legal Aid International Legal Defense Counsel, 111 S. 15th St., 24th Floor, Packard Building, Philadelphia, PA 19102 (© 215/977-9982), is a law firm specializing in legal difficulties of Americans abroad. See also "Embassies/Consulates" and "Emergencies," above.

Liquor Laws The legal drinking age in Mexico is 18; however, it is extremely rare that anyone will be asked for ID or denied purchase. Grocery stores sell everything from beer and wine to national and imported liquors. Authorities are beginning to target drunk drivers more aggressively. It's a good idea to drive defensively.

Mail Postage for a postcard or letter is 59¢; it may arrive anywhere between 1 to 6 weeks later. A registered letter costs $1.90. To send a package can be quite expensive—the Mexican Postal service charges $8.00 per kilo (2.20 lbs.)—and unreliable; it takes between 2 and 6 weeks, if it arrives at all. Packages are frequently lost within the Mexican postal system, although the situation has improved in recent years. The recommended way to send a package or important mail continues to be through Federal Express, DHL, UPS, or any other reputable international mail service.

Newspapers/Magazines In Puerto Vallarta, the English-language *Vallarta Today* is published daily, and the *Tribune* is published weekly. The *Guadalajara Reporter* is an excellent English-language weekly that also has a Puerto Vallarta supplement. Newspaper kiosks will also carry a selection of English-language magazines.

Police In Mexico City, police are to be suspected as frequently as they are to be trusted; however, you'll find many who are quite honest and helpful. In the rest of the country, especially in the tourist areas, the majority are very protective of international visitors. Several cities, including Puerto Vallarta, have gone as far as to set up a special corps of English-speaking Tourist Police to assist with directions, guidance, and more.

Taxes There's a 15% IVA tax on goods and services in most of Mexico, and it's supposed to be included in the posted price. There is an exit tax of around $18 imposed on every foreigner leaving the country, usually included in the price of airline tickets.

Telephone/Fax As this book went to press, Mexico announced a country-wide change in area codes that will affect every phone number in this book. For more information, please see the box "Changes in Mexico's Phone Numbers Announced," earlier in this chapter. Unfortunately, courtesy messages telling you that the number you dialed has been changed do not exist. You can call operator assistance (040) for difficult-to-reach numbers. Many fax numbers are also regular telephone numbers; you have to ask whoever answers your call for the fax tone ("*tono de fax, por favor*").

Cellular phones are becoming more and more popular for small businesses. To dial a cellular number inside the same area code, dial 044 and then the number. To dial the cellular phone from anywhere else in Mexico, first dial 01, and then the 8-digit number. To dial it from the U.S., just dial 011-52 plus the 8-digit number.

The country code for Mexico is 52. International long-distance calls to the United States or Canada are accessed by dialing ⓒ **001** and then the area code and seven-digit number. You can reach an AT&T operator by dialing ⓒ **01-800-288-2872**, MCI by dialing ⓒ **01-800-021-8000**, Sprint by dialing ⓒ **001-800-877-8000**, and British Telecom (BT) by dialing

℃ **01-800-123-0244** (pay phones may sometimes require a coin deposit). To make a person-to-person or collect call to outside of Mexico, dial ℃ **090.** For other international dialing codes, dial the operator at ℃ **040.** Other international long distance calls to Europe, Africa, and Asia are accessed by dialing ℃ **00,** then the country code, the city code, and the number. For further assistance dial ℃ **090.**

Time Zone Central standard time prevails throughout most of Mid-Pacific Mexico, but the state of Nayarit, including Nuevo Vallarta, is on Mountain Standard Time. Mexico observes daylight saving time, but during 2001, changed the dates of its observation to be from the first Sunday in May to the last Sunday in October. It is not known if this new custom will continue, or if they will revert to observing the same dates as the U.S. and Canada once again.

Tipping Most service employees in Mexico count on tips for the majority of their income—especially true for bellboys and waiters. Bellboys should receive the equivalent of 50¢ to $1US per bag; waiters generally receive 10% to 20% depending on the level of service. In Mexico, it is not customary to tip taxi drivers, unless they are hired by the hour, or provide touring or other special services.

Water Most hotels have decanters or bottles of purified water in the rooms, and the better hotels have either purified water from regular taps or special taps marked agua purificada. Some hotels will charge for in-room bottled water. Virtually any hotel, restaurant, or bar will bring you purified water if you specifically request it, but you'll usually be charged for it. Bottled purified water is sold widely at drugstores and grocery stores (popular brands include Santa Maria, Ciel, Agua Pura, Pureza, and Bonafit). Evian and other imported brands are widely available.

2

Settling into Puerto Vallarta

Puerto Vallarta was never the "sleepy little fishing village" that many proclaim. It began life as a port for processing silver brought down from mines in the Sierra Madre—then was forever transformed by a movie director and two star-crossed lovers. In 1963 John Huston brought stars Ava Gardner and Richard Burton here to film the Tennessee Williams play *Night of the Iguana*. Burton's new love, Elizabeth Taylor, came along to ensure the romance remained in full bloom—despite the fact both were married to others at the time. Titillated, the international paparazzi arrived, and when they weren't shooting photos of the famous couple—or of Ava Gardner water-skiing back from the set, surrounded by a bevy of beach boys—they photographed the beauty of Puerto Vallarta. This seaside town was never the same, and the later additions of a highway and airport helped it mature into the resort it is today.

Luxury hotels and shopping centers have sprung up to the north and south of the original town, allowing Vallarta to grow to a sizable city of 250,000 without sacrificing its considerable charms. Today, it boasts the services and infrastructure of a modern city as well as the authenticity of a colonial Mexican village.

Cool breezes flow down from the mountains along the Río Cuale, which runs through the center of town. The main waterfront street, or *malecón,* is graced with fanciful public sculptures and bordered by lively restaurants, shops, and bars. The *malecón* is a magnet for both residents and visitors, who stroll the broad walkway to take in an ocean breeze, a multihued sunset, or a moonlit, perfect wave.

If I sound partial, it's not just because Puerto Vallarta is my favorite of Mexico's sunny resorts; this has been my home for the past 10 years. I live here in good company—there's a considerable colony of American and Canadian residents. Perhaps they feel as I do, that the surrounding mountains offer the equivalent of a continual, comforting embrace, adding to that sense of welcome that so many visitors feel as well.

Tips **Watch for Area Code Changes**

As this book went to press, Mexico announced a country-wide change in its long-distance area codes. The new plan will affect every phone number in this book; for details, please consult the box "Changes to Mexico's Phone Numbers Announced," in chapter 1.

1 Puerto Vallarta Essentials

620 miles (1000km) NW of Mexico City; 260 miles (419km) W of Guadalajara; 175 miles (282km) NW of Manzanillo

GETTING THERE & DEPARTING

BY PLANE For a list of international carriers serving Mexico, see chapter 1. Some local numbers of international carriers serving Puerto Vallarta are **Alaska Airlines** (© 3/221-1350 or 3/221-1353), **American Airlines** (© 3/221-1799), **America West** (© 3/221-1333 or 001/880-235-9292 inside Mexico), and **Continental** (© 3/221-1025).

From other points in Mexico, **Aeromexico** (© 3/224-2777 or 3/221-1055) flies from Aguascalientes, Guadalajara, La Paz, León, Mexico City, Morelia, and Tijuana. **Mexicana** (© 3/224-8900 or 3/221-1266) has direct or nonstop flights from Guadalajara, Mazatlán, and Mexico City.

BY CAR The coastal **Highway 200** is the only choice between Mazatlán to the north (6 hr. away) or Manzanillo to the south (3½–4 hr.). The 6-hour journey from Guadalajara through Tepic can be shortened to 4 to 5 hours by taking Highway 15A from Chapalilla to Compostela (this bypasses Tepic and saves as much as 2 hr.), then continuing south on Highway 200 to Puerto Vallarta.

BY BUS The bus station, **Central Camionera de Puerto Vallarta,** opened in early 1998 and has centralized bus travel in and out of Puerto Vallarta. Located just north of the airport, approximately 7 miles from downtown, it offers ticketing, long-distance telephone, restaurants, overnight guarded parking, baggage storage, and local transportation into town. A large, marble-floored waiting area offers ample seating in air-conditioned comfort. Most major first-class bus lines operate from here, with transportation to points throughout Mexico including Mazatlán, Tepic, Manzanillo,

Guadalajara, and Mexico City. Taxis into town cost approximately $7 and are readily available; public buses have a regular stop in front of the arrivals hall, operating from 7am to 11pm.

ORIENTATION

ARRIVING BY PLANE   The airport is close to the north end of town near the Marina Vallarta, about six miles from downtown. **Transportes Terrestres** minivans and **Aeromovil** taxis make the trip. Costs for both are determined by zones—clearly posted at the respective ticket booths. Fares start at $8 for a ride to Marina Vallarta and go up to $25 for a trip to the south shore hotels. **Airport taxis** are federally licensed taxis that operate exclusively to provide transportation from the airport. Their fares are almost three times as high as city (yellow) taxis. A trip to downtown Puerto Vallarta costs $12, whereas a return trip using a city taxi costs only $4.50. Yellow cabs are restricted to picking up passengers leaving the airport. However, if you don't have too much baggage, you can cross the highway via the new overpass, and there you'll find yellow cabs lined up and ready to take you anywhere for a third of the price of the airport cabs.

VISITOR INFORMATION   The **Municipal Tourism Office,** at Juárez and Independencia (© **3/223-2500,** ext. 230; ask for the Tourism Office), is in a corner of the white Presidencia Municipal building (city hall) on the northwest end of the main square. In addition to offering a listing of current events and a collection of promotional brochures for local activities and services, they can also assist with specific questions—there's usually an English-speaking person on staff. This is also the office of the tourist police. It's open Monday through Friday from 9am to 8pm. During low season it has been known to close for lunch between 1 and 3pm or 2 and 4pm.

The **State Tourism Office,** at Plaza Marina L 144, 2nd floor (© **3/221-2676,** 3/221-2677, or 3/221-2678), also offers promotional brochures and can assist with specific questions about Puerto Vallarta and other points within the state of Jalisco, including Guadalajara, the Costa Alegre, and the town of Tequila. It's open Monday through Friday from 9am to 7pm and Saturday from 9am to 1pm.

CITY LAYOUT   The seaside promenade is called the *malecón,* and is frequently used as a reference point for giving directions. It borders the street **Paseo Díaz Ordaz,** which runs north to south through the central downtown area. From the waterfront, the town stretches back

Puerto Vallarta: Hotel Zone & Beaches

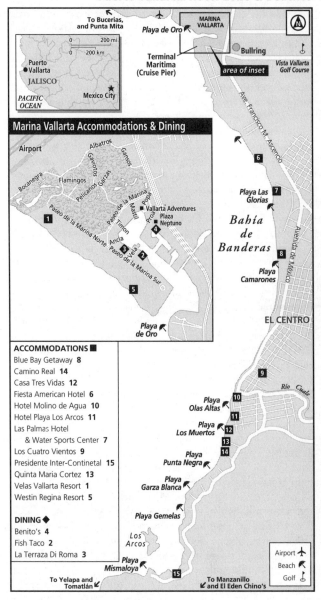

Marina Vallarta Accommodations & Dining

ACCOMMODATIONS ■

Blue Bay Getaway **8**
Camino Real **14**
Casa Tres Vidas **12**
Fiesta American Hotel **6**
Hotel Molino de Agua **10**
Hotel Playa Los Arcos **11**
Las Palmas Hotel
    & Water Sports Center **7**
Los Cuatro Vientos **9**
Presidente Inter-Continental **15**
Quinta Maria Cortez **13**
Velas Vallarta Resort **1**
Westin Regina Resort **5**

DINING ◆

Benito's **4**
Fish Taco **2**
La Terraza Di Roma **3**

into the hills a half-dozen blocks. The areas bordering the **Río Cuale** are the oldest parts of town—the original Puerto Vallarta. The area immediately south of the river, called **Olas Altas** after its main street (and sometimes Los Muertos after the beach of the same name), is now home to a growing selection of sidewalk cafes, fine restaurants, espresso bars, and hip nightclubs, many with live music. Once you're in the center of town, you'll find nearly everything within walking distance both north and south of the river. The two sections of downtown are linked by **bridges** on Insurgentes (northbound traffic) and Ignacio Vallarta (southbound traffic).

Beyond downtown, Puerto Vallarta has grown along the beach to the north and south. Linking downtown to the airport is **avenida Francisco Medina Ascencio** (sometimes still referred to by its previous name, Avenida de las Palmas). Along this main thoroughfare are many luxury hotels (in an area called the **Zona Hotelera,** or Hotel Zone), plus several shopping centers with casual restaurants.

Marina Vallarta, a resort city within a city, is at the northern edge of the Hotel Zone not far from the airport—you pass it on the right as you come into town from the airport. It boasts the most modern luxury hotels plus condominiums and residential homes, a huge marina with 450 yacht slips, a golf course, restaurants and bars, a water park, and several shopping plazas. Because the area began life as a swamp, filled in for development, the beaches are the least desirable in the area, with darker sand and seasonal inflows of cobblestones. They are, however, more than made up for by exquisite pools at the oceanfront hotels. Here, you're on a peninsula facing the bay and looking south to the town of Puerto Vallarta—yet feeling like a world apart.

Nuevo Vallarta is a planned resort, north of the airport, across the Ameca River in the state of Nayarit (about 8 miles north of downtown). It also has hotels, condominiums, and a yacht marina, but very little in the way of restaurants, shopping, or other attractions. (Although a new shopping mall opened in mid-2000, so far, it's done little to change this.) Most hotels there are all-inclusive, and guests usually plan to travel the distance into Puerto Vallarta (about a $15 cab ride) for anything other than poolside or beach action—however, these hotels do enjoy some of the finest beaches in the bay. There is regularly scheduled public bus service for about $1.20, which runs until 10pm.

Bucerías, a small beachfront village of cobblestoned streets, villas, and small hotels, is farther north along Banderas Bay, 19 miles beyond the airport. Past Bucerías, following the curved coastline of

Banderas Bay, is **Punta Mita.** Once a truly rustic village of fishermen and bamboo houses, it is in the process of development as a luxury destination of its own identity—in the works are a total of five super-exclusive luxury boutique resorts, private villas, and three golf courses. The site of an ancient celestial observatory, you cannot imagine a more exquisite setting, with white sand beaches and clear waters—a departure from other beaches in the area.

Going in the other direction from downtown is the southern coastal highway, home to more luxury hotels. Immediately south of town lies the exclusive residential and rental district of **Conchas Chinas.** Six miles south, on **Playa Mismaloya** (where *Night of the Iguana* was filmed), lies the Jolla de Mismaloya Resort. There's no road servicing the southern shoreline of Banderas Bay, but three small coastal villages are popular attractions for visitors to Puerto Vallarta: **Las Ánimas, Quimixto,** and **Yelapa,** all accessible only by boat. Many mistakenly believe these are islands; they are actually located along the same coast. Yelapa, located on a beautiful sheltered cove, has been a popular haven for long-term ex-pat visitors and artists due to its seclusion, natural beauty, and simplicity of life. Offering a selection of primitive accommodations, Yelapa—which has only solar-powered electricity—also offers beachside restaurants and hikes to one of two jungle waterfalls. Quimixto and Las Ánimas are popular day excursions aboard tour boats or water taxis. The tiny, pristine cove of **Caletas,** site of John Huston's former home, is a popular day or nighttime excursion (see "Boat Tours," in chapter 3).

GETTING AROUND

BY TAXI Taxis are plentiful and relatively inexpensive. Most trips from downtown to the northern Hotel Zone and Marina Vallarta cost between $3.50 and $5; to or from Marina Vallarta to Mismaloya Beach to the south costs $8. Rates are charged by zone, and are generally posted in the lobbies of hotels. Taxis can also be hired by the hour or day for longer trips, when you'd prefer to leave the driving to someone else. Rates run between $10 and $12 per hour, with discounts available for full-day rates—consider this as an alternative to renting a car.

BY CAR Rental cars are available at the airport and through travel agencies, but unless you're planning a distant side trip, don't bother. Car rentals are expensive, averaging $60 per day, and parking around town is difficult. If you see a sign for a $10 jeep rental, or $20 car rental, be aware that these are lures to get people to attend

---

Tips Steer Clear of the Rambo Bus!

Buses in Vallarta tend to be rather aggressive, and some even sport names—including "Terminator," "Rambo," and "Tornado." Don't tempt fate by assuming these buses will stop for pedestrians. Although Vallarta is an extremely low-crime city, bus accidents are frequent—and frequently fatal.

---

timeshare presentations. Unless you are interested in a timeshare, stopping to inquire will be a waste of your time.

BY BUS & *COLECTIVO*   City buses are easy to navigate and inexpensive. They run from the airport through the Hotel Zone along Morelos Street (1 block inland from the *malecón*), across the Río Cuale, and inland on Vallarta, looping back through the downtown hotel and restaurant districts on Insurgentes and several other downtown streets. To get to the northern hotel strip from old Puerto Vallarta, take the Zona Hoteles, Ixtapa, or Las Juntas bus. These same buses may also post the names of hotels they pass, such as Krystal, Fiesta Americana, Sheraton, and others. Buses marked MARINA VALLARTA will travel inside this area, stopping at the major hotels there. These buses, costing about 30¢, will serve just about all your transportation needs frequently and inexpensively.

Buses run generally from 6am to 11pm, and it's rare to wait more than a few minutes for one. Another bus route travels south every 10 to 15 minutes to either Mismaloya Beach or Boca de Tomatlán (the destination will be indicated in the front window) from Plaza Lázaro Cárdenas, a few blocks south of the river at Cárdenas and Suárez, and along Basilio Badillo, between Piño Suárez and Insurgentes.

BY BOAT   The cruise ship pier (*muelle*), also called Terminal Marítima, is where **excursion boats** to Yelapa, Las Ánimas, Quimixto, and the Marietas Islands depart. It's north of town near the airport and an inexpensive taxi or bus ride from town. Just take any bus marked IXTAPA, LAS JUNTAS, PITILLAL, or AURORA and tell the driver to let you off at the Terminal Marítima. *Note:* Odd though it may seem, there is a $1.50 fee that must be paid to access the pier—and your departing excursion boat.

Water taxis offering direct transportation to Yelapa, Las Ánimas, and Quimixto leave at 10:30 and 11am from the pier at Los Muertos Beach (south of downtown) on Rodolfo Rodríguez next to the Hotel Marsol. Another water taxi departs at 11am from the beachfront pier

---

 Don't Let Taxi Drivers Steer You the Wrong Way

Beware of restaurant recommendations offered by taxi drivers—many receive a commission from restaurants where they discharge passengers. Be especially wary if a driver tries to talk you out of a restaurant you've already selected.

---

at the northern edge of the *malecón.* A round-trip ticket to Yelapa (the farthest point) costs $12. Return trips usually depart between 3 and 4pm, but confirm the pickup time with your water taxi captain. Other water taxis depart from Boca de Tomatlán, located about 30 minutes south of town by public bus. These water taxis are the better option if you want more flexible departure and return times from the southern beaches. Generally, they leave on the hour for the southern shore destinations, or more frequently if there is traffic. Price is about $10 round-trip, with rates now clearly posted on a sign on the beach. A private boat taxi can be hired for between $35 and $50 (depending on your destination), allowing you to choose your own return time. They'll take up to eight people for that price, so often people band together at the beach to hire one.

 ### Fast Facts: Puerto Vallarta

American Express The local office is located in town at Morelos 660, at the corner of Abasolo (© **01-800/333-3211** in Mexico, or 3/223-2955). It's open Monday through Friday from 9am to 6pm and Saturday from 9am to 1pm, and offers excellent, efficient travel agency services in addition to money exchange and traveler's checks.

Area Code As this book went to press, Mexico was preparing for a wholesale change to the country's area codes. Puerto Vallarta's area code is slated to change from **3** (old) to **322** (new). But don't be confused; almost every seven-digit local number in Vallarta begins with "22," so if you were dialing a Puerto Vallarta number from outside the area code, you would first dial the area code (322) and then the local number (22X-XXXX). To compound the confusion, back in 1999 phone numbers abruptly changed from five to seven digits with the addition of the "22." This means people still frequently quote five-digit numbers, so just add a "22" at the beginning to get the local seven-digit phone number. For more information, see the box "Changes to Mexico's Phone Numbers Announced," in chapter 1.

Climate It's warm all year, with tropical temperatures; however, evenings and early mornings in the winter months can turn quite cool. Summers are sunny, but with an increase in humidity during the rainy season, between May and October. Rains come almost every afternoon in June and July, and are usually brief, but strong—just enough to cool off the air for evening activities. September is the month in which heat and humidity are least comfortable and rains are the heaviest.

Consumer Assistance Tourists with complaints about taxis, stores, abusive timeshare presentations, or other matters should contact **PROFECO,** the consumer protection office (© **3/225-0000** or 3/225-0018). The office is open Monday through Friday from 9am to 5pm.

Currency Exchange Banks are found throughout downtown and in the other prime shopping areas of Vallarta. Most banks are open Monday through Friday from 9am to 5pm, with partial-day hours on Saturday. ATMs are commonly found throughout Vallarta, including the central plaza downtown, and are increasingly becoming the most favorable way to exchange currency, as they offer bank rates plus 24-hour self-service convenience. Money exchange houses (*casas de cambio*) are also located throughout town and offer longer hours than the banks with only slightly lower exchange rates.

Embassies/Consulates Both the U.S. and Canadian consulates maintain offices here, in the building on the southern border of the central plaza (you'll see the U.S. and Canadian flags). The **U.S. Consular Agency** office (© **3/222-0069;** fax 3/ 223-0074, 24 hours a day for emergencies) is open Monday through Friday 10am to 2pm. The **Canadian Consulate** (© **3/ 222-5398** or 3/223-0858; 24-hr. emergency line 01-800-706-2900) is open Monday through Friday from 9am to 5pm.

Emergencies Police emergency, © 060; **local police,** © 3/ 221-2588 or 3/221-0759; **intensive care ambulance,** © 3/ 225-0386 (*note:* English-speaking assistance is not always available at this number); **Ameri-Med Urgent Care** (U.S.-standards health care service, available 24 hr.), © 3/221-0023 (fax 3/221-0026; www.amerimed-hospitals.com); the new San Javier Marina Hospital (also with U.S.-standards health care service, available 24 hr.), ⓒ 3/226-1010; **Red Cross,** ⓒ 3/222-1533.

Internet Access Puerto Vallarta is probably the best cyberconnected destination in Mexico. Of the numerous cybercafes around town, one of the most popular is **The Net House,** Ignacio L. Vallarta 232, two blocks past the southbound bridge (ⓒ 3/222-6953; info@vallartacafes.com), open daily from 7am to 2am. Rates are $4 per hour, and there are 21 computers with fast connections and English keyboards. **Café Net** (ⓒ 3/222-0092) has become a social hub, located at 250 Olas Altas, at the corner of Basilio Badillo. Rates run $2 for 30 minutes, and there are also complete computer services, a full bar, and food service. It's open daily from 8am to 2am. Some hotels are also offering e-mail kiosks in their lobbies, but this is a more expensive option than the Net cafes.

Newspapers & Magazines Vallarta Today, a daily English-language newspaper (ⓒ 3/225-3323 or 3/224-2829), is a good source for local information and upcoming events. The quarterly city magazine *Vallarta Lifestyles* (ⓒ 3/221-0106) is also very popular, but provides listings only of services that advertise, so is not comprehensive. Both are available for sale at area newsstands and hotel gift shops. The weekly *P.V. Tribune* (ⓒ 3/223-0585) is distributed free throughout town and offers a more objective local viewpoint.

Pharmacies (late night) **CMQ Farmacia,** Basilio Badillo 365 (ⓒ 3/222-1330), is open 24 hours and can also deliver to your hotel free of charge with a minimum purchase of $10. **Farmacia Guadalajara,** Emiliano Zapata 232 (ⓒ 3/224-1811), is also open 24 hours a day.

Post Office The post office (*correo*) is at Mina 188 (ⓒ 3/222-1888). It's open Monday through Friday from 9am to 6:30pm, Saturday from 9am to 1pm.

Safety Puerto Vallarta enjoys a very low crime rate. Public transportation is perfectly safe to use, and Tourist Police (dressed in white safari uniforms with white hats) are available to answer questions, give directions, and offer assistance. Most crime or encounters with the police are linked to using or purchasing drugs—so simply don't do it (see chapter 1). *Note:* the tourist police are making a more frequent habit of conducting random personal searches for drugs. Although there is some question about their right to do this, the best course of action if they want to frisk you is to comply—as objecting will likely result in a free tour of the local jail. Report any unusual incidents to the local consular office.

2 Where To Stay

Beyond a varied selection of hotels, Puerto Vallarta has many other types of accommodations. Oceanfront or marina-view condominiums or elegant private villas are also available; both can offer a better value and more ample space for families or small groups. For more information on short-term rentals, check out www. virtualvallarta.com, where a wide array of rental options are available. Prices start at $99 a night for non-beachfront condos and go to $1,000 for penthouse condos or private villas. **Vicki Skinner's Doin' it Right in Puerto Vallarta** (© **800/936-3646** or 619/ 297-3642; e-mail: GayPVR@aol.com) is a special service that rents gay-friendly condos and villas for individuals and groups (up to 75 people) and can package private chef and tour services with accommodations.

The following listings of the hotels are provided in directional order, moving south along Banderas Bay from the airport.

MARINA VALLARTA

Marina Vallarta is the most modern and deluxe area of hotel development in Puerto Vallarta. Located immediately south of the airport and just north of the Maritime (cruise-ship) Terminal, it's a planned development whose centerpiece is a 450-slip modern marina. The boardwalk surrounding the marina is filled with excellent restaurants, bars, galleries, and shops. A stay here is a world apart from the quaintness of downtown Puerto Vallarta.

The hotels reviewed below are located on the beachfront of the peninsula. The beaches here are much less attractive than beaches in other parts of the bay; the sand is darker and firmly packed, and, during certain times of the year, also quite rocky. The hotels in this zone make up for this shortfall with oversized pool areas and exotic landscaping. Still, if you're longing for a beautiful beach, try one of the southern hotel options. This area is better for families or for those looking for lots of centralized activity. Marina Vallarta is also home to an 18-hole **golf course** designed by Joe Finger and the **Mayan Palace Aquapark** (© **3/221-1500,** ext. 824), with water slides and tubes, pools, inner-tube canal, and snack-bar facilities. Open to the public daily from 11am to 6pm, it costs $15 for adults, $12 for kids, and is across from the Mayan Palace Resort.

In addition to the hotels reviewed below, another reliable choice is the **Hacienda Cora,** located on the golf course at Pelicanos 311 (© **3/221-0800;** fax 3/221-0801). This elegant, boutique-style hotel has extra-large rooms plus an on-site Spa, and lovely pool with shade cabanas. High season rates average $285.

Because of traffic, more than distance, a taxi from the Marina to downtown takes 20 to 30 minutes.

Velas Vallarta Grand Suite Resort 🌟🌟🌟 *Kids* The beachfront Velas Vallarta is an excellent choice for families since each suite offers a full-size, fully equipped kitchen, ample living and dining areas, separate bedroom(s), and a large balcony with seating. The apartments are tastefully decorated with light wood furnishings, cool terrazzo floors, bright fabrics, and marble tub/shower-combination bathrooms. This property is actually part hotel, part full-ownership condominiums, which means each suite is the size of a true residential unit, offering the feeling of a home away from home. The suites all have partial ocean views, as they face onto a central area where three freeform swimming pools, complete with bridges and waterfalls, meander through tropical gardens. A full range of services—including restaurants, minimarket, deli, tennis courts, spa, and boutiques—means you'd never need to leave the place if you didn't want to. The Marina Vallarta Golf Club is across the street, and special packages are available to Velas guests.

Paseo de la Marina 485, Marina Vallarta, Puerto Vallarta, Jal., 48354. © **800/ 659-8477** in the U.S. and Canada, or 3/221-0091. Fax 3/221-0755. www.velas vallarta.com. 361 units. High season $220 double, $300–$540 suite; low season $150 double, $220–$380 suite. AE, DC, MC, V. Free indoor parking. **Amenities:** Two restaurants, poolside snackbar, lobby bar; pool; golf privileges at Marina Vallarta Golf Club; three lighted tennis courts; fitness center with spa and massage services; beachfront with watersports equipment rental; bicycle rentals; activities program for children and adults; car rental; concierge; travel agency; new, expansive meeting facility with its own catering kitchen; salon; room service; laundry; minimarket; deli. *In room:* A/C, TV, dataport, full kitchen with coffeemaker, hair dryers, irons, safe.

Westin Regina Resort 🌟🌟🌟 Stunning architecture and vibrant colors are the hallmark of this award-winning property, considered Puerto Vallarta's finest. Although the grounds are large—over 21 acres with 850 feet of beachfront—the warm service and gracious hospitality is more befitting of an intimate resort. The central freeform pool is spectacular with hundreds of tall palms surrounding it. Frequently you'll find hammocks strung between the palms closest to the beach, where there's a wooden playground for kids. Rooms are contemporary in style, brightly colored in textured fabrics with oversize wood furnishings, tile floors, original art, tub/shower-combination bathrooms, and in-room safes. Balconies have panoramic views. Eight junior suites have whirlpools, and the five grand suites and presidential suite are two-level, with ample living areas. Two floors of rooms are designated as their Royal Beach Club, with VIP services, including private concierge, plush bathrobes, continental breakfast, newspaper, cocktails, and canapés. The fitness center here is one of the most modern, well-equipped facilities of its kind in Vallarta.

Paseo de la Marina Sur 205, Marina Vallarta, Puerto Vallarta, Jal., 48321. © 800/228-3000 in the U.S., or 3/221-1100. Fax 3/221-1121. www.westinpv.com. 280 units. High season $195–$295 double, $415–$520 suite; low season $160–170 double, $335–$420 suite. AE, DC, MC, V. Free parking. **Amenities:** Two restaurants, two poolside bars, lobby bar; oceanside pool; golf privileges at Marina Vallarta Golf Club; three grass tennis courts (lighted for night play); full-service state-of-the-art health club with treadmills, Stairmasters, resistance equipment, sauna, steam room, solarium, whirlpool, massage services, and salon; Kid's Club; travel agency; car rental; shopping arcade; 24-hour room service; laundry. *In room:* A/C, TV, dataport, minibar, coffeemaker, hair dryer, iron, safe deposit boxes.

THE HOTEL ZONE

The main street running between the airport and town is named avenida Francisco Medina Ascencio, but is commonly referred to as avenida de las Palmas, for the stately palm trees that line the dividing strip. The hotels built along this road were the result of the tourism boom that Vallarta enjoyed in the early 1980s, and most have been exceptionally well maintained. All offer excellent, wide beachfronts with generally tranquil waters for swimming. From here it's a quick taxi or bus ride into downtown Vallarta.

Blue Bay Getaway *Value*   The newest hotel in Vallarta, this all-inclusive hotel caters to adults only and has an outstanding location just minutes from town on a wide, beautiful stretch of beach. It's also an exceptional value, with all meals, beverages, activities, and entertainment included in the price of your room. Blue Bay is becoming known for really working to offer good value for all-inclusive stays—the buffets are varied, and you have the option of an a la carte restaurant.

Three types of rooms are available, but all are decorated in sunny golden and yellow hues with vibrant blue accents. The four-story Coral tower has the best rooms (double superior), with tile floors, small balconies with ocean or mountain views, and bathrooms with showers and tubs. The 11-story Arcos tower houses the deluxe and standard rooms. Deluxe rooms in the Arcos tower are the most spacious, with private balconies and ocean views. The standard rooms are the least expensive and are smaller, do not have balconies, and have showers without tubs. These rooms offer mountain views only, through small, curtained windows, but are a great value, especially since you probably won't spend too much time in your room, with all the activities they offer.

It's next door to the Sheraton Buganvilias. Guests staying at the Blue Bay Getaway may also enjoy the facilities at the Blue Bay Club, located on the southern shore of Puerto Vallarta. Shuttles run between the two resorts every hour. The Sheraton is larger, offers family activities and a disco, but doesn't have as nice of a beach as the Getaway has.

Av. Francisco Medina Ascencio km 1.5, Puerto Vallarta, Jal. 48330 ℂ 3/223-3600. Fax 3/223-3601. www.bluebayresorts.com. 358 units. High season $115 per person double standard, $125 per person double superior, $130 per person deluxe, all-inclusive; low season $80 per person double standard, $90 per person double superior, $95 per person deluxe, all-inclusive. AE, MC, V. Ample free parking. Adults only. **Amenities:** Two restaurants, snack bar, five bars, plus nightly entertainment and shows; large beachfront pool with activities, plus smaller quieter pool with wet bar; tennis court; spa with sauna, whirlpool tub, and massage service; non-motorized water-sports equipment; bikes; tour desk; car-rental desk; gift shop and small shopping strip with art and crafts shops; salon; laundry and dry cleaning services. *In room:* A/C, TV, hair dryer. Safe deposit boxes in the reception area are free of charge; in-room safe deposit boxes are available for a daily $2 charge.

Fiesta Americana Puerto Vallarta ⊛ The Fiesta Americana's towering, three-story, thatched *palapa* lobby is a landmark in the Hotel Zone, and the hotel is known for its excellent beach and friendly service. An abundance of plants, splashing fountains, constant breezes, and comfortable sitting areas in the lobby evoke a casual South Seas ambience. The nine-story terra-cotta–colored building embraces a large plaza with a pool facing the beach. Marble-trimmed rooms in neutral tones with pastel accents come with carved headboards and comfortable rattan and wicker furniture. All have private balconies with ocean and pool views.

Av. Francisco Medina Ascencio km 2.5, Puerto Vallarta, Jal., 48300. ℂ 800/FIESTA-1 in the U.S., or 3/224-2010. Fax 3/224-2108. www.fiestaamericana.com. 291 units. High season $180 double, $250–$700 suite; low season $120–$160 double, $180–$430 suite. AE, DC, MC, V. Limited free parking. **Amenities:** Three restaurants, lobby bar with live music nightly; large pool with cushioned lounges and towel service, pool activities; children's activities in high season; travel agency; modern meeting center; salon; room service; laundry. *In room:* A/C, TV, minibar, hair dryers, safes.

DOWNTOWN TO LOS MUERTOS BEACH

This part of town has recently undergone a renaissance; accommodations here are dominated by economically priced hotels and good-value guesthouses. Several blocks off the beach you can find numerous budget inns offering clean, simply furnished rooms; most will discount long-term stays. The neighborhood is older, but very friendly and generally safe. Most of Vallarta's nightlife activity is now centered in the areas south of the Río Cuale and along Olas Altas Avenue.

Hotel Molino de Agua ♠   With an unrivaled location adjacent to both the Río Cuale and the ocean, this hotel is a mix of stone and stucco-walled bungalows and small beachfront buildings, spread out among winding walkways and lush tropical gardens. It's located immediately past the Río Cuale—after crossing the southbound bridge, it's on your right. Although centrally located on a main street, open spaces, big trees, birds, and lyrical fountains lend it tranquillity. The individual bungalows are located in the gardens between the entrance and the ocean. They are well-maintained and simply furnished, with a bed, wooden desk and chair, Mexican tile floors, beamed ceilings, and beautiful tile bathrooms. Wicker rocking chairs grace their private patios. Rooms and suites in the two small two- and three-story buildings on the beach have double beds and private terraces.

Vallarta 130 (Apdo. Postal 54), Puerto Vallarta, Jal., 48380. ℂ 3/222-1957. Fax 3/222-6056. www.molinodeagua.com. 58 units, including bungalows and suites. High season garden bungalows $92, oceanfront rooms and suites $128–$150; low season bungalows $58, suites $83–$95 (all double). AE, MC, V. Free secured parking. **Amenities:** Restaurant/bar; beachside pool, plus a second pool with whirlpool beside the Lion's Court restaurant; tour desk; car-rental desk. *In room:* A/C.

Hotel Playa Los Arcos ♠♠   This is one of Vallarta's perennially popular hotels and a favorite of mine, with a stellar location in the heart of Los Muertos Beach, central to the Olas Altas sidewalk-cafe action and close to downtown. The four-story structure is U-shaped, facing the ocean, with a small swimming pool in the courtyard. Rooms with private balconies overlook the pool, while the 10 suites have ocean views and 5 of these have kitchenettes. The standard rooms are small but pleasantly decorated and immaculate, with carved wooden furniture painted pale pink. On the premises are a *palapa* beachside bar with occasional live entertainment, a gourmet coffee shop, and the popular Maximilian's gourmet restaurant. It's 7 blocks south of the river.

Olas Altas 380, Puerto Vallarta, Jal., 48380. ℂ 800/648-2403 in the U.S., or 3/222-1583. Fax 3/222-2418. www.playalosarcos.com. 175 units. High season

$92–$120 double, $150 suite; low season $65 double, $95 suite. AE, MC, V. Limited street parking available. **Amenities:** Two restaurants, lobby bar; pool; tour desk; car rental services; baby-sitting services; laundry; safe-deposit boxes and money exchange at the front desk. *In room:* A/C, TV.

Los Cuatro Vientos ⍟ This quiet, secluded inn is in the center of downtown on a hillside overlooking Banderas Bay and features rooms built around a small central patio and pool. A short flight of stairs takes you to the second-floor patio, pool, flowering trees, and the cozy Chez Elena restaurant, open in the evenings. The cheerful, spotless, colorful rooms have fans, small tiled bathrooms, brick ceilings, red-tile floors, and glass-louvered windows. Each is decorated with simple Mexican furnishings, folk art, and antiques. The rooftop, with a panoramic view of the city, is great for sunning, and it's the best place in the city for sunset drinks. Continental breakfast is served in the restaurant for guests only from 7 to 11am.

The hotel is favored by solo women travelers, and even offers weeklong "Women's Getaway" packages several times a year, with cultural discussions and recreational activities.

Matamoros 520, Puerto Vallarta, Jal., 48300. ☎ **3/222-0161.** Fax 3/222-2831. www.cuatrovientos.com. 14 units. High season $80 double, $130 suite; low season $55 double, $69 suite (up to 4 people). Rates include continental breakfast. MC, V. Very limited street parking available. **Amenities:** Restaurant, rooftop bar; small courtyard pool.

SOUTH TO MISMALOYA

Camino Real ⍟⍟⍟ The original luxury hotel in Puerto Vallarta, the Camino Real has retained its place as a premier property here despite newer arrivals. Scores of loyal guests think only of staying here, and its free monthly classical concerts (held the first Thurs of each month) have earned an integral place in the local community. It has unquestionably the nicest beach of any Vallarta hotel, with soft white sand in a private cove. Set apart from other properties, with a lush mountain backdrop, it retains the exclusivity that made it popular from the beginning—yet it's only a 5- to 10-minute ride to town. The hotel consists of two buildings: the 250-room main hotel, which curves gently with the shape of the Playa Las Estacas, and a newer 11-story Camino Real Club tower, also facing the beach and ocean. An ample pool fronts the main building, facing the beach. Standard rooms in the main building are large, some with sliding doors opening onto the beach and others with balconies. A two-story Presidential suite in the main building has a large private pool. Royal Beach Club rooms from the sixth floor up feature balconies with whirlpool tubs. The top floor is divided among six two-bedroom Fiesta Suites, each with a private swimming pool. All rooms have the signature vibrant colors of Camino Real hotels. With a new owner, this hotel is scheduled for some major renovations and upgrades over the coming year, though it's remarkably well-maintained as it exists now.

Carretera Barra de Navidad, km 3.5, Playa Las Estacas, Puerto Vallarta, Jal., 48300. © 800/722-6466 in the U.S. and Canada, or 3/221-5000. Fax 3/221-6000. www. caminoreal.com. 337 units. High season $180–$200 double, $500–$1,000 suite; low season $135–$150 double, $400–$880 suite. AE, DC, MC, V. Free secured parking. **Amenities:** Four restaurants, lobby bar, pool bar; swimming pool; beach *palapas* with chair, towel, and dining service; two lighted grass tennis courts; fitness room with weights; children's program during Easter and Christmas vacations; travel agency; car rental; 24-hour room service; laundry. *In room:* A/C, TV, dataport, minibar, hair dryer, iron, safe-deposit boxes.

Casa Tres Vidas 🌟🌟 *Value*   Terraced down a hillside to Conchas Chinas Beach, Casa Tres Vidas is actually three individual villas that make a great—and affordable—place to stay for families or groups of friends. Set on a stunning private cove, Tres Vidas gives you the experience of your own private villa—complete with service staff. Under new ownership since 2000, Tres Vidas has been upgraded in furnishings and amenities, and is an outstanding value for the location—close to town, and with sweeping panoramic views from every room—as well as for the excellent personal service. Each of the three villas has at least two levels, and over 5,000 square feet of mostly open living areas, plus a private swimming pool, heated whirlpool, and air-conditioned bedrooms. The Villa Alta penthouse villa has three bedrooms, plus a rooftop deck with pool and bar. Vida Sol, the center villa, has an 18-foot high domed living room with fireplace, along with graceful arches and columns. Although it has three bedrooms, it can sleep ten, as two of the rooms have two king-size beds in each. Directly on the ocean, Vida Mar is a four-bedroom villa, accommodating eight guests. An added bonus is that gourmet meals are prepared in your villa twice a day—you only pay the cost of the food, and you choose the menu. Casa Tres Vidas is now owned and managed by the same owners of the adjacent Quinta María Cortez, below.

Sagitario 134, Playa Conchas Chinas, Puerto Vallarta, Jal., 48300. © 888-640-8100 or 801/531-8100 in the U.S., or 3/221-5317. Fax 3/221-53-27. www. casatresvidas.com. 3 villas. Prices are per night, for complete villa with services: High season: Villa Alta $510; Villa Sol $485; Villa Mar $510. Low season: Villa Alta $375; Villa Sol $350; Villa Mar $375. Special summer 1-2 bedroom rates are available, three night minimum stay. AE, MC, V. Very limited street parking available. **Amenities:** Two meals per day prepared in your villa; private pool for each villa;

concierge; tour desk; auto rental. *In room:* A/C (bedrooms only), full kitchen facilities, safe deposit boxes.

Presidente Inter-Continental ✿   This hotel is taking the all-inclusive concept upscale. Meals, drinks, and sports are included here—a convenient necessity, as this welcoming hotel is 20 minutes south of Puerto Vallarta, secluded from the activity of town. Backed by a jungle mountain landscape and fronted by a beautiful white-sand beach, the 11-story building is draped in flowering bougainvillea. Deluxe rooms all have large furnished balconies with ocean views, tile floors, white wood furnishings, and muted colored textiles. Marble tub/shower-combination bathrooms are extra large with separate vanity areas. The 19 suites have in-room whirlpools; the three Master suites have two separate bedrooms and whirlpools; and the Presidential suite has its own swimming pool. A large mosaic pool with swim-up bar is on a terrace overlooking the beach, adjacent to the grass tennis court and small fitness room. Guests aren't limited to buffet dining, but can order a la carte from a selection of two restaurants, plus enjoy premium drinks at their choice of bars. It's a top choice for honeymooners looking for romantic seclusion.

Carretera Barra de Navidad, km 8.5, Puerto Vallarta, Jal., 48300. ℂ **800/327-0200** in the U.S., or 3/228-0507. Fax 3/228-0609. www.basshotels.com. 120 units. High season $330–$350 double, $470–$750 suite; low season $260–$300 double, $380–$650 suite. Rates are all-inclusive. AE, DC, MC, V. Limited free parking. **Amenities:** Two restaurants, poolside restaurant/bar; There are also two theme nights every week: a Mexican Fiesta and a poolside barbecue, both with live music. beachfront pool with watersports equipment for rent; lighted grass tennis court; fitness room with sauna and steam; full adults' activities program; year-round Kid's Club; game room; travel agency; car rental; laundry and valet. *In room:* A/C, TV.

Quinta María Cortez ✿✿✿ *(Finds)*   An eclectic, sophisticated, and imaginative B&B on the beach, this is Puerto Vallarta's most original place to stay—and one of Mexico's most memorable inns. Seven large suites, uniquely decorated in antiques, whimsical curios, and original art, all feature a private bathroom, and most include a kitchenette and balcony. Sunny terraces, a small pool, and a central gathering area with fireplace and *palapa*-topped dining area (where an excellent full breakfast is served) occupy different levels of this seven-story house. A rooftop terrace offers yet another alternative for taking in the sun—and is among the very best sunset-watching spots in town. Located on a beautiful cove on Conchas Chinas beach, the rocks just offshore form tranquil tide pools, perfect for wading and snuggling. A terrace fronting the beach supports Roman columns and accommodates chairs for taking in the sunset.

For years this intimate inn was owned and run by a legendary Vallarta resident and Texan named Silver, who welcomed celebrity guests and allowed the house to be used as a location for fashion shoots and several films, including *Revenge,* starring Kevin Costner. The new owners have lovingly maintained its singular sense of style while significantly upgrading amenities and remodeling common areas. The Quinta María wins my highest recommendation (in fact, I enjoyed living here for a few years when it still accepted long-term stays), but admittedly it's not for everyone. Air-conditioned areas are limited, due to the open nature of the suites and common areas, but then, that's a large part of the charm. Breakfast is served under a midlevel thatched-roof area, overlooking the pool and ocean below. Those who love it return year after year, charmed by this remarkable place, and by the consistently gracious service. Not appropriate for children.

Sagitario 132, Playa Conchas Chinas, Puerto Vallarta, Jal., 48300. ℂ **888-640-8100** or 801/536-5850 in the U.S., or 3/221-5317. Fax 3/221-53-27. www.quinta-maria.com. 7 units. High season $150–$250 double; low season $100–$185 double. Rates include breakfast. AE, MC, V. Very limited street parking available. **Amenities:** Breakfast service; small pool; concierge. *In room:* CD players, telephone with dataport, mini-refrigerators, coffeemaker, hair dryer, safe deposit boxes.

3 Where To Dine

Puerto Vallarta has the most exceptional dining scene of any resort town in Mexico. Over 250 restaurants serve cuisine from around the world in addition to fresh seafood and regional dishes. Chefs from France, Switzerland, Germany, Italy, and Argentina have come for visits and then stayed on to open restaurants of their own. In celebration of the diversity of dining experiences available, Vallarta's culinary community hosts a 2-week-long Gourmet Dining Festival as part of its annual SeaFest each November.

Nonetheless, dining is not limited to high-end options—there are plenty of small, family-owned restaurants, local Mexican kitchens, and vegetarian cafes. Vallarta also has its branches of the imported world food-and-fun chains: Hard Rock Cafe, Planet Hollywood, Outback Steakhouse, and even Hooters. I won't bother to review these restaurants, as the consistency and decor are so familiar.

Of the inexpensive local spots, one of the long-standing favorites for light meals and fresh fruit drinks is **Tutifruti,** Morelos 552 (ℂ **3/222-1068**). It's open Monday through Saturday from 8am to 8pm. No credit cards. A favorite for cheap eats is **Archi's,** serving only (great) chargrilled hamburgers, chicken burgers, fish fillet burgers, hot dogs, and homemade fries in a surfer-inspired atmosphere. It's located at Morelos 799 at Pípila, behind Carlos O'Brian's (© 3/222-4383). Open Tuesday through Sunday from 11am to 1am; cash only, and now they deliver, too! An inexpensive, bountiful, and delicious vegetarian lunch buffet is served daily at **Planeta Vegetariano,** Iturbide 270, just down from the main church (© 3/223-3073). The buffet is offered from 11am to 5:30pm, and costs $4.50, no credit cards. A la carte dinners are served from 6 to 10pm. Closed Sundays.

MARINA VALLARTA

Contrary to conventional travel wisdom, most of the best restaurants in the Marina are located in hotels. Especially notable are **Andrea,** at Velas Vallarta for fine Italian cuisine, and **Garibaldi,** on the beachfront of the Westin Regina Resort, for exceptional seafood. (See "Where to Stay," earlier in this chapter for more information.) Other choices are found along the boardwalk bordering the marina yacht harbor. My pick for the best "cheap eats" in the area are the fish tacos served at **Marina Fish Taco,** located in the Las Palmas II commercial center at the eastern entrance to the marina *malecón* (no phone). A variety of fish and seafood tacos are just $1.50 per order. Open Monday through Saturday from noon to 8pm. Also notable is the new **Café Gourmet,** next to the Vallarta Adventure offices in Condominiums Marina Golf, Local 11 (© 3/221-0362). It serves excellent coffee and espresso drinks.

Benitto's 𝕽𝕽 CAFE   Wow! What a sandwich! Benitto's food would be reason enough to come to this tiny yet terrific cafe inside the Plaza Neptuno—but added to this are the original array of sauces and the very personable service. This has quickly become popular with locals for light breakfasts, filling lunches, or even fondue and wine in the evenings. It's the best place in town to find pastrami, corned beef, or other traditional (gringo!) sandwich fare, all served on your choice of gourmet breads. Draft beer and wine are available, as are Benitto's specialty infused waters.

Inside Plaza Neptuno. © 3/209-0288. Breakfast $2–$5; main courses $2.50–$7. No credit cards. Daily 8am–11pm.

La Terraza di Roma 𝕽 ITALIAN   One of the first restaurants in the marina, this remains a favorite here, serving authentically flavorful Italian dishes and excellent breakfasts in a casual atmosphere with exceptional service. For starters, the fried calamari is delicately seasoned, and the grilled vegetable antipasto could easily serve as a full meal. Signature pasta dishes include fusilli prepared with fresh mushrooms, olive oil, and garlic, and fettuccini carbonara. It also has a selection of shrimp dishes as well as brick-oven pizzas. Most people prefer seating on the wooden dock situated over the marina, or the gazebo-like terrace bordering the marina *malecón.* Indoor dining is air-conditioned, and there is occasionally live piano music in the evenings.

Puesta del Sol, Local 2 (Marina Vallarta *malecón*). ℰ **3/221-0560.** Main courses $4–$14. AE, MC, V. Daily 8am–11pm.

DOWNTOWN

It's not that I'm particularly partial to Italian or more continental cuisine; it just happens that the best restaurants here happen to fall into these categories. Although Vallarta has over 250 restaurants to choose from, it lacks in the categories of Mexican cuisine and seafood. It does boast an exceptional community of European chefs who have come here to live and open up places that serve their own native specialties—our good fortune!

EXPENSIVE

Café des Artistes ✿✿ FRENCH/INTERNATIONAL   This sophisticated dinner-only restaurant is known as the place in town for that very special evening. Located in a restored house that resembles a castle, and with an interior that combines murals, lush fabrics and an array of original works of art, Café des Artistes is the creation of award-winning Chef Thierry Blouet, a member of the French Academie Culinaire and Maitre Cuisinier de France. The Nobel prize-winning Mexican novelist Carlos Fuentes wrote of this restaurant, "At Café des Artistes, there is no dish that is not a work of art, nor a work of art that does not feed the spirit."

There are three distinct dining areas—the streetside balcony, the various interior dining rooms, and my personal favorite, the terraced garden. Despite the attention giving to the decorative setting, the real star here is the food. The menu is highly original, with dishes drawing heavily on Chef Blouet's French training, yet using regional specialty ingredients. A few of the noteworthy entrees include shrimp sautéed with mushrooms, *guajillo chile* and *raicilla* sauce, and the renowned roasted duck glazed with honey, soy, ginger, lime sauce, served with a pumpkin risotto. And speaking of pumpkin, don't miss the signature starter, pumpkin and prawn soup served from a carved gourd. Chef Blouet started his culinary career as a pastry chef, so be sure to save room for one of his desserts, which are as lovely to look at as they are to savor. The only downside here is that it is easily the most expensive meal in town, but worth the splurge.

Guadalupe Sanchez 740. © 3/222-3228/29/30. Main courses $9–$24. AE, MC, V. Mon–Sat 6–11:30pm.

MODERATE

de Santos ✸✸ MEDITERRANEAN   Opened just over a year ago, de Santos quickly became the hot spot in town for late night dining and bar action. Although the dining aspect initially didn't live up to the atmosphere and music, now it does. Fare is Mediterranean-inspired, with best bets including lightly breaded calamari, seafood casserole, and excellent thin crust pizzas. The cool, refined interior, with exposed brick walls, crisp white-clothed tables, and lots of votive candles, feels more urban than resort, and it boasts the most sophisticated sound system in town—including its own DJ who spins to match the mood of the crowd. It probably helps that one of the partners is also a member of Mana, the chart-topping, wildly popular Latin group. Prices are extremely reasonable for the quality and overall experience of an evening here. Start with dinner here—then stay on and enjoy the town's favorite bar.

Morelos 771, Centro. © 3/223-3052. Main courses $5–$15; wine and mixed drinks $3–$5. AE, MC, V. Dinner 5pm–1am; bar open until 4am on weekends.

La Bodeguita del Medio ✸ CUBAN   This authentic Cuban restaurant and bar has quickly become a local favorite for its casual energy, terrific live Cuban music, and the *mojitos*—a stiff rum-based drink with fresh mint and lime juice. Food is as authentic as the atmosphere, with black beans and rice, a variety of styles of plantains, and delicious seafood casseroles. It is a branch of the original Bodeguita in Havana (reportedly Hemingway's favorite restaurant there), opened in 1942, and if you can't get to that one, the Vallarta version has successfully imported the essence—plus, there's a small souvenir shop with Cuban cigars, rum, and other items for sale. The downstairs dining area has large wooden windows that open up to the *malecón* street action, while the upstairs offers terrific views of the bay. Walls throughout are decorated with old photographs and the scrawled signatures of the many patrons who have beaten a path here—if you can, find a spot and add yours!

Malecón (at Allende). © 3/223-1585. Main courses $5–$19. AE, MC, V. Daily 11:30am–3am.

La Dolce Vita ✸✸ ITALIAN   This popular eatery combines good food, a casually upbeat atmosphere, attentive service, and great entertainment. Overlooking the *malecón,* La Dolce Vita offers excellent views and prime people-watching through its oversized windows and second-floor balcony. Despite its choice location and superb food, prices remain more than reasonable. Owned by an engaging group of Italian friends, the food is authentic in preparation and flavor, from the thin crust, brick-oven pizzas to savory homemade pastas—my favorite is the "Braccio de Fiero," topped with spinach, black olives, and fresh tomatoes. Sultry jazz by house band The Sweet Life plays Thursday and Friday evenings.

Paseo Díaz Ordaz 674, Centro. (✆) **3/222-3852.** Main courses $5–$15; wine and mixed drinks $2–$3.60. AE, MC, V. Mon–Sat noon–2am; Sun 6pm–1am.

Las Palomas MEXICAN   One of Puerto Vallarta's first restaurants, this is the power-breakfast place of choice for local movers and shakers—and a generally popular hangout for everyone else throughout the day. Authentic in atmosphere and menu, it's one of Puerto Vallarta's few genuine Mexican restaurants, with the atmosphere of a gracious home. Breakfast is the best value here, with mugs of steaming coffee spiced with cinnamon poured as soon as you're seated. Try the classic *huevos rancheros* or *chilaquiles* (tortilla strips, fried and topped with a red or green spicy sauce, cream, cheese, and fried eggs). Lunch and dinner offer other traditional Mexican specialties, plus a selection of stuffed crêpes. The best place for checking out the *malecón* and watching the sun set while sipping an icy margarita is in the spacious bar or upstairs terrace.

Paseo Díaz Ordaz 594. (✆) **3/222-3675.** Breakfast $3.50–$7; lunch $5–$12; main courses $6–$18. AE, MC, V. Daily 8am–11pm.

Rito's Baci 🐠🐠 ITALIAN   If the food weren't reason enough to come here (and it definitely is!), then Rito himself would be, with his gentle, devoted way of caring for every detail of this cozy trattoria. His grandfather emigrated from Italy, so the recipes and tradition of Italian food come naturally to him. So does his passion for food—obvious as he describes the specialties, which include lasagna (vegetarian, *verde,* or meat-filled); ravioli stuffed with spinach and ricotta cheese; spaghetti with garlic, anchovy, and lemon zest; or a side of homemade Italian sausage. Everything, in fact, is made by hand from fresh ingredients. Pizza-lovers favor the Piedmonte, with that famous sausage and mushrooms, and the Horacio, a cheeseless pizza with tomatoes, oregano, and basil. Sandwiches come hot or cold; but arrive hungry, as they're a two-handed operation. Because Rito offers home and hotel delivery, I enjoy his food more than any other restaurant in town! It's 1½ blocks off the *malecón*, on Josefa O. de Domínguez between Morelos and Juárez.

Domínguez 181. ⓒ 3/222-6448. Pasta $6.50–$9.50; salads and sandwiches $2–$5.60; pizza $13–$14.50. MC, V. Daily 1–11:30pm.

Trio ⓐⓐⓐ *(Finds* INTERNATIONAL   Trio is the current darling of Vallarta restaurants, with diners beating a path to this modest but stylish cafe because chef/owner Bernhard Güth's undeniable passion for food imbues each dish. Partners Güth and Chef Peter Lodes have combined local ingredients with impressive culinary experience; the result is such memorable entrees as San Blas shrimp in a roasted red pepper and mango sauce, risotto with wild mushrooms, ricotta ravioli with sun-dried tomatoes, and grilled seabass with vegetables, served in a black olive salsa—but these dishes may not be on the menu when you arrive, as it's a constantly changing work of art! Trio is noted for the perfected melding of Mexican and Mediterranean flavors. What's great about this restaurant is that despite a sophisticated menu, the atmosphere is always comfortable and welcoming, and Bernhard is regularly seen chatting with guests at the end of an evening. There is also a rooftop bar area for a more comfortable wait for a table or for enjoying an after dinner coffee. A real treat!

Guerrero 264. ⓒ 3/222-2196. Reservations recommended. Main courses $6.50–$19. AE, MC, V. Lunch (high season only) Mon–Sat noon–4pm; dinner daily 6pm–midnight.

SOUTH OF THE RÍO CUALE TO OLAS ALTAS

South of the river is the most condensed restaurant area, with the street Basilio Badillo nicknamed "Restaurant Row." A second main dining drag has emerged along calle Olas Altas, where you can find all variety of food types and price categories. Its wide sidewalks are lined with cafes and espresso bars, generally open from 7am to midnight.

EXPENSIVE

Café Maximilian ⓐⓐ INTERNATIONAL   This bistro-style cafe has a casually elegant atmosphere with a genuinely European feel to it. It's the prime place to go if you want to combine exceptional food with great people-watching. Austrian-born owner Andreas Rupprechter is always on hand to ensure that the service is as impeccable as the food is delicious. Indoor, air-conditioned dining is at cozy tables dressed in crisp white linens; sidewalk tables are larger and great for groups of friends. The cuisine merges old-world European preparations with regionally fresh ingredients. My personal favorite is the filet of trout with almonds and white wine sauce, served on a bed of spinach—so much so that I've never tried any other dish, although friends tell me the mustard chicken with mashed potatoes is excellent, and the braised baby lamb with rosemary and poblano peppers is simply divine. It also offers northern European classics like *Rahmschnitzel*, sautéed pork loin and homemade noodles in a creamy mushroom sauce. Desserts are especially tempting, as are its gourmet coffees—Maximilian has its own Austrian café and pastry shop next door. It's at the intersection of Basilio Badillo and Olas Altas streets, in front of the Playa los Arcos Hotel.

Olas Altas 380, Zona Romantica. (*C*) **3/223-0760.** Reservations recommended in high season. Main courses $7–$18. AE, MC, V. Mon–Sat 6–11pm.

Los Pibes *R*R* ARGENTINIAN/STEAKS   You won't find a better steak anywhere in Vallarta—or many other places. Los Pibes offers signature thick cuts, exceptional quality, and a variety of preparations. Argentinean Cristina Juhas opened this restaurant in 1994, for her *pibes* (children), and the rave reviews have just grown over the years. You select your steak cut from a tray of fresh meat (portions are huge, all imported from the U.S.). While it's being prepared, try one of the wonderful *empanadas* filled with meat or corn and cheese, or savor an order of *alubias,* marinated beans served with bread. The homemade sausage is also delicious, and you won't find a better *chimichutri* sauce. In addition to beef, Los Pibes has an ample selection of salads, side dishes, chicken, and pastas, as well as an excellent wine list. This slice of Argentina is on Basilio Badillo, across from Adobe Café. A second location, equally delicious, is located on the Marina Vallarta *malecón* ((*C*) **3/221-0669**).

Basilio Badillo 261. (*C*) **3/223-1557.** Reservations recommended in high season. Main courses $12–$22. AE, MC, V. Wed–Mon 2pm–2am.

MODERATE

Adobe Café *R*R* INTERNATIONAL   Adobe Café offers a classically chic atmosphere in which to enjoy innovative cuisine based on traditional Mexican specialties. A Santa Fe–style decor with rustic wood accents provides a serene backdrop, and tables are comfortably large for enjoying a leisurely meal. Waiters possess that ideal skill of being attentive without being intrusive. The menu features imaginative dishes, including grilled jumbo shrimp battered in coconut and served with homemade apple sauce, penne pasta with Italian sausage in a creamy tequila sauce, and tenderloin of beef stuffed with *huitlacoche* in a cheese sauce—to name just a few specialties. Owner Rodolfo Choperena is almost always on hand, which accounts for the consistently fine food and service. Adobe Café is at the corner of Calles Basilio Badillo and Ignacio Vallarta, opposite Los Pibes restaurant, on the "Calle de los Cafés," or Restaurant Row.

Basilio Badillo 252. (C) **3/222-6720** or 3/223-1925. www.adobecafe.com.mx. Reservations recommended in high season. Main courses $11–$19. MC, V. Wed–Mon 6–11pm. Closed Aug–Sept.

Archie's Wok ⟨⟨⟨ *Finds* ASIAN/SEAFOOD   Since 1986, Archie's has been legendary in Puerto Vallarta for serving original cuisine influenced by the intriguing flavors of Thailand, China, and the Philippines. Archie was Hollywood director John Huston's private chef during the years he spent in the area. Today his wife Cindy continues his legacy as she welcomes guests to this tranquil retreat. Their Thai Mai Tai and other tropical drinks are made from only fresh fruit and juices, and they are a good way to kick off a meal here, as are the Filipino spring rolls, consistently crispy and delicious. The popular Singapore fish filet features lightly battered fillet strips in a sweet-and-sour sauce, while the Thai garlic shrimp are prepared with fresh garlic, ginger, cilantro, and black pepper. Vegetarians have plenty of options, including the broccoli, tofu, mushroom, & cashew stir-fry in a black bean and sherry sauce. Finish things off with the signature Spice Islands coffee or a slice of lime cheese pie. Thursday through Saturday from 8 to 11pm, live classical guitar and flute set the atmosphere in Archie's Oriental garden.

Francisco Rodríguez 130, ½ block from the Los Muertos pier. (C) 3/222-0411. awok@pvnet.com.mx. Main courses $6–$12. AE, MC, V. Mon–Sat 2–11pm. Closed Sept–Oct.

La Palapa ⟨ SEAFOOD/MEXICAN   This colorfully decorated, open-air, *palapa*-roofed restaurant on the beach is a decades-old local favorite. Enjoy a tropical breakfast by the sea, lunch on the beach, cocktails at sunset, or a romantic dinner—at night the staff sets cloth-covered tables in the sand. For lunch and dinner, seafood is the specialty, with featured dishes including grilled shrimp in a *guajillo* (chile) and mango sauce, and poached red snapper with fresh cilantro sauce. Its location in the heart of Los Muertos Beach makes it an exceptional place to either start or end the day; I favor it for breakfast or, even better, a late-night sweet temptation and specialty coffee, enjoyed while watching the moon over the bay with the sand at your feet. A particular favorite is their all-you-can-enjoy Sunday brunch, which entitles you to a spot on popular Los Muertos beach for the day! There are acoustic guitars and vocals nightly from 8 to 11pm, generally performed by Alberto himself.

Pulpito 103. ℂ 3/222-5225. Reservations recommended for dinner in high season. Breakfast $2.50–$7; main courses $7–$25; salad or sandwiches $5–$10. AE, MC, V. Daily 8am–11pm.

INEXPENSIVE

Café San Angel CAFE   This comfortable, classic sidewalk cafe has become a local gathering place from sunrise to sunset. For breakfast, choose between a *burrito* stuffed with eggs and *chorizo* sausage, a three-egg Western omelet, crêpes filled with mushrooms, or a tropical fruit plate. Deli sandwiches, crêpes, and pastries round out the small but ample menu. It also has exceptional fruit smoothies, like the Yelapa—a blend of mango, banana, and orange juice—and perfectly made espresso drinks. Note that the service is reliably slow and frequently frustrating, so choose this place if you have time on your side. Bar service and Internet access are available.

Olas Altas 449, corner of Francisco Rodríguez. ℂ 3/223-2160. Breakfast $3.50–$5; main courses $3.50–$6. Daily 8am–midnight.

Fajita Republic 𝕽𝕽 MEXICAN/SEAFOOD/STEAKS   Since opening a few years ago, this place has been consistently popular—and deservedly so. Fajita Republic has hit on a winning recipe: delicious food, ample portions, welcoming atmosphere, and low prices. The specialty is, of course, *fajitas*, grilled to perfection in every variety: steak, chicken, shrimp, combo, and vegetarian. All come with a generous tray of salsas and toppings. This "tropical grill" also serves sumptuous BBQ ribs, Mexican *molcajetes* with incredibly tender strips of marinated beef fillet, and grilled shrimp. Starters include fresh guacamole served in a giant spoon and the ever-popular Mayan cheese sticks (cheese, breaded and deep-fried). Try a "Fajita Rita Mango Margarita"—or one of the other spirited temptations—served in oversized mugs or by the pitcher. It's a casual, fun, and festive atmosphere in a garden of mango and palm trees. Located on Basilio Badillo, Restaurant Row, 1 block north of Olas Altas.

Pino Suárez 321, corner of Basilio Badillo. ℂ 3/222-3131. Main courses $9–$17. MC, V. Daily 4–11pm.

Red Cabbage Café (El Repollo Rojo) 𝕽𝕽 *Finds* MEXICAN The tiny, hard-to-find cafe is worth the effort—a visit here will reward you with not only exceptional traditional Mexican cuisine, but also with a whimsical crash course in the contemporary culture of this country. The small room is covered wall to wall and table to table with photographs, paintings, movie posters, and news clippings about the cultural icons of Mexico. Frida Kahlo figures prominently in the decor, and there's a special menu that duplicates dishes she and husband Diego Rivera prepared for guests.

Specialties from all over Mexico are featured, including the divine *chiles en nogada* (*poblano chiles* stuffed with ground beef, pine nuts, and raisins, topped with a sweet cream sauce and served cold), an intricate chicken *mole* from Puebla, and the hearty *carne en su jugo* (steak in its juice). In addition, chef-owner Lola serves probably the most diverse, tasty vegetarian menu in town (she offers cooking classes for interested groups of four or more). There's a piano with occasional live music; talented (and not so talented!) diners are also welcome to play. This is not the place for an intimate conversation, however—the poor acoustics cause everyone's conversations to blend together, although generally what you're hearing from adjacent tables are raves about the food.

Calle Rivera del Río 204A, across from the Río Cuale. ✆ 3/223-0411. Main courses $3–$10. No credit cards. Daily 5–11pm.

JUNGLE RESTAURANTS

One of the unique attractions of Puerto Vallarta is its "jungle restaurants," located to the south of town toward Mismaloya. Each offers open-air dining in a tropical setting by the sea or beside a mountain river. A stop for swimming and lunch is included in the many varieties of "Jungle" or "Tropical" tours (see "Organized Tours," in chapter 3). If you travel on your own, a taxi is the best transportation, as they are all located quite a distance from the main highway. Taxis are usually waiting for return patrons. The restaurants up the hill from the entrance to Mismaloya are **Chino's Paraíso** and **El Edén** (no phones). Both are located up the mountain road at Highway 200 km 6.5, and feature mediocre restaurants in once-beautiful natural settings of tropical jungle next to a stream. El Edén, further up the road from Chino's, was the site of several key scenes in the Arnold Schwarzenegger film *Predator.* Both are somewhat unkempt, and during summer months swimming in the river here can be extremely dangerous—flash floods come without warning and take several lives each year. I cannot in good conscience recommend El Edén; the place is dirty and the staff has repeatedly abused and mistreated animals in attempts to assemble a makeshift "zoo" attraction.

Just past Boca de Tomatlán, at Highway 200 km 20, is **Chico's Paradise** (✆ 3/222-0747 or 3/223-0413; chicos@prodigy.net), a better option, offering spectacular views of massive rocks—some marked with petroglyphs—and the surrounding jungle and mountains. There are natural pools and waterfalls for swimming, plus a small *mercado* selling pricey trinkets. The menu features excellent seafood (the seafood platter for two is excellent, with lobster, clams, giant shrimp, crab, and fish fillet) as well as Mexican dishes. The quality is quite good, and the portions are generous, although prices are higher than in town—remember, you're paying for the setting. It's open daily from 10am to 7pm.

The newest and most recommendable of the jungle restaurants is **El Nogalito** ✻ (©/fax **3/221-5225**). Located beside a clear jungle stream, this exceptionally clean, beautifully landscaped ranch serves lunch, beverages, and snacks on a shady terrace in a very relaxing atmosphere. There are also several hiking routes that depart from the grounds. If you're accompanied by one of El Nogalito's guides, they'll point out the native plants, birds, and wildlife of the area. To find it, a taxi can easily take you, or travel to Punta Negra, just about 5 miles south of downtown Puerto Vallarta. There's a well-marked sign that leads up Calzada del Cedro, a dirt road, to the ranch. It's much closer to town than the other jungle restaurants mentioned above, and it's open daily from noon to 5:30pm.

3

Exploring Puerto Vallarta & Beyond

Beyond the cobblestoned streets, graceful cathedral, and welcoming atmosphere, Puerto Vallarta offers a wealth of natural beauty and man-made pleasures.

Ecotourism activities are gaining ground—from mountain biking the Sierra foothills to whale-watching, ocean kayaking, or diving with giant mantas in Banderas Bay. Twenty-six miles of beaches extend from the center of town around the bay, many tucked in pristine coves accessible only by boat. High in the Sierra Madre Mountains the mystical Huichol Indians still live in relative isolation in an effort to protect their centuries-old culture from outside influences. Their art is both intricate and highly prized; in the "Shopping" section, later in this chapter, I've given some tips for how to spot the best works.

Villages such as **San Blas, Rincon de Guayabitos, Barra de Navidad,** and **Melaque** are still laid-back, almost undiscovered, and offer travelers a glimpse into the local culture. Excursions to these smaller villages make easy day trips or extended stays and are starkly different from the spirited resort towns.

1 Beaches, Activities & Excursions

Travel agencies can provide information on what to see and do in Puerto Vallarta and can arrange tours, fishing, and other activities. Most hotels have a tour desk on-site. Of the many travel agencies in town, I highly recommend **Tukari Servicios Turísticos,** av. España 316 (© 3/224-7177; fax 3/224-2350), which specializes in ecological and cultural tours. Another source for information is **Xplora Adventours** (© 3/223-0661), located in the Sierra Madre shop on the *malecón*. It has books of all locally available tours with photos, explanations, and costs; however, be aware that this company is owned by a timeshare resort, so an invitation to a presentation, which you may decline, will be part of receiving your tour information. **American Express Travel Services,** Morelos 660 (© 3/223-2955), also has a varied selection of high-quality, popular tours. One of the

---

Tips Watch for Area Code Changes

As this book went to press, Mexico announced a country-wide change in its long-distance area codes. The new plan will affect every phone number in this book; for details, please consult the box "Changes to Mexico's Phone Numbers Announced," in chapter 1.

---

tour companies with the largest—and best quality—selection of boat cruises and land tours is **Vallarta Adventures** (© **3/297-1212,** ext. 3; www.vallarta-adventures.com). I can highly recommend any of their offerings. Book with them directly and get a discount of 10% when you mention you read it in Frommer's.

THE BEACHES

For years, beaches were Puerto Vallarta's main attraction. Although visitors today are exploring more of the surrounding geography, the sands are still a powerful draw. Over 26 miles of beaches extend around the broad Bay of Banderas, ranging from action-packed party spots to secluded coves accessible only by boat.

IN TOWN   The easiest to reach is **Playa Los Muertos** (also known as Playa Olas Altas or Playa del Sol), just off calle Olas Altas, south of the Río Cuale. The water can be rough here, but the wide beach is home to a wide array of *palapa* restaurants with food, beverage, and beach-chair service. The two most popular are the adjacent El Dorado and La Palapa, located at the end of Pulpito Street. On the southern end of this beach is a section known as "Blue Chairs"—the most popular gay beach. Vendors stroll the length of Los Muertos, and beach volleyball, parasailing, and jet skiing are all popular pastimes. The **Hotel Zone** is also known for its broad, smooth beaches, accessible primarily through the associated hotel lobbies.

SOUTH OF TOWN   **Playa Mismaloya** is in a beautiful sheltered cove about 6 miles south of town along Highway 200. The water here is clear and beautiful, ideal for snorkeling off the beach. Entrance to the public beach is just to the left of the Jolla de Mismaloya Hotel. Colorful *palapa* restaurants dot the small beach and you can rent beach chairs for sunning. You can also stake out a table under a *palapa* for the day. Using a restaurant's table and *palapa* is a reciprocal arrangement—they let you be comfortable, and you buy your drinks, snacks, and lunch there. *Night of the Iguana* was filmed at Mismaloya. **La Jolla de Mismaloya Resort**

and Spa (© 3/228-0660) has a restaurant on the restored film set—**La Noche de la Iguana Set Restaurant,** open daily from noon to 11pm. The movie runs continuously in a room below the restaurant, and photo stills from the filming hang in the restaurant. The restaurant is accessible by land on the point framing the south side of the cove. Just below the restaurant is **John Huston's Bar & Grill,** serving drinks and light snacks from 11am to 6pm.

La Jolla de Mismaloya Resort and Spa is to the right of the public beach, and restaurants there are available to outsiders as well. The beach at **Boca de Tomatlán,** just down the road, is similar in setup to Mismaloya, but without a large resort looming in the backdrop. The two are accessible by public buses that depart from the corner of Basilio Badillo and Insurgentes every 15 minutes from 5:30am to 10pm, costing just 50¢.

Las Ánimas, Quimixto, and **Yelapa** beaches offer a true sense of seclusion; they are accessible only by boat (see "Getting Around," in chapter 2, for information about water-taxi service). They are each larger than Mismaloya, offer intriguing hikes to jungle waterfalls, and are similarly set up with restaurants fronting a wide beach. Overnight stays are available only at Yelapa (see "Side Trips from Puerto Vallarta," later in this chapter).

NORTH OF TOWN The beaches at **Marina Vallarta** are the least desirable in the area, with darker sand and seasonal inflows of stones.

The entire northern coastline from Bucerías to Punta Mita is a succession of sandy coves alternating with rocky inlets. For years the beaches to the north, with their long, clean breaks, have been the favored locale for surfers. The broad sandy stretches at **Playa Anclote, Playa Piedras Blancas,** and **Playa Destiladeras,** along with their *palapa* restaurants, have made them favorites with local residents looking for a quick but meaningful getaway from town. The stellar white sand beach at Punta Mita, home of the new Four Seasons, is closed off from road access, except for guests of the hotel.

ORGANIZED TOURS

BOAT TOURS Puerto Vallarta offers a number of different boat trips, including sunset cruises and trips for snorkeling, swimming, and diving. They generally travel one of two routes: to the **Marietas Islands,** which are about a 30- to 45-minute boat ride off the northern shore of Banderas Bay, or to **Yelapa, Las Ánimas,** or **Quimixto** along the southern shore. The trips to the southern beaches make a

---

Moments Special Events in Puerto Vallarta

Each November, **Fiestas del Mar** (SeaFest) is celebrated with a Gourmet Dining Festival, Cultural Festival, art exhibitions, tennis tournaments, regattas, and more. Dates vary; call the Tourism Board (© **888/384-6822** from the U.S.) for dates and schedule. From December 1 through December 12, the **Festival of the Virgin of Guadalupe** *®*—Mexico's patron saint—is celebrated in one of the most authentic displays of culture and community in Mexico. Each business, neighbor-hood, association, or group makes a pilgrimage (called *pere-grinaciones*) to the church, where offerings are exchanged for a brief blessing by the priest. These processions, especially those offered by hotels, often include floats, Aztec dancers, and mariachis, and are followed by fireworks. Hotels fre-quently invite guests to participate in the walk to the church. It's an event not to be missed.

---

stop at **Los Arcos,** an island rock formation south of Puerto Vallarta, for snorkeling. Don't base your opinion of underwater Puerto Vallarta on this, though—with dozens of tour boats daily dumping quantities of snorkelers overboard at the same time each day, this is exactly when the fish know *not* to be there. It is, however, an excellent site for night diving. When comparing all these boat cruises, note that some include lunch, while most provide music and an open bar on board. Most leave around 9:30am, stop for 45 minutes of snorkeling, and arrive at the beach destination around noon for a 2½-hour stay before returning around 3pm. At Quimixto and Yelapa, visitors can take a half-hour hike to a jungle waterfall or rent a horse for the ride. Prices range from $20 for a sunset cruise or a trip to one of the beaches with open bar to $70 for an all-day outing with open bar and meals.

One boat, the *Marigalante* (© 3/223-0309), is an exact replica of Columbus's ship the *Santa Maria,* built in honor of the 500-year anniversary of his voyage to the Americas. It features a daytime "pirate's cruise" complete with picnic barbecue and treasure hunt or a sunset dinner cruise with folkloric dance and fireworks. The day tour is $55 per person and the sunset dinner cruise is $70 per person.

One of the best trips is the day trip to **Caletas** *®®*, the cove where John Huston made his home for years. **Vallarta Adventures** (© 3/297-1212, ext. 3; www.vallarta-adventures.com) holds the

Downtown Puerto Vallarta

Bahia de Banderas

Playa Los Muertos
Pier (water taxi)

exclusive lease on this private cove and has done an excellent job of restoring Huston's former home, adding exceptional day-spa facilities and landscaping the beach, which is wonderful for snorkeling. The quality facilities, combined with the relative privacy this excursion offers, has made it one of the most popular, at $65 per person. It also offers an evening cruise, complete with dinner and a spectacular contemporary dance show, "Rhythms of the Night" (see "Puerto Vallarta After Dark," below.)

Travel agencies have tickets and information on all cruises. If you prefer to spend a longer time at Yelapa or Las Ánimas without taking time for snorkeling and cruise entertainment, note the information about travel by water taxis, under "Getting Around," in chapter 2.

Whale-watching tours are becoming more popular each year, since viewing humpback whales is almost a certainty from mid- to late November to March. The majestic whales have migrated to this bay for centuries (in the 1600s, it was called "Humpback Bay") to reproduce and bear calves. The noted local authorities are **Open Air Expeditions,** Guerrero 339 (©/fax **3/222-3310;** openair@viva

Moments   Art Along the *Malecón*

One of the great pleasures of strolling Puerto Vallarta's *malecón* is to take in the fanciful sculptures that line this seaside promenade. Among the notable works on display is *Nostalgia*, across from Carlos O'Brian's restaurant. Created by Ramiz Barquett, it depicts a couple sharing a romantic moment while gazing out to the bay. Farther south is the sculpture group at the *Rotonda del Mar*, locally known as *Fantasy by the Sea*. It's an array of sculpture "chairs" by renowned Mexican artist Alejandro Colunga. This wildly creative series—one chair is topped by a large octopus head, another bench has two giant ears for backrests—seems to always draw a crowd. Closer to the main square is the *Boy on the Seahorse* sculpture, an image that has come to represent this resort town. Photo ops abound—and don't miss the fountain across from the main square; its three bronze dolphins seem ready to leap right into the bay.

mexico.com), who offer ecologically oriented tours (of up to 12 people) in small boats, for $65. These are specially designed soft boats, and the twice-daily tours (8:30am or 1:30pm) last 4 hours, and include a healthful snack and T-shirt. They also spearhead a photo-ID project to track returning whales—each one has unique markings on its fluke, or tail. **Vallarta Adventures** (© 3/297-1212, ext. 3) offers whale-watching photo excursions for $70, with travel in small boats, and includes a pre-departure briefing on whale behaviors. This company also features whale-watching on tours to the Marietas Islands. For $60 you get lunch, time at a private beach, and a more festive than educational ambience aboard the large catamaran boats.

LAND TOURS   **Tukari Tours** travel agency can arrange bird-watching trips to the fertile birding grounds near **San Blas,** 3 to 4 hours north of Puerto Vallarta in the state of Nayarit; shopping trips to **Tlaquepaque and Tonalá** (6 hr. inland near Guadalajara); or a day trip to **Rancho Altamira,** a 50-acre, hilltop working ranch for a barbecue lunch and horseback riding, then a stroll through **El Tuito,** a small nearby colonial-era village. They can also arrange an unforgettable morning at **Terra Noble Art & Healing Center**

(© 3/223-3530 & 223-3531), a mountaintop day spa and center for the arts where participants can get a massage or treatment, work in clay and paint, and have lunch in a heavenly setting overlooking the bay.

Hotel travel desks and travel agencies, including Tukari and American Express, can also book the ever-popular **Tropical Tour** or **Jungle Tour** ($21 each), a basic orientation to the area. These tours are really expanded city tours that include a drive through the workers' village of Pitillal, the affluent neighborhood of Conchas Chinas, the cathedral, the market, the Taylor-Burton houses, and lunch at a jungle restaurant. Any stop for shopping usually means the driver picks up a commission for what you buy.

The **Sierra Madre Expedition** is another excellent tour offered by **Vallarta Adventures** (© 3/297-1212, ext. 3). This daily excursion travels in special Mercedes all-terrain vehicles north of Puerto Vallarta through jungle trails, stopping at a small town, into a forest for a brief nature walk, and winding up on a pristine secluded beach for lunch and swimming. The $65 outing is worthwhile because it takes tourists on exclusive trails into scenery that would otherwise be off-limits.

AIR TOURS   Speaking of off-limits, you can explore some of the most remote and undiscovered reaches of the Sierra Madre Mountains in Vallarta Adventure's **San Sebastián Air Adventure.** A 15-minute flight aboard a 14-seat turbo prop Cessna Caravan takes you into the heart of the Sierra Madre. The plane is equipped with raised wings, which allows you to admire—and photograph—the mountain scenery below. The plane arrives on a gravel landing strip in the old mining town of San Sebastián, a beautiful, antiquated village dating back to 1605. One of the oldest mining towns in Mexico, it reached its prosperous peak in the 1700s with over 30,000 inhabitants. Today, San Sebastián remains an outstanding example of how people lived and worked in a remote Mexican mountain town—it's a living museum. The half-day adventure costs $125, and includes the flight, a walking tour of the town (including a stop at the old Hacienda Jalisco, a favored getaway of John Huston, Liz and Dick, and their friends), plus brunch in town. Reserve by calling (© 3/297-1212, ext. 3) or e-mailing (info@ vallarta-adventures.com). For those who would like to spend more time in San Sebastián, other excursions have overnight stays and returns by bike or horseback. A longer bus tour is available through Celebrity Travel, but involves more time traveling up and down the mountain and about the same amount of time in town. There's also a **Jeep tour** to San Sebastián available for $65, for up to four people per jeep, including a guide. You can choose to drive or the guide can. This tour departs at 9am and returns at 5pm. Call Pacific Travel (© 3/225-2270) to reserve.

Anyone for a taste of tequila? We're talking about the town, along with a sampling of the best of the spirit of Mexico. Vallarta Adventures offers a half-day trip that takes you at a comfortable pace to the classic town of Tequila, where you visit one of the original haciendas and tequila fields.

It's just a comfortable 35-minute flight aboard a private 16-passenger plane to the town of Tequila. This is the only region in the world where this legendary spirit is distilled, much like the exclusive champagne region in France. The visit centers around Herradura Tequila's impressive 18th-century Hacienda San Jose, where you learn about the myth and the tradition of producing tequila from the stately plants that line the hillsides of this town—an experience comparable to California's winery tours.

Departures are every Thursday at 1pm from the Aerotron private airport (adjacent to the PV International Airport); returning to Puerto Vallarta by 8pm. Cost is $255, which includes all air and ground transportation, tours, lunch, and beverages. Reserve by calling (© 3/297-1212, ext. 3) or e-mailing (info@vallarta-adventures.com).

Day-Off Hot-Air Balloon Tours, Morelos 56 at Corona (© 3/223-2002), offers two hot-air balloon trips a day at 7am and 5pm (weather permitting) for $175 per person. The balloons glide along the coast, over beaches, jungle, and farmland; the trip ends with a round of champagne.

TOURS IN TOWN   Every Wednesday and Thursday in high season (from late November to Easter), the **International Friendship Club** (© 3/222-5466) offers a **private home tour** of four private villas in town for a donation of $25 per person, with proceeds donated to local charities. Tour arrangements begin at 10am at the Hotel Molino de Agua, av. Ignacio L. Vallarta no. 130, adjacent to the southbound bridge over the Río Cuale, where you can buy breakfast while you wait for the group to gather—and arrive early, because this tour sells out quickly! The tour departs at 11am and lasts approximately 2½ hours.

You can also tour the **Taylor/Burton villas** (Casa Kimberley; © 3/222-1336), located at 445 calle Zaragoza. Tours of the two houses owned by Elizabeth Taylor and Richard Burton cost $6. Just ring the bell between 10am and 6pm, and if the manager is available, he will take you through the house.

A TASTY TOUR   There's a new, spirited tour in town—the **Don Porfidio Tequila Distillery Tour** (© 3/221-2543 or 3/221-2545) at Porfidio's facility just 10 minutes north of town. For an entry fee of $10, you can see how agave plants are juiced, fermented, distilled, and bottled for shipping. Entrance to the facility is also available through Celebrity Tours (© **3/221-1909;** fax 3/221-1236). The entry fee includes a glass of Porfidio, reputed to be one of Mexico's finest tequilas, but in reality a blend of other premium tequilas with exceptional packaging and marketing. It doesn't quite compare to a visit to the actual tequila fields and traditional tequila-making haciendas, but if you don't have time to do the half-day tour outlined above, this is an interesting—albeit abbreviated—glimpse at the tequila-making process.

STAYING ACTIVE

DIVING   Underwater enthusiasts from beginner to expert can arrange scuba diving through **Vallarta Adventures** (© **3/297-1212,** ext. 3; www.vallarta-adventures.com), a five-star PADI dive center. Dives take place at Los Arcos, a company-owned site at Caletas Cove, Quimixto Coves, the Marietas Islands, or the offshore El Morro and Chimo reefs. A full range of certification courses up through Instructor are also available. **Chico's Dive Shop,** Díaz Ordaz 772–775, near Carlos O'Brian's (© **3/222-1895;** www. chicos-diveshop.com), offers similar dive trips and is also a PADI five-star dive center. Chico's is open daily from 8am to 10pm, and has branches at the Marriott, Vidafel, Villa del Palmar, Camino Real, Paradise Village, and Playa Los Arcos hotels.

ECOTOURS & ACTIVITIES   Open Air Expeditions (©/fax **3/222-3310;** openair@vivamexico.com) offers other nature-oriented trips, including bird-watching as well as ocean kayaking in Punta Mita. **Ecotours de México,** Ignacio L. Vallarta 243 (©/fax **3/222-6606**), has eco-oriented tours, including seasonal (Aug–Nov) trips to a turtle preservation camp where you can witness hatching baby Olive Ridley turtles.

FISHING   A fishing trip can be arranged through travel agencies or through the **Cooperativa de Pescadores** (Fishing Cooperative) on the *malecón* north of the Río Cuale, next door to the Rosita Hotel (© **3/222-1202** or 3/224-7886). Fishing charters cost $180 to $350 a day for four to eight people; the price varies with the size of the boat. Although the posted price at the fishing cooperative is the same as what you'll find through travel agencies, you may be able to negotiate a lower price at the cooperative. No credit cards. It's open Monday through Saturday from 7am to 10pm, but make arrangements a day ahead. You can also arrange fishing trips at the Marina Vallarta docks, or by calling **Fishing with Carolina** (© 3/ **224-7250,** or cellular (044) 3/292-2953, fishingwithcarolina@ hotmail.com), aboard a 30-foot Unitlite sportsfisher, fully equipped with an English-speaking crew. Fishing trips generally include equipment and bait, but drinks, snacks, and lunch are optional, so check to see what the price includes.

GOLF Puerto Vallarta has two long-standing golf courses, one stunning newcomer, and more on the horizon. The Joe Finger–designed course at the **Marina Vallarta Golf Club** (© 3/ **221-0073**) is an 18-hole, par-74, private course that winds through the Marina Vallarta peninsula with ocean views. It's for members only, but most of the luxury hotels in Puerto Vallarta have memberships that their guests can use. A bar, restaurant, golf pro, and pro shop are on the premises. The greens fees are $125 in high season (depending on the type of membership your hotel has) and $85 during low season. Fees include golf cart, range balls, and tax. A caddy costs $5 to $10. Club rentals, lessons, and special packages are available.

North of town in the state of Nayarit, about 10 miles beyond Puerto Vallarta, is the 18-hole, par-72 **Los Flamingos Club de Golf** (© 329/8-0606 or 329/8-0280). The older of the two courses, it's open to the public and has beautiful jungle vegetation, but is not as well maintained. It's open from 7am to 5pm daily, with a snack bar (but no restaurant) and full pro shop. The greens fee is $60; add $34 for use of a golf cart, $12 for a caddy, and $22 for club rental. A free shuttle service is available from downtown Puerto Vallarta; call for pickup times and locations.

The new Jack Nicklaus Signature course at the **Four Seasons Punta Mita** (© 3/291-6000; fax 3/291-6060) is breathtaking, and reportedly the current personal favorite of this renowned golf pro. It has eight ocean-facing holes, but you can see the ocean from every hole on the course. Its hallmark is Hole 3B, the "Tail of the Whale," with a long drive to a green located on a natural island—the only natural island green in the world. It requires an amphibious golf cart to take you over when the tide is high, and the management has thoughtfully added an alternative play hole for when the ocean or tides are not accommodating. It's open only to guests of the Four Seasons resort or to members of other golf clubs with a letter of introduction from their pro. Selected other Vallarta-area hotels also have guest privileges—ask your concierge. Greens fees for non-guests of the Four Seasons are $135, with cart rentals an extra $25 and club rentals (Calloway) $45. Golf lessons are also available.

A Jack Nicklaus Signature–design course is located at Punta Mita, and a second Jack Nicklaus course, Vista Vallarta 9 (© 3/ 290-0030), just opened in April 2000 in the foothills of the Sierra Madre behind the bullring in Puerto Vallarta. A round of golf at Vista Vallarta costs just $125 per person, including cart.

Professionally guided golf tours to area courses and down the Costa Alegre are offered by **American Golf Tours** (© 3/225-2056; www.mexicogolftours.com). Prices vary according to number of golfers and optional overnight stays. Personalized packages can be arranged, and club and shoe rentals are available.

HORSEBACK-RIDING TOURS   Guided horseback rides can be arranged through travel agents or directly through one of the local ranches. The two best are **Rancho Palma Real,** Carretera Vallarta, Tepic 4766 (© 3/221-2120). The office is 5 minutes north of the airport, and the ranch is in Las Palmas, approximately 40 minutes northeast of Vallarta. It is by far the nicest horseback riding tour in the area. The horses are in excellent health and condition, plus you enjoy an added tour of local farms on your way to the ranch. Breakfast and lunch are included for the $45 fee. American Express only. **Rancho El Charro,** av. Francisco Villa 895 (© 3/224-0114 or 329/2-0122; www.ranchoelcharro.com), and **Rancho Ojo de Agua,** Cerrada de Cardenal 227, Fracciónamiento Las Aralias (©/fax 3/224-0607), also offer high-quality tours. Both of these ranches are about a 10-minute taxi ride north of downtown toward the Sierra Madre foothills. The morning or sunset rides last 3 hours and take you up into the mountains overlooking the ocean and town. The cost is $30. They also have their own comfortable base camp for serious riders who want to stay out overnight.

Rancho El Charro also offers an exclusive **"Fly-away to a Hide-away in San Sebastián"** day trip from 9:30am to 5pm. A 15-minute flight takes you to this 17th-century mining town (see "Side Trips from Puerto Vallarta," later in this chapter). A bilingual guide meets you at the airstrip, well-tended horses in tow; after a short ride to the Hacienda Jalisco, you'll get a light breakfast and a tour of the hacienda. The ride continues into town along a riverside trail used by the locals since mining days. A thorough tour of the town is provided, touching on the historical buildings, church, carpenter shop, and coffee plantation, before heading back to the Hacienda for a gourmet lunch. Overnight stays can be arranged. The cost is $160 per person, minimum four people, and advance reservations are required.

For a unique getaway, try **Horseback on Mexico**'s Hacienda Trail from Sea to Sierra Madre, several 3- to 7-day journeys by horseback into the mountains. Trips are offered from November 1 to April 30; there's a four-person minimum and a 15-person maximum. The cost of $270 per person per day includes food, horses, camping en route, and stays in centuries-old haciendas. They can arrange hotels in Puerto Vallarta and provide complete details on the quality of horses and accommodations. For details, contact Pam Aguirre of Rancho El Charro (see above). No credit cards are accepted.

MASSAGE If you overstress yourself staying active, or just need a relaxing massage, Karl Winkler is a professional massage therapist who offers relaxation or deep tissue massage, as well as acupressure, reflexology, aroma therapy, and body scrubs with sea salt—all this in the comfort of your hotel or villa. Rates are $50 per hour for outcall service, with special package rates available (© **3/222-5639;** www. pilitas.com).

MOUNTAIN BIKING & HIKING Bike Mex ⟨⟨, calle Guerrero 361 (© **3/223-1834** or 3/223-1680; www.bikemex.com), offers expert guided biking and hiking tours up the Río Cuale canyon and to outlying areas. The popular Río Cuale bike trip costs $42 for 4 hours and includes bike, helmet, gloves, insurance, water, lunch, and an English-speaking guide. Trips take off at either 9am or 2pm, but starting times are flexible; make arrangements a day ahead.

Who says Yelapa is accessible only by boat? I've traveled with Bike Mex on its all-day, advanced-level bike trip to this magical cove (see "Side Trips from Puerto Vallarta," later in this chapter). Riders depart at 7:30am in a van, traveling to your starting point in the town of El Tuito. The 33-mile ride includes 18½ miles of climbs to a peak elevation of 3,600 feet. The journey consists of switchbacks, fire roads, single tracks, awesome climbs, and steep downhills before ending up at a beachfront *palapa* restaurant in Yelapa. You have the option of staying the night in Yelapa or returning that afternoon by small boat. This tour costs $150, takes 4 to 6 hours, includes all bike gear, drinks, lunch, boat and land transportation, guide, and *ample* encouragement. Other bicycle trips, such as those along the beach-front of Punta Mita, are also available. Guided **hiking tours** are available along the same routes, with prices starting at $30, depending on the route.

SAILING   Sail Vallarta, Club de Tenis Puesta del Sol, Local 7-B, Marina Vallarta (© **3/221-0096;** fax 3/221-0097; sail@pnet. puerto.net.mx), offers a diverse variety of sailing vessels for hire. A group day sail, including crew, use of snorkeling equipment, drinks, food, and music, plus a stop at a beach for swimming and lunch, costs $82. Most trips include a crew, but you can make arrangements to sail yourself on a smaller boat. Prices vary for full boat charters, depending on the vessel and amount of time desired. **Vallarta Adventures** (© **3/297-1212**, ext. 3; www.vallarta-adventures.com) also offers two beautiful sailboats for charter or small group sails (up to 12 people). Their service is superb, as is the quality of the food and beverages served on board, and the company is known for having the boats that are most frequently under sail—many of the other sailing charters prefer to simply motor around the bay.

SWIMMING WITH DOLPHINS   Ever been kissed by a dolphin? Take advantage of a unique and absolutely memorable opportunity to swim with Pacific bottlenose dolphins in a clear lagoon. **Dolphin Adventure** 🐬🐬 (© **3/297-1212**, ext. 3; www.vallarta-adventures.com) operates an interactive dolphin-research facility—considered the finest in Latin America—that allows limited numbers of people to swim with dolphins Monday through Saturday at scheduled times. Cost for the swim is $170, with advance reservations required—they are generally sold out at least a week in advance. You may prefer the **Dolphin Encounter** ($75), at the same facility, which allows you to touch and learn about these dolphins in smaller pools, so you're ensured up-close and personal time with them. Dolphin Adventures now has two facilities—one in the lagoon of Nuevo Vallarta, and a new, more expansive home and headquarters of Vallarta Adventures. I give this my highest recommendation. Not only does the experience leave you with an indescribable sensation, but it's a joy to see these dolphins—they are well cared for, happy, and spirited. The program is about education and interaction, not entertainment or amusement, and is especially popular with children 10 and older.

TENNIS   Many hotels in Puerto Vallarta offer excellent tennis facilities, many with clay courts. There are also two full-service tennis clubs. The **Continental Plaza Tennis Club** (© **3/**

A Spectator Sport

Bullfights are held December through April beginning at 5pm on Wednesday afternoons at the La Paloma bullring across the highway from the town pier. Tickets can be arranged through travel agencies and cost around $21.

224-0123), located at the Continental Plaza hotel in the Hotel Zone, offers indoor and outdoor courts (including a clay court), full pro shop, lessons, clinics, and partner matchups. The **Iguana Tennis Center** (© 3/221-0683), located on the main highway, just south of the entrance to Marina Vallarta, offers covered courts and clinics.

WATER-SKIING & PARASAILING Water-skiing, parasailing, and other watersports are available at many beaches along the Bay of Banderas. Best known for watersports equipment rental is **Club Bananas Water Sports Center** at the beach of the Las Palmas Hotel, av. Francisco Medina Ascencio km 2.5, Hotel Zone (© 3/224-0650; ask for the Water Sports Center). WaveRunners, banana boats, parasailing, and water-skiing are all available here, for hourly, half-day, or full-day rentals.

A STROLL THROUGH TOWN

Puerto Vallarta's cobblestoned streets are a pleasure to explore; they're full of tiny shops, rows of windows edged with curling wrought iron, and vistas of red-tile roofs and the sea. Start with a walk up and down the *malecón,* the seafront boulevard.

Among the sights you shouldn't miss is the **municipal building** on the main square (next to the tourism office), which has a large Manuel Lepe mural inside in its stairwell. Nearby, up Independencia, sits the **Parrish of Nuestra Señora de Guadalupe church,** Hidalgo 370 (© 3/222-1326), topped with its curious crown held in place by angels—a replica of the one worn by Empress Carlota during her brief time in Mexico as Emperor Maximilian's wife. On its steps, women sell religious mementos, and across the narrow street stalls sell native herbs for curing common ailments. Services in English are held Sunday at 10am. Regular parish hours are 7am until 9:30 or 10pm daily.

Three blocks south of the church, head east on Libertad, lined with small shops and pretty upper windows, to the **municipal market** by the river. After exploring the market, cross the bridge to the island in the river; sometimes a painter is at work on its banks. Walk down the center of the island toward the sea and you'll come to the tiny **Museo Río Cuale** (no phone), which has a small but impressive permanent exhibit of pre-Columbian figurines. It's open Monday through Saturday from 10am to 4pm. Admission is free.

Retrace your steps back to the market and Libertad and follow calle Miramar to the brightly colored steps up to Zaragoza. Midway is a magnificent view over rooftops to the sea, plus a cute cafe, **Graffiti** (no phone), where you can break for a cappuccino and a snack. Up Zaragoza to the right 1 block is the famous **pink arched bridge** that once connected Richard Burton's and Elizabeth Taylor's houses. This area, known as **"Gringo Gulch,"** is where many Americans have houses.

2 Shopping

Shopping in Puerto Vallarta is generally concentrated in small, eclectic, and independent shops rather than impersonal malls. You can find excellent-quality **folk art,** original **clothing** designs, and fine home accessories at great prices. Vallarta is known for having the most diverse and impressive selection of **contemporary Mexican fine art** available outside Mexico City. There is also an abundance of tacky T-shirts and the ubiquitous **silver jewelry.**

THE SHOPPING SCENE

There are a few key areas where the best shopping is concentrated: central downtown, the Marina Vallarta *malecón,* the popular *mercados,* and on the beach—where the merchandise comes to you. Some of the more attractive shops are found 1 to 2 blocks in **back of the malecón.** Start at the intersection of Corona and Morelos streets—interesting shops are found in all directions from here. **Marina Vallarta** does offer two shopping plazas, but both have a limited selection of shops: Plaza Marina and Neptuno Plaza, both on the main highway coming from the airport into town. **Neptuno Plaza** has become the better option in the past year, now anchored by a new Radio Shack and Internet cafe. Although still home to a few interesting shops, the marina boardwalk (*marina malecón*) is dominated by real estate companies, timeshare vendors, restaurants, and boating services.

Puerto Vallarta's **municipal market** is just north of the Río Cuale where Libertad and A. Rodríguez meet. The *mercado* sells clothes, jewelry, serapes, shawls, leather accessories and suitcases, papier-mâché parrots, stuffed frogs and armadillos, and, of course, T-shirts. Be sure to do some comparison shopping and definitely bargain

---

Tips **Beware the Silver Scam**

Much of the silver sold on the beach is actually alpaca, a lesser-quality silver metal (even though many pieces are still stamped with the designation "9.25," supposedly indicating that it is true silver). The prices for silver on the beach are much lower, as is the quality. If you're looking for a more lasting piece of jewelry, you're better off in a true silver shop.

---

before buying. The market is open daily from 9am to 7pm. Upstairs, a **food market** serves inexpensive Mexican meals—for more adventurous diners, it's probably the best value and most authentic dining experience in Vallarta. An **outdoor market** can be found along Río Cuale Island, between the two bridges. Stalls sell crafts, gifts, folk art, and clothing.

Along any public beach, it's more than likely that you'll be approached by walking **vendors** selling merchandise that ranges from silver jewelry to rugs, T-shirts to masks. "Almost free!" they'll call out, in seemingly relentless efforts to attract your attention. If you're too relaxed to think of shopping in town, this can be an entertaining alternative for picking up a few souvenirs. *Remember:* Bargaining is expected. The most reputable beach vendors are concentrated at Los Muertos Beach in front of the El Dorado and La Palapa restaurants (calle Pulpito).

In most of the better-quality shops and galleries, shipping, packing, and delivery services to Puerto Vallarta hotels are available, while some will also ship to your home address.

THE LOWDOWN ON HUICHOL INDIAN ART

Puerto Vallarta offers the best selection of Huichol art in Mexico. Descendants of the Aztecs, the Huichol Indians are one of the last remaining indigenous cultures in the world that has remained true to its ancient traditions, customs, language, and habitat. The Huichol live in adobe structures in the high Sierras (at an elevation of 4,600 ft.) north and east of Puerto Vallarta. Due to the decreasing fertility (and therefore productivity) of the land surrounding their villages, they have come to depend more on the sale of their artwork for sustenance.

Huichol art has always been cloaked in a veil of mysticism— probably one of the reasons this form of *artesanía* is so sought after by serious collectors. Huichol art is characterized by colorful, symbolic yarn "paintings," inspired by visions experienced during spiritual ceremonies. In these ceremonies, artists ingest peyote, a hallucinogenic cactus, which induces brightly colored visions; these are considered to be messages from their ancestors. The symbolic and mythological imagery seen in these visions is reflected in the art, which encompasses not only yarn paintings but fascinating masks and bowls decorated with tiny colored beads.

The Huichol might be geographically isolated, but they have business savvy and have adapted their art to meet consumer demand—original Huichol art, therefore, is not necessarily traditional. Iguanas, jaguars, sea turtles, frogs, eclipses, and eggs are a result of popular demand. For more traditional works, look for pieces that depict deer, scorpions, wolves, or snakes.

The Huichol have also had to modify their techniques to create more pieces in less time and meet the increased demand. The detailed designs that used to fill the pieces are sometimes replaced by patterned fill-work that is faster to produce. The same principle applies to yarn paintings. While some are beautiful depictions of landscapes and even abstract pieces, they are not traditional themes.

Huichol Indians may also be seen on the streets of Vallarta—they are easy to spot, dressed in white clothing embroidered with colorful designs. A number of fine Huichol galleries are located in downtown Puerto Vallarta (see individual listings under "Crafts & Gifts" and "Decorative & Folk Art," below).

A notable place for learning more about the Huicholes is **Huichol Collection,** Morelos 490, across from the sea-horse statue on the *malecón* (© 3/223-2141). Not only does this shop offer an extensive selection of Huichol art in all price ranges, but it also has a replica of a Huichol adobe hut, informational displays explaining more about their fascinating way of life and beliefs, and usually a Huichol Indian at work creating art.

CLOTHING

Vallarta's single true department store is **LANS,** Juárez 867 (© 3/223-2829), plus a new location in the Hotel Zone, in front of the Gigante shopping center (© 3/225-4242), offering a wide selection of name-brand clothing, accessories, footwear, cosmetics, and home furnishings. Along with the nationally popular **LOB, Carlos 'n' Charlie's,** and **Bye-Bye** brands, Vallarta offers several distinctive shops featuring original designs.

Adriana Gangoiti   Elegant, European-style fashions and made-

Fun Fact **A Huichol Art Primer:
Tips for What to Buy**

Huichol art falls into two main categories: yarn paintings and beaded pieces. All other items you might find in Huichol art galleries are either ceremonial objects or items used in their everyday lives.

Yarn paintings are made on a wood base covered with wax that is meticulously overlaid with colored yarn. Designs represent the magical vision of the underworld, and each symbol gives meaning to the piece. Paintings made with wool yarn are more authentic than those made with acrylic; however, acrylic yarn paintings are usually brighter and have more detail because the threads are thinner. It is normal to find empty spaces where the wax base shows. Usually the artist starts with a central motif and works around it, but it's common to have several independent motifs that, when combined, take on a different meaning. A painting with many small designs tells a more complicated story than one with only one design and fill-work on the background. Look for the story of the piece on the back of the painting. Most Huichol artists will write in pencil in Huichol and Spanish.

Beaded pieces are made on carved wooden shapes depicting different animals, wooden eggs, or small bowls made from gourds. The pieces are covered with wax and tiny *chaquira* beads are applied one by one to form different designs. Usually the beaded designs represent animals; plants; the elements of fire, water, or air; and certain symbols that give a special meaning to the whole. Deer, snakes, wolves, and scorpions are traditional elements; other figures such as iguanas, frogs, and any animals not indigenous to Huichol territory are incorporated by popular demand. Beadwork with many small designs that do not exactly fit into one other is more time consuming and has a more complex symbolic meaning. This kind of work has empty spaces where the wax shows.

to-order clothing are the specialties of this combination boutique and designer studio. The emphasis is on women's wear, but men's casual clothing is also available, with prices much less than you'd expect to pay for such quality fabrics and workmanship. Open Monday through Saturday from 10am to 2pm and 6 to 10pm. Marina las Palmas II, Local 13, Marina Vallarta malecón. ℂ 3/221-2343. AE.

Laura López Labra Designs ⍟ The most comfortable clothing you'll ever enjoy—LLL is renowned for her trademark all-white (or natural) designs in 100% cotton or lace. Laura's fine gauze fabrics float in her designs of seductive skirts, romantic dresses, blouses, beachwear, and baby-dolls. Men's offerings include cotton drawstring pants and lightweight shirts. New designs include a line of precious children's clothing and some pieces with elaborate embroidery based on Huichol Indian designs. Personalized wedding dresses are also available. It's open Monday through Saturday from 10am to 2pm and 5 to 9pm. Basilio Badillo 324. ℂ3/222-3074. No credit cards.

CONTEMPORARY ART

Known for sustaining one of the stronger art communities in Latin America, Puerto Vallarta has an impressive selection of fine galleries featuring quality original works of art. The several dozen galleries get together to offer art walks almost every week between November and April, alternating between galleries located in Marina Vallarta and those in central downtown. These are a social highlight of Vallarta during high season.

Arte de las Americas This gallery is an arm of the Galerí Uno (see below); it exhibits some of the same artists, but has a decidedly more abstract orientation. Open Monday through Saturday from 10am to 10pm. Marina Vallarta, between La Taberna and the Yacht Club. ℂ 3/221-1985.

Galería AL (Arte Latinoamericano) One of the newer gallery successes in town is this showcase of contemporary works created by young, primarily Latin American artists, as well as Vallarta favorite Marta Gilbert. Feature exhibitions take place every two weeks during high season. The historic building (one of Vallarta's original structures) has exposed brick walls; small rooms of exhibition spaces on the second and third floors surround an open courtyard. It's also rumored to have a friendly resident ghost, who partner Susan Burger says has been quite welcoming to this new, cultured environment. Open Monday through Saturday from 10am to 9pm. Josefa Ortiz Dominguez 155. ℂ/fax 3/222-4406. AE, MC, V.

Galería Dante This gallery-in-a-villa showcases contemporary sculptures and classical reproductions of Italian, Greek, and Art-Deco bronzes—all set against a backdrop of gardens and fountains. Located on the "calle de los cafés," the gallery is open daily during the winter from 10am to 5pm. Viewings by appointment are also welcome. Basilio Badillo 269. ⓒ 3/222-2477. Fax 3/222-6284. dante@pvnet.com.mx. MC, V.

Galería Pacífico   Since opening in 1987, Galería Pacífico has been considered one of the finest galleries in Mexico. On display is a wide selection of sculptures and paintings in various media by midrange masters and up-and-comers alike. The gallery expanded and changed locations in the fall of 1998; it's now 1½ blocks inland from the fantasy sculptures on the *malecón*. Among the artists whose careers they have influenced are rising international sensation Rogelio Díaz, Ramiz Barquet, and Patrick Denoun. The gallery is open Monday through Saturday from 10am to 9pm, and Sundays by appointment only. Between May and October, check for reduced hours or vacation closings. Aldama 174, 2nd floor. ⓒ 3/222-1982. www.art mexico.com. AE, MC, V.

Galería Rosas Blancas   This notable member of Puerto Vallarta's gallery community features contemporary painters from throughout Mexico. The downstairs courtyard exhibition space showcases a featured artist, while the upstairs offers a sampling of the artists who regularly exhibit here. A shop next door sells art supplies and books on Mexican art in English and Spanish. Owner Marcella Alegría also runs the adjacent folk-art store, Querubines (see "Decorative & Folk Art," below). Open Monday through Saturday from 9am to 9pm. Juárez 523. ⓒ 3/222-1168. AE, MC, V.

Galería Uno   One of Vallarta's first galleries, this features an excellent selection of contemporary paintings by Latin American artists, plus a variety of posters and prints. During the high season, featured exhibitions change every two weeks. Set in a classic adobe building with open courtyard, it's also a casual, *salón*-styled gathering place for friends of owner Jan Lavender. Open Monday through Saturday from 10am to 9pm. Morelos 561 at Corona. ⓒ 3/222-0908. AE, MC, V.

Studio Cathy Van Rohr   This lovely studio showcases the work of Cathy Von Rohr, one of the most respected artists in the area. For years, Cathy lived in the secluded cove of Majahuitas, on the bay's southern shore, and much of her work reflects the tranquillity and deep connection with the natural world that resulted from that time. Paintings, prints, and sculptures are featured. Open by appointment. Manuel M. Dieguez 321. ⓒ 3/222-5875. www.cathyvonrohr.com. No credit cards.

CRAFTS & GIFTS

Alfarería Tlaquepaque   Opened in 1953, this is Vallarta's original source for Mexican ceramics and decorative crafts, all at excellent prices. Talavera pottery and dishware, colored glassware, bird cages, baskets, and wood furniture are just a few of the many items found in this warehouse-style store. Open Monday through Sunday from 9am to 9pm. Av. México 1100. ℂ 3/223-2121. www.at.com.mx. AE, MC, V.

El Vuelo   You'll find a collection of ethnic and contemporary gifts here, including world music (the Cuban music recordings are outstanding), books, woven fabrics, jewelry, and decorative objects for the home. The shop is open Monday through Saturday from 10am to 10pm. Morelos 684, ½ block from American Express. ℂ 3/222-1822. AE, MC, V.

Safari Accents   Flickering candles glowing from within colored-glass holders welcome you into this highly original shop overflowing with creative gifts, one-of-a-kind furnishings, and reproductions of paintings by Frida Kahlo and Botero. Open from 10am to 11pm daily. Olas Altas 224, Local 4. ℂ3/223-2660. MC, V.

DECORATIVE & FOLK ART

Azul Siempre Azul   Religious figurative pieces, antique *retablos* (painted scenes on tin backgrounds depicting the granting of a miracle), artistic jewelry, and beeswax candles in grand sizes all come together in this tiny store brimming with captivating treasures. Open Monday through Saturday from 10am to 2pm and 5 to 10pm, and Sunday from 5 to 10pm. Located across from Club Roxy, just across the southbound bridge. Ignacio L. Vallarta 228. ℂ 3/223-0060. MC, V.

La Tienda   La Tienda sells fine antiques and decorative objects for the home, including unique furniture, religious-themed items (including *retablos*), glassware, and pewter. They have an outstanding selection of rustic candlesticks and beeswax candles, both in a variety of sizes. It's open Monday through Saturday from 10am to 2pm and 4 to 8pm. A second, smaller location is on "restaurant row," Basilio Badillo 276 (ℂ 3/223-0692), with the same hours. Rodolfo Gómez 122, near Los Muertos Beach. ℂ 3/222-1535. latienda@pvnet.com.mx. AE, MC, V.

Lucy's CuCu Cabaña and Zoo *Finds*   Owners Lucy and Gil Givens have assembled one of the most entertaining, eclectic, and memorable collections of Mexican folk art—about 70% of which is animal-themed. Each summer they travel and personally select the handmade works created by over 100 indigenous artists and artisans. Items include metal sculptures, Oaxacan wooden animals, *retablos* (commemorations of miracles), and fine Talavera ceramics. Five percent of all sales goes to benefit the Puerto Vallarta Animal

Protection Association, organized by the Givenses. It's open Monday through Saturday from 10am to 10pm. Closed from May 15 to October 15. Basilio Badillo 295. No phone. MC, V.

Olinala   Two floors of fine indigenous Mexican crafts and folk art, including an impressive collection of museum-quality masks and original contemporary art by Brewster Brockman, the gallery owner. It's open Monday through Friday from 10am to 2pm and 5 to 8pm, and Saturday from 10am to 2pm. Cárdenas 274. (3/222-4995. MC, V.

Querubines *Finds*   This is my personal favorite for the finest-quality artisan works from throughout Mexico. Owner Marcella García Alegría travels across the country to hand-select the items on sale, which include exceptional artistic silver jewelry, embroidered and handwoven clothing, bolts of loomed fabrics, tin mirrors and lamps, glassware, pewter frames and trays, high-quality wool rugs, straw bags, and Panama hats. It's open daily from 10am to 9pm. Marcella's has also opened a sister-shop to Querubines, called **Serafina** ((3/223-4594), located at Basilio Badillo 260, which features a more extensive selection of her cotton clothing and one-of-a kind handmade jewelry. Open daily from 10am to 9pm. Juárez 501A (corner of Galeana, behind Planet Hollywood). (3/223-1727. AE, MC, V.

JEWELRY & ACCESSORIES

Mosaiqe   It's a potpourri of global treasures—an extensive selection of silk, cotton, and cashmere pareos and shawls, plus resort bags, jewelry, and home decor items. After its first year, it was so successful it now has three locations—in addition to the Basilio Badillo location, others are found at Juarez 279 ((3/223-3146), and Corona 172 ((3/223-1177). Open daily from 10am to 7pm. Basilio Badillo 277. (3/223-3183. AE, MC, V.

Viva   At Viva, both the shop and the jewelry are stunning. You enter through a long corridor lined with displays showcasing exquisite jewelry from 72 international designers. The main room has a large glass pyramid-shaped skylight as its roof, with comfy couches surrounded by more memorable jewelry displays. They also feature the largest selection of authentic French espadrilles and ballet slippers in Latin America. Open daily from 10am to 10pm. Basilio Badillo 274. (3/222-4078. AE, MC, V.

TEQUILA & CIGARS

La Casa del Habano   This fine tobacco shop has certified quality cigars from Cuba, Mexico, and the Dominican Republic, along with humidors, cutters, elegant lighters, and other smoking accessories. It's also a local cigar club, with a walk-in humidor for regular clients. In the back, you'll find comfy leather couches, TV sports, and full bar service—in other words, a manly place to take a break from shopping. It's open Monday through Saturday from 10am to 10pm. Aldama 174. ℭ **3/223-2758**. AE, MC, V.

La Casa del Tequila   Here you'll find an extensive selection of premium tequilas, plus information and tastings to help guide you to an informed selection. Also cigars from Cuba and Veracruz, books, tequila glassware, humidors, and other tequila-drinking and cigar-smoking accessories. In the back, there's a garden patio with a bar for enjoying espresso drinks and tequila drinks. Open Monday through Friday from 9:30am to 11pm. Morelos 589. ℭ **3/222-2000**. AE, MC, V.

3 Puerto Vallarta After Dark

Puerto Vallarta's spirited nightlife reflects the town's dual nature: part resort, part colonial Mexican town. In the past few years, Vallarta's nightlife has seen an expansion of live music, especially in clubs along calle Ignacio L. Vallarta (the extension of the main southbound road) after it crosses the Río Cuale. Along one 3-block stretch you'll find a live blues club, sports bar, Harley Davidson–themed bar with live rock 'n' roll, live mariachi music, gay dance club, steamy-hot live salsa dance club, and the obligatory **Señor Frogs**. Walk from place to place and take in a bit of it all!

The *malecón,* which used to be lined with restaurants, is now known more for its selection of hip dance clubs and a few more relaxed options, all of which look out over the ocean. You can first walk along the broad walkway by the water's edge and check out the action at the various clubs, which extend from the new **Bodeguita del Medio** on the north end to **Hooters** just off the central plaza.

Marina Vallarta has its own array of clubs, with a more upscale, indoor, air-conditioned atmosphere. Also south of the Río Cuale, the Olas Altas zone literally buzzes with action pouring out of its wide selection of small cafes and martini bars. In this zone, there's also an active gay and lesbian club scene.

PERFORMING ARTS & CULTURAL EVENTS

Truth be told, there's a limited selection of cultural nightlife beyond the **Mexican Fiesta.** Culture in Vallarta centers on the visual arts, so the opening of an exhibition has great social and cultural significance. Puerto Vallarta's gallery community comes together to present almost weekly **art walks** where new exhibits are presented, featured artists are in attendance, and complimentary cocktails are served. These social events alternate between the galleries along the Marina Vallarta *malecón* and those in the central downtown area. Check listings in the daily English-language newspaper, *Vallarta Today*, upon arrival to see what may be on the schedule during your stay.

FIESTA NIGHTS

Major hotels in Puerto Vallarta feature frequent fiestas for tourists—open-bar, Mexican buffet dinner, and live-entertainment extravaganzas. Some are fairly authentic and good introductions for first-time travelers to Mexico; others can be a bit cheesy. Shows are usually held outdoors but move indoors when necessary.

Krystal Vallarta Hotel   One of the best Fiesta Nights is hosted by the Krystal Vallarta on Tuesday and Saturday at 7pm. These things are difficult to quantify, but Krystal's program is probably less tacky than most of its hotel counterparts. Av. de las Palmas, north of downtown off the airport road. (✆ 3/224-1041. kvallart@krystal.com.mx. Cover $37. AE, MC, V.

Rhythms of the Night (Cruise to Caletas) ★★★ *(Moments* This is an unforgettable evening under the stars at John Huston's former home at the pristine cove called Las Caletas. The smooth, fast Vallarta Adventure catamaran travels here, entertaining guests along the way until you're greeted at the dock by tiki torches and native drummers. There's no electricity here—you'll dine by the light of the multitude of candles, the stars, and the moon. The buffet dinner is delicious—steak, seafood, and generous vegetarian options. Everything is first class. The show, set to the music of native bamboo flutes and guitars, showcases indigenous dances in a contemporary style. Departs at 6pm, returns by 11pm. Departs from Terminal Marítima. (✆ 3/297-1212, ext 3. www.vallarta-adventures.com. Cost $75, includes boat cruise, dinner, open bar, and entertainment. AE, MC, V.

THE CLUB & MUSIC SCENE
RESTAURANT/BARS

de Santos ★★★   This is Vallarta's newest chic dining spot, but is really known more for the urban, hip crowd the bar draws. The atmosphere really rocks, and it's a great place for a late drink. The decor is minimalist, with lots of exposed brick walls, high ceilings, and, in the back, an open-air patio. The owners obviously put the bulk of their investment into the elegant lighting and outstanding sound system. One of the partners is a member of the super-hot Latin rock group Mana, who uses Vallarta as a home base for writing new songs. As the hour grows later, the music volume increases, and there is even a DJ to match the music to the crowd, which varies in age from 20s on up, but shares a common denominator of cool style. Open daily from 5pm to 2am, 4am weekends. Morelos 771. ℭ 3/223-3052 or 3/223-3053. No cover. AE, MC, V.

Kit Kat Club ✿✿ It's swank and sleek and reminiscent of a New York high-style club, but don't be fooled—it also has a terrific sense of humor. In the golden glow of candlelight, lounge around in cushy, leopard-patterned chairs or cream-colored, overstuffed banquettes listening to swinging tunes while you sip a martini. Not only is the place very hip, it also serves good food, with especially tasty appetizers—that can double as light meals—and scrumptious desserts. Michael, the owner, describes his lounge and cafe as cool, crazy, wild, jazzy, and sexy. I agree. Open daily from 11am to 2am. Martini T dances daily from 5 to 7pm. Pulpito 120, Playas Los Muertos. ℭ 3/223-0093. No cover. MC, V.

La Cantina ✿✿ It's a Mexican classic gone contemporary. *Cantinas* have been a centuries-old tradition in Mexico, and this one has retained the fundamentals while updating the concept to a hip club. Cantinas serve little complimentary plates of food as your table continues to order drinks. This is done here from 1pm to 5pm, and might include *carne con chile* (meat in a chile sauce), soup of the day, or *quesadillas*. In the evenings, enjoy a romantic, clubby atmosphere with recorded music alternating between sultry boleros and the hottest in Mexican rock, at levels that still permit conversation. If you require more stimulation, board games are available to play in one of the brightly colored, smaller rooms or on the larger open-air patio. Beers cost $1.50, with bar drinks priced at $2.50. It's open Sunday through Wednesday from noon to 2am, and Thursday through Saturday from noon to 4am. Morelos 709, downtown. ℭ 3/222-1734. No cover. No credit cards.

ROCK, JAZZ, & BLUES

Club Roxy ✿✿ Currently the most popular live-music club in Vallarta, Club Roxy features a hot house band led by club owner Pico, playing a mix of reggae, blues, rock, and anything by Santana. Live music jams between 10pm and 2am Monday through Saturday nights. It's south of the river between Madero and Cárdenas. Hours are nightly from 6pm to 2am. Ignacio L. Vallarta 217. No cover. ℭ 3/223-2402. AE, MC, V.

El Faro Lighthouse Bar ✿ El Faro is a circular cocktail lounge at the top of the Marina lighthouse and one of Vallarta's most romantic nightspots. Live or recorded jazz plays, and conversation is manageable. Drop by at twilight for the magnificent panoramic views. Open daily from 5pm to 2am. Royal Pacific Yacht Club, Marina Vallarta. ℂ 3/221-0541 or 3/221-0542. elfaropv@pvnet.com.mx. No cover. AE, MC, V.

Mariachi Loco   OK, so it's not rock, jazz, or blues, but this live and lively mariachi club also features singers belting out boleros and ranchero classics. By 10pm it gets going, with the mariachi show beginning at 9pm—the mariachis stroll and play as guests join in impromptu singing. After midnight the mariachis play for pay, which is around $3.50 for each song. They also serve Mexican food until 1am. The club itself is open daily from 1pm to 4am. Lázaro Cárdenas 254, at Ignacio Vallarta. ℂ 3/223-2205. No cover. AE, DC, MC, V.

DANCE CLUBS & DISCOS
A few of Vallarta's clubs or discos charge admission, but generally you pay just for drinks—$3 for a margarita, $2 for a beer, more for a whiskey and mixed drinks. Keep an eye out for the discount passes frequently available in hotels, restaurants, and other tourist spots. Most clubs are open from 10pm to 4am.

Christine   Proving that disco is alive and well, this dazzling club still draws a crowd with an opening laser-light show, pumped-in dry ice and oxygen, flashing lights, and a dozen large-screen video panels. The sound system is truly amazing, and the mix of music can get almost anyone dancing. Open nightly from 10pm to 4am; the light show begins at 11pm. *Note:* No shorts (for men, of course), tennis shoes, or thongs. In the Krystal Vallarta Hotel, north of downtown off av. Francisco Medina Ascencio. ℂ 3/224-0202. Cover varies depending on the night from free to $6. AE, DC, MC, V.

J& B Salsa Club ℛ   This is the locally popular place to go for dancing to Latin music—from salsa to samba, the dancing here is hot! Fridays, Saturdays, and holidays it features live bands. Open from 9pm to 6am. Av. Francisco Medina Ascencio, km 2.5 (Hotel Zone). ℂ 3/224-4616. Cover $5. MC, V.

Señor Frogs   The sheer size of this hot new outpost of the famed Carlos 'n' Charlie's chain is daunting, but it still fills up and rocks until the early morning hours. Those cute waiters remain a signature of the chain, and one never knows when they'll assemble on stage and call on a bevy of beauties to join them in a tequila-drinking contest. Occasionally live bands appear. Although mainly popular with the 20s set, all ages will find it fun. There's food service as well, but it's better known for its dance-club atmosphere. Open from noon to 4am. Ignacio L. Vallarta and Venustiano Carranza. © **3/222-5171** or 3/222-5177. Up to $5 cover, depending on the night. AE, MC, V.

Zoo ⩗   Your chance to be an animal and get wild in the night. The Zoo even has cages to dance in if you're feeling unleashed. This popular club has a terrific sound system and a great variety of dance music, including techno, reggae, and rap. Every hour's a happy hour here with two-for-one drinks. Open from 11:30am until the wee hours. Paseo Díaz Ordaz 630 (the malecón).© **3/222-4945.** Cover varies from free to $5. AE, MC, V.

A SPORTS BAR & A STRIP JOINT

Micky's No Name Cafe   With a multitude of TVs and enough sports memorabilia to start a mini-museum, Micky's is a great venue for catching your favorite game, with all NBA, NHL, NFL, MLB, and PPV broadcast sporting events. Mickey's also serves great BBQ ribs and USDA imported steaks. Open daily from 11am to midnight. Morelos 460 (malecón) at Mina. © **3/223-2508.** No cover. MC, V.

Q'eros   Adult nightclub featuring exotic dancers, private shows, and stripteases. Open nightly from 9pm to 6am. Av. Francisco Medina Ascencio, in front of Plaza Genovesa. © **3/222-4367.** Cover $5. MC, V.

GAY & LESBIAN CLUBS

Vallarta has a vibrant gay community with a wide variety of clubs and nightlife options, including special bay cruises and evening excursions to nearby ranches. The free **Southside PV Guide,** Amapas 325 (© **3/222-2517;** pvguide@hotmail.com), specializes in gay-friendly listings.

The two top clubs are:

Club Paco Paco   This combination disco, cantina, and rooftop bar also hosts a spectacular "Trasvesty" transvestite show every Friday, Saturday, and Sunday night at 1:30am. The club is open from noon to 6am daily and is air-conditioned. **Paco's Ranch,** around the corner at Venustiano Carranza 239, has nightly specials, including Western Night on Tuesdays and Leather Night on Thursdays. A nightly "Ranch Hand's Show" performs at 9pm and 12:30 and 3am. This club, which can be accessed from Club Paco Paco, is open from 8pm to 6am. Cover is the same at both clubs. Ignacio L. Vallarta 278. © **3/ 222-1899.** www.pacopaco.com. Cover $6, which includes a drink. (Cover applies at 10pm or before the first show, whichever is first.) AE, MC, V.

Los Balcones   One of the original gay clubs in town, this bi-level space with several dance floors and an excellent sound system earned a few chuckles when it was listed as one of the most romantic spots in Vallarta by *Brides* magazine. Air-conditioned, it's open from 9pm to 4am and posts nightly specials, including exotic male dancers. Juárez 182. © 3/222-4671. No cover. MC, V.

4 Side Trips From Puerto Vallarta

YELAPA: ROBINSON CRUSOE MEETS JACK KEROUAC

It's a cove straight out of a tropical fantasy, and only a 45-minute trip by boat from Puerto Vallarta. Yelapa ℛ has no electricity or cars, and has just had its first paved (pedestrian-only) road put in last year—it remains accessible only by boat. Its tranquillity, natural beauty, and seclusion have made it a popular home for hippies, hipsters, artists, writers (looking for inspiration), and a few ex-pats (looking to escape the stress of the rest of the world, or perhaps the law). A seemingly strange mix, but you're unlikely to ever meet a stranger there—Yelapa remains casual and friendly.

To get there, travel either by excursion boat or inexpensive water taxi (see "Getting Around," in chapter 2). Of course, there's also a challenging mountain bike trip with Bike Mex (see "Mountain Biking & Hiking," under "Staying Active," above). You can spend an enjoyable day, but a longer stay is recommended—and provides a completely different perspective of the place.

Once you're in Yelapa, you can lie in the sun, swim, snorkel, eat fresh grilled seafood at a beachfront restaurant, or sample the local moonshine, *raicilla*. The local beach vendors specialize in the most amazing pies you've ever tasted (coconut, lemon, or chocolate)—and equally amazing is how the pie ladies walk the beach while balancing the pie plates on their heads; they sell crocheted swimsuits, too. You can also tour this tiny town or hike up a river to see one of two waterfalls. The closest to town is about a 30-minute walk from the beach. *Note:* If you use a local guide, agree on a price before you start out. Horseback riding, guided bird-watching, fishing trips, and paragliding are also available.

For overnight accommodations, local residents frequently rent rooms, and there's also the rustic **Hotel Lagunita** (© **01-329/ 8-0554;** www.lalagunita.com.mx). With 27 cabanas (all with private bathroom, though only a few hours of power daily), plus a saltwater pool, massage services, and an amiable restaurant/bar, this is the most accommodating place for most visitors—although you may need to bring your own towel, as they are known to be in short supply. Rates run $70 during the season and $55 off-season per night, depending on the cabana and the time of year. They accept AE, MC, and V with a 10% surcharge. It's become quite popular for yoga students and other groups.

If you stay over on a Wednesday or Saturday night during winter months, don't miss the regular dance at the **Yelapa Yacht Club** 𝒜 (no phone). Typically tongue-in-cheek for Yelapa, the "yacht club" consists of a cement dance floor and a disco ball, but the DJ spins a great range of tunes from Glenn Miller to 'N Sync, attracting all ages and types to the dance. Dinner is a bonus—the food may be the best anywhere in the bay. The menu changes depending on what's fresh. Ask for directions; it's located in the main village, on the beach.

Also notable is the new **Café Vortex** (no phone), overlooking the juncture where the river meets Yelapa Bay. It serves espresso drinks, terrific breakfasts (including the bacon and egg burrito), snacks, and full bar service.

NUEVO VALLARTA & NORTH OF VALLARTA: ALL-INCLUSIVE

Many people assume Nuevo Vallarta is simply a suburb of Puerto Vallarta, but it's really a stand-alone destination located in Nayarit, a different state. Original plans called for a mega-resort development—complete with marina, golf course, and luxury hotels—but much of this remains to be built. Currently, it's a collection of mostly all-inclusive hotels, located on one of the widest, most attractive beaches in the bay. A lengthy entrance road from the highway passes by fields that are great for birding, and nearby lagoons that are great for kayaking. A marina has been finished, and its once-shallow draft can now accommodate bigger boats. The newly opened Paradise Plaza shopping center is adding much to the area in terms of shopping, dining, and services. It's open from 10am to 10pm, and is next to Paradise Village.

Also worthwhile is a day spent at the **Etc. Beach Club,** Paseo de los Cocoteros #38, Nuevo Vallarta (𝒞 **3/297-0174**). This beach club has a volleyball net, showers, rest room facilities, and food and drink service on the beach, both day and night. To get there, take the second entrance to Nuevo Vallarta coming from Puerto Vallarta and turn right on Paseo de los Cocoteros; it is past the Vista Bahia hotel. It's open daily during the winter from 11am to 10:30pm, summer from 11am to 7pm. Drinks range from $1 to $3.50, with entrees costing between $4.50 and $7; cash only.

A trip into downtown Puerto Vallarta takes about 30 minutes by taxi, costs about $15, and is available 24 hours a day. The ride is slightly longer by public bus, which costs 80¢ and operates from 7am to 11pm.

Hotel Club Marival   This all-inclusive hotel is located almost by itself at the northernmost end of Nuevo Vallarta. Done in Mediterranean style, it's a refreshing option next to the mega-resorts that tend to dominate the Nuevo Vallarta landscape. This smaller property has a large variety of rooms ranging from standard rooms with no balconies to large master suites with whirlpools. The master suites have minibars in the room and hair dryers in the bathroom. The beach is one of the real assets here—it stretches over 500 yards and is broad with white sand. There is also an extensive activities program, including fun for children. Club Marival is the first resort to your right on Cocoteros Avenue when you enter Nuevo Vallarta from the second entrance, if you are coming from the Puerto Vallarta airport.

Paseo de los Cocoteros y Blvd, Nuevo Vallarta s/n, Nuevo Vallarta, Nay. 63735. ℂ 3/297-0100. Fax 3/297-0160. www.clubmarival.com. 504 units. High season $123 per person double standard; low season $115 per person double standard. Upgrade to Jr. suite $50 per day, to Master suite w/o whirlpool $250 per day, to Master suite with whirlpool $300 per day. Request your upgrade when making reservations. Rates are all-inclusive. Ask for seasonal specials. AE, MC, V. **Amenities:** Four restaurants, seven bars; three pools and a whirlpool for adults, two pools for children; four lighted tennis courts; a tobacco shop, an arts and craft shop. *In room:* A/C, TV, safe-deposit boxes.

Paradise Village 🏨🏨   Truly a village, this self-contained resort on an exquisite stretch of beach has a full array of guest services, from an on-site disco to a full-service European spa and health club. Styled in a Mayan-influenced design, the collection of pyramid-shaped buildings houses all-suite accommodations in studio, one-bedroom, and two-bedroom configurations. All are well-designed, with a muted color scheme, sitting areas, and kitchenettes—making it ideal for families or groups of friends. The Mayan theme extends to both oceanfront pools with mythical creatures forming water slides and waterfalls. The exceptional spa is reason enough to book a vacation here, with treatments, hydrotherapy, massage (including massage on the beach), and fitness and yoga classes. Special spa packages are always available.

Paseo de los Cocoteros 001, Nuevo Vallarta, Nay. 63731. ℂ 800/995-5714 in the U.S., or 3/226-6770. Fax 3/226-6713. www.paradisevillage.com. 490 units. High season $182–$350 double; low season $140–$280 double. AE, DC, MC, V. **Amenities:** Two beachfront snack bars, two full-service restaurants, nightclub; two oceanfront swimming pools, lap pool; four tennis courts; European spa and complete fitness center; basketball court; beach volleyball; watersports center; Kid's Club; travel services desk for tours and excursions; fleet of rental cars for guests only; meeting facilities; petting zoo; full marina. *In room:* A/C, TV, dataport, minibar, coffeemaker, hair dryer, iron, safe-deposit boxes.

BUCERÍAS: A COASTAL VILLAGE

Only 11 miles north of the Puerto Vallarta airport, Bucerías (Boo-sayr-*ee*-ahs, meaning "place of the divers") ✿ is a small coastal fishing village of 10,000 people in Nayarit State on Banderas Bay. It's caught on as an alternative to Puerto Vallarta for those who find the pace of life there too hectic. Bucerías offers a seemingly contradictory mix of accommodations—trailer-park spaces and exclusive villa rentals tend to dominate, although there's a small selection of hotels as well.

To reach the town center by car, take the exit road from the newly widened highway and drive down the shaded, divided street that leads to the beach. Turn left when you see a line of minivans and taxis that service Bucerías and Vallarta. Go straight ahead 1 block to the main plaza. The beach, with a lineup of restaurants, is half a block farther. You'll see cobblestoned streets leading from the highway to the beach and hints of the villas and town homes behind high walls. Bucerías has already been discovered by second–home owners and by about 1,500 transplanted Americans as a peaceful getaway; tourists have discovered its relaxed pace as well.

If you are taking the bus to Bucerías, get off the bus when you see the minivans and taxis to and from Bucerías line up on the shaded, divided street that leads to the beach. To get here from Puerto Vallarta via public transportation, take a minivan or bus marked BUCERÍAS (they run 6am–9pm). The last minivan stop is Bucerías's town square. There's also 24-hour taxi service.

EXPLORING BUCERÍAS Come here for a day-trip from Puerto Vallarta just to enjoy the long, wide, and uncrowded beach, along with the fresh seafood served at the beachfront restaurants or at one of the unusually great cafes listed below. If you are inclined to stay a few days, you can relax inexpensively and explore more of Bucerías. Sunday is street-market day, but it doesn't get going until around noon, in keeping with the town's casual pace.

The **Coral Reef Surf Shop,** Heroe de Nacozari 114-F (© **3/ 298-0261**), offers not only a great selection of surfboards and gear for sale, but has surfboard and boogie board rentals, surf lessons, and ATV and other adventure tours to surrounding areas.

WHERE TO STAY   Several small hotels and condominiums rent rooms here. For advance planning, check out the Bucerías villa rental bulletin board at **www.sunworx.com**. Locally, **Las Palmas** in Bucerías (© **329/8-0060;** fax 329/8-1100) will book accommodations, including villas, houses, and condos. Call ahead or, when you get to Bucerías, ask for directions to their office, open Monday through Friday from 9am to 2pm and 4 to 6pm, and Saturday from 9am to 2pm. Unfortunately, I cannot recommend any of the hotels in Bucerías; they're run-down, and most people who choose to stay here opt for a private home rental.

WHERE TO DINE   Besides those mentioned below, there are many seafood restaurants fronting the beach. The local specialty is *pescado sarandeado,* a whole fish smothered in tasty sauce and slow-grilled.

Cafe Magaña BBQ RIBS   Famous for its BBQ ribs and chicken, Cafe Magaña gives you a choice of 10 original sauces, all home-made. Flavors have mythological names and contain creative ingredients like ginger, garlic, oranges, apples, cinnamon, and chiles. The sauces have been such a hit that British owner Jeff Rafferty also offers them bottled and for sale. This casual, colorful cafe and take-out restaurant also features TV sports and an occasional live band.

Lázaro Cárdenas 40. © **329/8-1091.** Main courses $7–$12. No credit cards. Fri–Wed 5–11pm.

Karen's Place ⊛ INTERNATIONAL/MEXICAN   This ocean-side casual restaurant offers classic cuisine, plus Mexican favorites in a style that appeals to North American appetites. Known for Sunday brunch (9am–3pm), it also is a great place to spend the day on the beach while enjoying a light lunch, and makes for a romantic dining spot. Their best-selling dinner is a Parmesan herb-crusted fish filet, with a salad of baby greens. This casual, comfortable restaurant also features live music on Tuesday and Saturday evenings.

Located on the beach at the Costa Dorada, Calle Lazaro Cardenas. © **329/8-1499.** Main courses $5–$12. No credit cards. Tues–Sun 9am–10pm; Sunday brunch served 9am–3pm.

Mark's ⊛⊛ *(Finds* ITALIAN/STEAK/SEAFOOD   It's worth a special trip to Bucerías just to eat at this covered-patio restaurant. The most popular American hangout in town, Mark's offers a great assortment of thin-crust pizzas and flat bread, baked in its brick oven and seasoned with fresh herbs grown in the garden. In fact, everything from the shrimp in angel-hair pasta to the pesto-crusted fish fillet and grilled pork tenderloin with mango basil sauce has a wonderfully fresh taste. The multi-talented Chef Jan Marie (Mark's charming wife and partner) runs an adjacent boutique, with the nicest selection of women's resort wear in town. All major sporting events are televised in the bar. Mark's is only half a block from the beach. From the highway, turn left just after the bridge where there's a small sign for Mark's. Then double back left at the next street (it's immediately after you turn left) and turn right at the next corner. Mark's is on the right, the block before the ocean.

Lázaro Cárdenas 56. ℂ **329/8-0303.** Pasta $6.50–$11.50; main courses $9–$16. MC, V. High season Wed–Mon noon–11pm; low season Wed–Mon 5:30–11pm.

PUNTA DE MITA: EXCLUSIVE SECLUSION

At the very northern tip of the bay is an arrowhead-shaped piece of land called Punta de Mita ☆☆☆. Considered a sacred place by the ancestral Indians of the area, this is the point where Banderas Bay, the Pacific Ocean, and the Sea of Cortez come together. The natural beauty here is magnificent, with white-sand beaches due to the coral reefs just offshore. Stately rocks jut out along the shoreline, and the water is a dreamy translucent blue. Today, it is evolving into one of Mexico's most exclusive developments. The master plan calls for a total of four luxury hotels plus several very high-end residential communities interspersed among three championship golf courses. It is the first luxury residential development in Mexico intended for the foreign market. Today, all you'll find is the elegant Four Seasons Resort and its Jack Nicklaus Signature golf course.

Four Seasons Resort Punta Mita ☆☆☆ *(Finds* The Four Seasons Resort has brought a new standard of luxury to Mexico's Pacific Coast. This boutique hotel, situated on 1,000 acres of land bordered on three sides by the ocean, artfully combines seclusion and pampered service with a welcoming sense of comfort. The 113 rooms and 27 suites are in three-story *casitas,* which surround the main building where the lobby, cultural center, restaurants, and pool are located.

Every guest room offers breathtaking views of the ocean from a large terrace or balcony. Most suites also offer a private plunge pool, as well as a separate sitting room, bar, and powder room. Two- and three-bedroom suites are available. Room interiors are typically Four Seasons—plush and spacious with a king or two double beds, plus a seating area and oversized bathroom with a deep soaking tub, separate glass-enclosed shower, and dual vanity sink.

More than the stylish luxury, this hotel boasts unerring service that is both warm and unobtrusive. It's a place to completely get away—bear in mind you are at least 45 minutes from Puerto Vallarta's activities—but then, most guests feel so relaxed and at ease here, it's hard to think of places beyond the resort. The centerpiece of the resort, of course, is the 19-hole (one hole is on a natural island) Jack Nicklaus Signature golf course. It has ocean views from every hole and eight holes that border the ocean (see "Golf" under "Staying Active," above, for complete details). A full-service spa, tennis center, and private championship golf course are options enough, it seems.

Bahía de Banderas, Nay. 63734. © 800/332-3442 in the U.S., or 3/291-6000. Fax 3/291-6060. www.fourseasons.com. 140 units. High season $360–$527 double, $680–$900 suite; low season $280–$360 double, $480–$650 suite. AE, DC, MC, V. Valet parking. **Amenities:** Two restaurants, lobby bar; heated infinity pool surrounded by private cabanas; tennis center with four courts of various surfaces; full-service fitness center; European-style spa; watersports equipment including sea kayaks, Windsurfers, surfboards, and sunfish sailboats; Daily activity agenda, Kids for All Seasons children's activity program; 24-hour concierge service; tour desk; cultural center with lectures and activities. 24-hour room service; complimentary video library. *In room:* A/C, TV/VCR, dataport, minibar, coffeemaker, hair dryer, iron, safe-deposit boxes.

SAN SEBASTIÁN: AN AUTHENTIC MOUNTAIN HIDEAWAY

If you haven't heard about San Sebastián ✫✫✫ yet, it probably won't be long—its remote location and historic appeal have made it the media's new darling destination in Mexico. Originally discovered in the late 1500s and settled in 1603, the town peaked as a center of mining operations, swelling to a population of over 30,000 by the mid-1800s. Today, with roughly 600 year-round residents, San Sebastián retains all the charm of a village locked in time, with an old church, a coffee plantation, an underground tunnel system—and without a T-shirt shop to be found.

GETTING THERE You can arrive by car—it's a 2½-hour drive up the Sierra Madre from Puerto Vallarta on an improved road, but this can be difficult during the summer rainy season, as the road washes out frequently. **Vallarta Adventures** (© 329/7-1212, ext. 3) runs a daily plane service there for half-day tours, but can occasionally accommodate overnight visitors. The small private airport can arrange flights, for about $100 round-trip, depending on the type of plane and number of passengers traveling.

WHERE TO STAY There are two places to stay in San Sebastián. The first is the very basic **El Pabellon de San Sebastián,** which faces the town square. Its nine rooms are clean and simply furnished, surrounding a central patio. Don't expect extras here, but the rates run $12 per double, or $7.50 for singles. Reservations are handled through the town's central phone lines—you call and leave a message or send a fax, and hopefully the hotel will receive it. On any given day, either of the following can serve as the fax line: © **329/7-0332** or 329/7-0333. More secure is by ssb@pvnet.com.mx. Except on holidays, there is generally room at this inn. No credit cards.

A more enjoyable option is the stately **Hacienda Jalisco** (reserve through ssb@pvnet.com.mx, or through the town telephones listed above), built in 1850 and once the center of mining operations in this mining town. Located near the airstrip a 15-minute walk from town, the beautifully landscaped, rambling old Hacienda has walls that seem to whisper stories of its past. If proprietor Bud Acord is feeling social, his stories will probably outshine any the Hacienda has to tell. He's welcomed John Huston, Liz Taylor, Richard Burton, Peter O'Toole, and a cast of local characters as his guests.

The extra-clean rooms have wood floors, rustic furnishings and antiques, and working fireplaces; some are decorated with pre-Columbian reproductions. The ample bathrooms are beautifully tiled and have skylights. Hammocks grace the upstairs terrace, while a sort-of museum on the lower level attests to the celebrity guests and importance the Hacienda has enjoyed over the years. Because of its remote location, all meals are included. Rates are $120 per couple per night, including meals; alcoholic beverages are extra. Group rates are available and discounts can be had for longer stays. No credit cards accepted. Guided horseback, walking, or mine tours can be arranged through the Hacienda.

SAN BLAS: FOR BIRD-WATCHERS & SURFERS

San Blas is a rather nondescript Pacific Coast fishing village of 10,000 people in Nayarit State, but it's one of the country's premier birding spots. Birding enthusiasts come often for long stays. Surfers do too, since some of Mexico's best surfing waters are at Las Islitas Beach.

Only 150 miles from Puerto Vallarta, San Blas is an easy 3½-hour trip along a new two-lane paved highway that starts at Las Varas off Highway 200 (a sign announces LAS VARAS), goes through the villages of Santa Cruz and Aticama, then connects with the two-lane highway into San Blas. Signs are few, so if you're driving, keep asking directions. Buses depart from Puerto Vallarta's new central bus station (1km/.6mi north of Puerto Vallarta's airport) and travel regularly to San Blas. Day-trips and bird-watching excursions run regularly from Puerto Vallarta, available through most hotel tour desks.

As you enter the village you'll be on avenida Juárez, the principal street, which leads to the main plaza on the right. At its far end sits the old church, with a new church next to it. Across the street from the church is the bus station, and on the other side of the churches is the market. After you pass the square, the first one-way street to your left is Batallón, an important street that passes a bakery, a medical clinic, several hotels, and Los Cocos Trailer Park, and ends up at Borrego Beach, with its many outdoor fish restaurants. Nearly everything is within walking distance, and there are public buses that go to the farther beaches—Matanchen and Los Cocos—on their way to Santa Cruz, the next village to the south.

EXPLORING SAN BLAS   Like Acapulco, San Blas was once a very important port for New Spain's trade with the Philippines, and the town was fortified against pirates. Ruins of the fortifications, complete with cannons, the old church, and houses all overgrown with jungle, are still visible atop La Contadura Hill. The fort settlement was destroyed during the struggle for independence in 1811 and has been in ruins ever since. Also, it was from San Blas that Fr. Junípero Serra set out to establish missions in California in the 18th century.

The view from La Contadura is definitely worth the walk there—a panorama of coconut plantations, coastline, town, and the lighthouse at Playa del Rey. To reach the ruins from San Blas, head east on avenida Juárez about half a mile, as if going out of town. Just before the bridge, take the stone path that winds up the hill to your right.

BEACHES & WATERSPORTS   One of the closest beaches is **Borrego Beach;** to reach it, head south from the town plaza on Batallón until it ends. Half a mile past the settlement is a dirt road to **Las Islitas Beach,** a magnificent stretch of sand extending for miles with a few beach-shack restaurants. This is a famous surfing beach with mile-long waves, especially during September and October when storms create the biggest swells. If you don't have a surfboard, you can usually rent one from one of the local surfers. The bodysurfing at Islitas is good, too. A taxi to Islitas costs about $5 from downtown San Blas.

JUNGLE CRUISE TO TOVARA SPRINGS   Almost the moment you hit San Blas, you'll be approached by a guide offering a boat ride into the jungle. This is one of Mexico's unique tropical experiences. To make the most of it, find a guide who will leave at 6:30 or 7am, since the first boat on the river encounters the most birds and the Tovara River is like glass early in the morning, unruffled by breezes. Around 9am boatloads of groups start arriving and the serenity evaporates like the morning mist.

The cost is about $40 for a boatload of one to four people for the 3- to 4-hour trip from the bridge at the edge of town on Juárez. It's less (about $30) for the shorter, 2-hour trip from the embarcadero near Matanchen Bay, out of town. Either way, you won't regret taking the early-morning cruise through shady mangrove mazes and tunnels, past tropical birds and cane fields to the beautiful natural springs, **La Tovara,** where you can swim. There's a restaurant here, too, but it's much more costly than what's available in town. *Note:* The guide may also offer to take you to "The Plantation," which refers to pineapple and banana plantations on a hill outside of town. The additional cost of this trip is not worth it for most people.

BIRD-WATCHING   As many as 300 species of birds have been sighted around San Blas, one of the highest counts in the Western Hemisphere. Birding is best from mid-October to April. Birders and hikers should go to the **Hotel Garza Canela** (✆ 3/285-0307 or 3/285-0480) in San Blas (see "A Place to Stay & Dine," below) to buy a copy of the booklet *Where to Find Birds in San Blas, Nayarit,* by Rosalind Novick and Lan Sing Wu. With maps and directions, it details all the best birding spots and walks, including hikes to some lovely waterfalls where you can swim. Ask the staff at Hotel Garza Canela to put you in touch with the bilingual guide they currently recommend. A half-day tour costs around $100 for up to four people, with an extra charge of $5 per additional person.

A PLACE TO STAY & DINE   There aren't many good accommodations and dining options in San Blas. The **Hotel Garza Canela** 𝕲 (✆ 3/285-0307, 3/285-0480, or 3/285-0112) is still one of the most comfortable places to stay on the coast. A block inland from the waterfront and nestled among pretty gardens of palms, hibiscus, and other tropical plants are the cottagelike fourplexes and other buildings of this resort. You'll find a tranquil ambience, two pools (one for toddlers), and the best restaurant/bar in town. Pets are welcome. The 45 rooms and minisuites ($91 double, $130 to $198 suite, breakfast included; American Express, MasterCard, and Visa accepted) are modern, bright, airy, and immaculate, with well-screened windows, fans, and air-conditioning. Several rooms have kitchens and come with king-size beds; otherwise, most have two double beds, and a few have an extra single bed. Each room has satellite TV and an in-room safe-deposit box. The hotel's **El Delfín** restaurant (main courses $6 to $12; open daily 8am–10am and 1–9pm) serves the best food in San Blas in an air-conditioned dining room with soft lights, soft music, and comfortable captain's chairs. Try the exquisite shrimp with creamy *chipotle* pepper sauce. The spaghetti dishes include pasta with shrimp in lime, roasted garlic, and basil sauce. The homemade soups and desserts are also quite good. Find the hotel and restaurant on calle Paredes Sur 106.

To get here, walk south from the square on Batallón about 6 blocks, turn right on Campeche across from the Marino Inn, then turn left on the next street, Paredes Sur. The hotel, which accepts major credit cards, has a fax (3/285-0308) and toll-free telephone number from within Mexico (© **800/713-2313**).

4

The Costa Alegre: From Puerto Vallarta to Barra de Navidad

Costa Alegre is one of Mexico's most spectacular coastal areas, a 145-mile stretch that connects tropical forests with a series of dramatic cliff-lined coves. The road is lined with tiny outpost towns while dirt roads trail down to a succession of magical coves with pristine beaches, most of them steeped in privileged exclusivity. Considered one of Mexico's greatest undiscovered treasures, this area is becoming a favored hideaway for publicity-fatigued celebrities and those in search of natural seclusion.

The area is alternately referred to as **Costa Alegre** (Happy Coast)—the marketer's term for the area—and **Costa Careyes** (Turtle Coast), after the many sea turtles that nest here annually. Today, it is home to an eclectic array of the most unique, captivating, and exclusive places to stay in Mexico, with a selective choice of activities that includes championship golf and polo. Along the line, however, you will encounter those funky beach towns that provided the original lure to travelers who discovered the area.

Stops along Highway 200, as it meanders between Puerto Vallarta to the north and Manzanillo to the south, can be an enjoyable daytrip, but the drive is usually made en route to an ultimate destination along the coast.

EXPLORING THE COSTA ALEGRE The Costa Alegre is really more an ultimate destination than a place to rent a car and

---

Tips **Watch for Area Code Changes**

As this book went to press, Mexico announced a country-wide change in its long-distance area codes. The new plan will affect every phone number in this book; for details, please consult the box "Changes to Mexico's Phone Numbers Announced," in chapter 1.

---

take a drive, as most of the beaches are tucked in coves accessed by dirt roads that can extend for miles inland. If you do drive along this coast, Highway 200 is safe, but it's not lit and it curves through the mountains, so travel only during the day. A few buses travel this route, but stop only at the towns that line the highway, and many of them are several miles inland from the resorts tucked in along the coast.

1 Along The Costa Alegre (from North to South)

CRUZ DE LORETO & ITS LUXURY ECO-RETREAT

Hotelito Desconocido ✰✰✰ *Moments* The fact that the Hotelito Desconocido (little unknown hotel) is ecologically minded is a bonus in my opinion, but it's not the principal appeal. A cross between *Out of Africa* and *Blue Lagoon,* it is among my favorite places to stay in Mexico. Think camping out with luxury linens, romantic candles everywhere and a symphony performed by cicadas, birds, and frogs.

The rooms, called *palafitos,* are in cottages perched on stilts over a lagoon. The rustic, open-air rooms seem to extend out beyond the bamboo-planked doors and wooden terraces. A grouping of suites—with inviting daybeds that practically cry out *siesta*—are located on the ample sand bar that separates the tranquil estuary from the rousing Pacific Ocean. Their ingenious saltwater pool is also here, a clever diversion since the ocean is too aggressive for even seasoned swimmers.

Inside each of the 24 rooms, you'll find white cotton sheets, oversized bath towels, and gauzy mosquito nets draped seductively over the beds—necessary or not. A housekeeper performs a ritualistic turndown and light up (candles, that is) service each evening at sundown. There is also an inventive system for morning room service— from the comfort of your bed, pull a rope and a flag is hoisted, signaling that you're ready for coffee. Ceiling fans cool the air, and water is solar-heated. It's easy to disconnect here. In fact, it's mandatory: There's no electricity, no phones, no neighboring restaurants, nightclubs, or shopping—only delicious tranquillity for those in search of seclusion. What service lacks in polished professionalism is made up for in enthusiasm.

Part Polynesia and *muy* Mexicano, each room revels in singular style. Marcello Murzilli, the Italian designer who owns the place, traveled throughout Mexico to assemble an admirable collection of antiques, curios, and "so tacky they're classy" knickknacks. The

The Costa Alegre & Central Pacific Coast

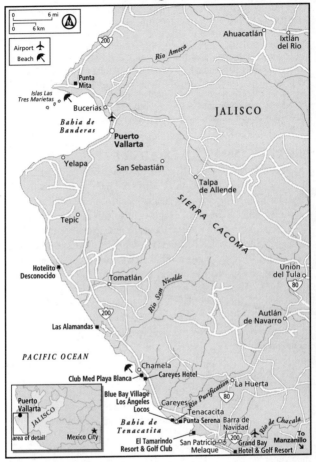

resort has been prominently featured in an admirable collection of travel, fashion, and style magazines, including *Architectural Digest* and *Travel & Leisure*. With a generous creative dash, this *hotelito* is a conscious respite from an overly revved up world.

To get here, take Highway 200 south for one hour, then turn off at the exit for Cruz de Loreto and continue on the unpaved road for about 25 minutes to the Hotelito Desconocido. The signs are clearly marked.

Playón de Mismaloya s/n, Cruz de Loreto, Tomatlán, Jal. 48360. © **877/486-3372** in the U.S. and Canada. Fax 310/385-1908. (For reservations, call © 310/385-1395 in the U.S., 01-800/851-1143 in Mexico, or 3/222-2526, 3/222-2546, or [fax] 3/ 223-0293.) www.hotelito.com. 24 units. High season *Palafito* room $674; Palafito beachfront $740; *Palafito* suite $820. Low season *Palafito* room $420; *Palafito* beachfront $450; *Palafito* suite $500. All meals and activities included; all drinks— including bottled water and soft drinks—extra. AE, MC, V. **Amenities:** Two restaurant/bars; primitive-luxury spa with massage and spa treatments (for extra charge) plus sauna, whirlpool; beach volleyball, bird-watching tours, windsurfing, billiards, kayaking, mountain biking, hiking, and horseback riding (included in room price).

LAS ALAMANDAS: AN EXCLUSIVE LUXURY RESORT

Las Alamandas 𝕽𝕽𝕽   Almost equidistant between Manzanillo (1½ hr.) and Puerto Vallarta (1¾ hr.) a small sign points in the direction of the ocean to Las Alamandas, an ultra-exclusive resort owned by Isabel Goldsmith, daughter of British financier Sir James Goldsmith. A dirt road winds for about a mile through a tiny village to the guardhouse of Las Alamandas, part of a 1,500-acre estate and itself set on 70 acres against low hills. The resort is composed of villas and *palapas* spread among four beaches, gardens, lakes, lagoons, and a bird sanctuary. It's designed for privacy to the point that guests rarely catch a glimpse of one another. The resort recently added air-conditioning and telephones, giving way to the demands of today's travelers, yet still manages to keep the experience as natural as possible. Its architecture is a mix of Mediterranean, Mexican, and southwestern United States, while furnishings are a stunning blend of Mexican handcrafted furniture, pottery, and folk art, and sofa beds and pillows are covered in bright textiles from Mexico and Guatemala. Although exquisite, the furnishings still exude a relaxed feel. Only 22 guests can be accommodated at any one time, so the threat of crowds is nonexistent.

All the villas are spacious and have high-pitched tiled roofs, cool tiled floors, and tiled verandas with ocean views. They have several bedrooms (each with its own bathroom) and can be rented separately or as a whole house; preference for reservations is given to guests who rent whole villas. Some villas are on the beach, while others are set back from the beach across a cobblestoned plaza. Transportation in the hotel's van to and from Manzanillo ($180 one way) and Puerto Vallarta ($180 one way) can be arranged when you reserve your room. Air transport from Puerto Vallarta is also available; call for details and prices.

Mailing address: Domicilio Conocido Costa Alegre QUEMARO Jalisco, Apdo Postal 201, San Patricio Melaque, Jal. CP 48980. Location address: Hwy. 200,

Manzanillo–Puerto Vallarta, Jal. 48800. ((*©* **800/223-6510** or 888/882-9616 in the U.S. and Canada, or 3/285-5500. Fax 3/285-5027. www.las-alamandas.com. 6 villas containing 11 suites. High-season $390–$1,200 suite, $1,150–$2,598 villa; low season $290–$780 suite, $1,610–$1,820 villa. Meal plans also available. AE, MC, V. **Amenities:** Restaurant with room service; 60-foot swimming pool with massage jets; lighted tennis court; weight room; horses; hiking trails; boat tours to Río San Nicolás for birding; mountain bikes; boogie boards; concierge; tour desk; library of books and videos. A private 3,000-foot paved landing strip capable of accommodating a King Air turbo prop is on the premises; make advance arrangements for landing. *In room:* A/C, dataport, minibar. Rooms may have TVs with VCRs, upon request only, but s no television reception from the outside.

CAREYES

The resorts **Club Med Playa Blanca** and **The Careyes Hotel** are roughly 100 miles south of Puerto Vallarta. They're about a 2-hour drive north of Manzanillo on Highway 200, but only about a 1-hour drive from the Manzanillo airport. If you haven't arranged for transportation through either hotel, taxis from the Manzanillo airport charge around $100 one way for the trip. There are also car rentals at both the Manzanillo and Puerto Vallarta airports. These resorts are completely self-contained, and a car would be useful only for exploring the coast—Barra de Navidad and other resorts, for example—although the hotels can also make such touring arrangements.

Club Med Playa Blanca *֍*   On a beautiful cove separated by grand bluffs from The Careyes Hotel, this sienna-colored resort climbs up, around, and down a lovely, lushly landscaped hillside to the beach. Accommodations are in basic, yet comfortable adobe brick *casitas,* with large, bright rooms with a choice of two full beds or one king bed.

This Club Med has always been popular with active singles and young couples, as the extensive, innovative program of activities would indicate. No facilities are available for children, as this is an adults-only club. Numerous special-interest activities are included in the prices. You can avail yourself of the circus workshop and learn to fly from a high trapeze, jump on a trampoline, juggle, and walk the high wire. There is a PADI scuba-certification class for beginning divers (extra charge), but no exploration dives. Usually, there are twice-daily boat excursions that include snorkeling and a picnic at a nearby, secluded beach.

Other special-interest activities are offered at an additional charge, including an intensive horseback riding program and a rock-climbing wall. There are daily excursions to nearby Bird Island (a natural habitat for nesting boobies), out into the ocean for deep-sea fishing, and to nearby Manzanillo, Barra de Navidad, and more. Massages are available, as well as arts-and-crafts workshops, with a small charge for materials.

Cihuatlán, Careyes, Jal., 48980. ℂ **800/CLUBMED** in the U.S. and Canada, or 3/351-0001 or 3/351-0002. Fax 3/351-0004. www.clubmed.com. 295 units. Weekly all-inclusive rates include airfare and are based on departure city. Shorter stays and stays without air are only available space permitting, and all prices must be quoted through Club Med. AE, MC, V. Closed May–Nov. **Amenities:** Three restaurants, two bars, disco, plus nightly shows and entertainment; Olympic-size pool; six tennis courts (four lit for night play); fitness center with aerobics and calisthenics; equipment for sailing, kayaking, snorkeling, archery, volleyball, basketball, Ping-Pong, bocce, and billiards;; token-operated washers and dryers; infirmary. *In room:* A/C, irons and ironing boards available, safes.

The Careyes Hotel ⟨⟩

The Careyes is a gem of a resort nestled on a small, pristine cove between dramatic cliffs that are home to the super-exclusive villas of Careyes. This area has practically defined the architectural style that defines Mexico beach chic today—bold washes of vibrant colors, open spaces, and gardens that showcase the tropical flowers and palms indigenous to the area.

The hotel, whose management was just taken over by Starwood Hotels, is in the process of undergoing some significant upgrades in services and facilities. The pampered accommodations all face the ocean and are stylishly simplistic. Although guests come here for its isolation, you can still enjoy many services, including a full European spa and polo. It's both rustic and sophisticated, with the room facades awash in scrubbed pastels forming a U around the center lawn and freeform pool. Earthy but elegant Mexican tiles and decorative accents give each room a dramatic feel, from the colony shutters and white-tile floors to the handsome loomed bedspreads and colorful pillows. Some rooms have balconies; all have ocean views. Twenty rooms have private pools, and affiliated full villas are also available for rent through the hotel. The hotel is a member of the Small Luxury Hotels of the World group and has become popular for small corporate retreats.

The hotel offers a number of special-interest activities for guests. Named after the hawksbill turtle (*carey* in Spanish), the hotel sponsors a Save the Turtle program in which guests can participate between July and December.

Km 53.5 Hwy. 200, Careyes (mail to Apdo Postal 24, Cihuatlán), Jal., CP 48970. ℂ **800/525-4800** in the U.S. and Canada, or 3/351-0000. Fax 3/351-0100. www.grupoplan.com. 48 units. High season $250 double, $395–$460 suite; low season $225 double, $350–$450 suite. AE, MC, V. **Amenities:** Restaurant/bar, deli; large oceanfront pool; privileges at the super-exclusive El Tamarindo Resort,

25 miles south, with 18-hole mountaintop golf course overlooking the ocean; two tennis courts; paddle court; fully equipped state-of-the-art spa with massage, loofah scrub, wax, hot and cold plunge pools, steam, sauna, weight equipment; kayaks, windsurf boards, Aquafins; "Just for Kids" children's activity program offered during Christmas and Easter vacation periods; room service; laundry; tobacco shop; library of books and videos. *In room:* A/C, TV, minibars, small refrigerators, hair dryers, robes.

TENACATITA BAY

Located 60 minutes (33 miles) north of Manzanillo airport, this jewel of a bay is accessed by a 5-mile dirt road, passing through a small village set among banana plants and coconut palms. Sandy, serene beaches are tucked into coves around the bay (frolicking dolphins along the beachfront are a common sight), and a coastal lagoon is filled with exotic birds. Swimming and snorkeling are good here, and the bay is a popular stop for luxury yachts cruising down the coast. Just south of the entrance to Tenacatita is a sign directing you to the area's accommodations: the all-inclusive **Blue Bay Los Ángeles Locos** and **Punta Serena** resorts, as well as the exclusive **El Tamarindo Resort and Golf Club.** There is no commercial or shopping area, and dining options outside your hotel are limited to a restaurant or two that may emerge during the winter months (high season). Relax—that's what you're here for.

Blue Bay Village Los Ángeles Locos 𝒜   Set on a 3-mile stretch of sandy beach, Blue Bay Village Los Ángeles Locos offers an abundance of activities and entertainment in the midst of the seclusion of Tenacatita Bay. An extensive activities program and an ample selection of dining and entertainment options offer guests excellent value. It's a good choice for families and groups of friends. All rooms have ocean views, with either balconies or terraces. The three-story hotel is basic in its decor and amenities, but it's clean and comfortable. The attraction here is the wide array of on-site activities, plus a Jungle River–cruise excursion (included in the price of your stay). **La Largata Disco** is a little on the dark and smoky side, but can really rock, depending on the crowd—it's basically the only option on the bay.

Km 20 Carretera Federal 200, Tenacatita 48989, Municipio de la Huerta, Jal. ℭ **800/BLUE BAY** in the U.S., or 3/351-5020 or 3/351-5100. Fax 3/351-5050. www.bluebayresorts.com. 204 units. High season $85 double; low season $75 double. Rates are all-inclusive. AE, MC, V. **Amenities:** Two restaurants, snack bar, three bars, disco; one pool for adults and one for kids adjacent to the beach; tennis (three courts) available for an extra charge; exercise room; windsurfing, kayaks, Hobie Cats; horseback riding; basketball court; Kid's Club; pool tables; massage; babysitting; laundry. *In room:* A/C, TV.

Punta Serena 𝄞𝄞 Punta Serena is a refuge for relaxation and renewal. Set on a mountain overlooking this virgin bay, it's an adults-only holistic resort with a complete offering of services aimed at either putting you into a total state of relaxation or awakening new energy inside.

Punta Serena is one of the only resorts in Mexico truly geared for spiritual renewal, and does an excellent job of offering enough without making non-enthusiasts feel uncomfortable. Yoga, tai chi, and chi kung classes, native Aztec *Temazcal* (sweat lodge) ceremonies, and guided meditation sessions are offered over a daily-changing schedule. Too much introspection for your taste? It's also perfectly OK to simply immerse yourself in a mindless read while lolling in one of the two hot tubs nestled into the side of the cliff overlooking the Pacific blue, below.

All rooms and suites are set in two-story bungalows, with ocean views and either balconies or large terraces with hammocks. Smoke-free and spacious, the rooms are very basic but both comforting and comfortable. The open-air restaurant serves three meals daily featuring excellent buffets of healthful selections, fresh juices, and vegetarian cuisine—it's the one buffet that I've really enjoyed. *Palapa*-topped, it has a stunning view of the bay and a constant breeze. Yes, drinks (including wine and other spirits) are served with meals, also included in your stay.

There is a private beach—one of the only nude (optional) beaches in Mexico. Get a massage in the open-air massage area or in a more private room. A library and video corner are part of the common areas. Guests have access to the facilities at the neighboring Blue Bay Village, if things here get too quiet.

Km 20 Carretera Federal 200, Tenacatita 48989, Municipio de la Huerta, Jal. ℂ 800/551-2558 in the U.S., or 3/351-5013. www.puntaserena.com. 21 smoke-free units. High season $85–$110; low season $65–$110 double. Rates are all-inclusive. AE, MC, V. **Amenities:** Restaurant; small but striking pool; small well-equipped gym; two cliff-side hot tubs; sauna; schedule of relaxation-inducing activities and classes. *In room:* A/C.

The Tamarindo 𝄞𝄞𝄞 *Finds* El Tamarindo is the area's most luxurious resort, complete with its own golf course. For years, it was invitation-only for one of these oceanfront villas, each set in its own private cove. Now under management by Starwood hotels, it may finally gain the recognition it deserves.

The bungalows exude an air of exclusivity—guests each have their own thatched-roof bungalow complete with splash pool and whirlpool, plus lounging and dining areas that complement the stunning bedrooms. Details like bouquets of tropical flowers, fresh plums, and a basket filled with rolled white towels is standard fare here. Meals can be served "en suite," thus pampering you like you have your own private staff to serve every whim. The bedrooms—with dark hardwood floors and furnishings—can be closed off for air-conditioned comfort, but the remaining areas are delightfully open to the sea breezes and heady tropical air.

The different categories of bungalows denote their location—Beachfront, Palm Tree, Garden, and Forest. The non-beachfront bungalows all have the same quality decor and amenities, but feature more closed-in areas—after all, you are in the tropical jungle. Anyone squeamish about creepy crawlies may be uncomfortable in the beginning, as the rain forest brings in the occasional land crab or bug, but really, it's a spectacular sensation to listen to the life around you. The bungalows circle back from a calm, private cove. Situated amid 2,000 acres of tropical rain forest bordering the Pacific Ocean, you'll feel as if you've found your own personal, tropical bit of heaven.

Tamarindo has its own championship 18-hole golf course; the approach to the first hole is through a forest of palms so tall they block the sun. The golf course has seven oceanside holes, with fairways and greens gently worked into the mountainous terrain and dramatic views. It's heavenly, and you'll often be the only one on the course.

El Tamarindo is located about 3 hours south of Puerto Vallarta, or 40 minutes north of Manzanillo airport. To get there, take Highway 200, then turn west at the clearly market exit for El Tamarindo, where you'll continue down a smoothly paved but winding road for about 25 minutes to the resort. The signs are clearly marked.

Km 7.5 Carretera Melaque–Puerto Vallarta, Cihuatlan, Jal., CP 48970. ✆ 335/15032. Fax 335/15070. www.starwood.com. 28 bungalows. High season Beachfront Bungalow $475, 2-bedroom Palm Tree Bungalow $550, Forest Bungalow $300; low season Beachfront Bungalow $425, 2-bedroom Palm Tree Bungalow $525, Forest Bungalow $275. AE, MC, V. **Amenities:** Restaurant/bar, en-suite dining; large beachfront pool with whirlpool; tennis (two clay courts); spa services available; estuary bird-watching tours; windsurfing, kayaking, aquafin sailboats; horseback riding; mountain biking; hiking along well-kept trails. *In room:* A/C, dataport, hair dryer, safe, bathrobes.

2 Barra De Navidad & Melaque

This pair of rustic beach villages (only 3 miles apart) has been attracting long-time travelers to Mexico for decades. Only 30 minutes north of Manzanillo's airport by car, or 65 miles north of downtown, Barra has a few bricked or cobblestoned streets, good budget hotels and restaurants, and funky beach charm. All of this lies incongruously next to the super-luxurious Grand Bay Hotel, which sits on a bluff across the inlet from Barra. Melaque offers a lineup of budget hotels both on and off the beach, fewer restaurants, and little in the way of funky charm, although the beach is as wide and more beautiful than Barra's. Both villages appeal to those looking for a quaint, quiet, and inexpensive retreat, rather than a modern, sophisticated destination. The Grand Bay Hotel, with its five-star quality and 27-hole golf course, provides a whole new dimension to vacationing in Barra—just as Barra adds a whole new dimension to vacationing in a luxury resort.

In the 17th century Barra de Navidad was a harbor for the Spanish fleet, and it was from here that galleons first set off in 1564 to find China. Located on a crescent-shaped bay with curious rock outcroppings, Barra de Navidad and neighboring Melaque are connected by a continuous beach on the same wide bay, and they revel in their very relaxed pace. It's safe to say that the only time Barra and Melaque hotels are full is during Easter and Christmas weeks. **Barra de Navidad** has the most charm, the most tree-shaded streets, best restaurants, most stores, and the best conviviality between locals and tourists. Barra is very laid-back; faithful returnees adore its lack of flash. Other than the new Grand Bay Hotel, on the cliff across the waterway in what is called Isla Navidad (although it's not on an island), nothing is new or modern. But there's a bright edge to Barra now, with more good restaurants and a limited—but existent— nightlife.

Melaque, on the other hand, is larger, rather sun-baked, treeless, and lacking in attractions. It does, however, have plenty of cheap hotels available for longer stays and a few restaurants. Although the beach between the two is continuous, Melaque's beach, with deep sand, is more beautiful than Barra's, where the sand is more packed down by the wave action.

Although **Isla de Navidad Resort** has a manicured 27-hole golf course and the super-luxurious Grand Bay Hotel, the area's pace hasn't quickened as fast as expected. The golf is challenging and also delightfully uncrowded, with another exceptional course at nearby Tamarindo. Simply put, it's become a serious golfer's dream.

ESSENTIALS
GETTING THERE   Buses from Manzanillo frequently run the route up the coast along Highway 200 on their way to Puerto Vallarta and Guadalajara (for about $2.60). Most stop in the central

Barra de Navidad Bay Area

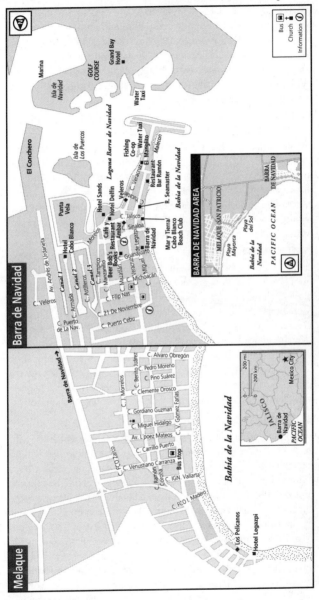

villages of both Barra de Navidad and Melaque. From the Manzanillo airport, it's only around 30 minutes to Barra, and taxis are available to take you there. Puerto Vallarta is a 3-hour (by car) to 5-hour (by bus) ride north on Highway 200 from Barra. From Manzanillo, the highway twists through some of the Pacific Coast's most beautiful mountains covered in oak and coconut palm and acres of banana plantations.

VISITOR INFORMATION   The **tourism office** for both Barra de Navidad and Melaque is in Barra on Jalisco 67 between Veracruz and Mazatlán (©/fax **3/355-5100**). The office is open Monday through Friday from 9am to 5pm. The **Travel Agency Isla Navidad Tours** at Veracruz 204-A (© **3/355-5666** or 3/355-5667) can handle arrangements for plane tickets and sells bus tickets from Manzanillo to Puerto Vallarta and Guadalajara. It's open Monday through Saturday from 10am to 8pm. American Express, MasterCard, and Visa are accepted.

ORIENTATION   In Barra, the main beachfront street, **Legazpi,** is lined with hotels and restaurants. From the bus station, beachfront hotels are 2 blocks straight ahead across the central plaza. Two blocks behind the bus station and to the right is the lagoon side. More hotels and restaurants are located on its main street, **Morelos/ Veracruz.** Few streets are marked, but 10 minutes of wandering will acquaint you with the village's entire layout. There's a taxi stand at the intersection of Legazpi and Sinaloa streets. Posted rates for trips to Manzanillo run $25. Barra's **central plaza** is bordered by Legazpi, Jalisco, Sinaloa, and Veracruz streets. It seems active with playing kids, and there's an occasional market set up selling fresh flowers.

ACTIVITIES ON & OFF THE BEACH

Swimming and enjoying the attractive beach and views of the bay take up most tourists' time. Hiring a small boat for a coastal ride or fishing can be done in two ways. Go toward the *malecón* on calle Veracruz until you reach the tiny boatmen's cooperative with fixed prices posted on the wall, or you can walk two buildings farther to the water taxi ramp. The inexpensive ($1) water taxi is the best option for going to Colimilla (5 min. away) or across the inlet (3 min., 50¢) to the Grand Bay Hotel. The water taxis make the rounds regularly, so if you're at Colimilla, all you have to do is wait and a water taxi will be along shortly. At the Cooperative, a 30-minute **tour around the lagoon** costs $15, and a tour out on the sea costs $18. **Sportfishing** $75 for up to four people for half a day in a small *panga* (open fiberboats like the ones used for the water taxis).

Unusual **area tours; house, condo, and apartment rentals;** and **sports-equipment rental** can all be arranged through **The Crazy Cactus,** Jalisco 8 (©/fax **3/355-6099**), operated by Trayce Ross and located half a block inland from the town church on Legazpi. She rents cars, bicycles, boogie boards, snorkeling equipment, life jackets, and kayaks—as well as handles real estate rentals and sales. The adjoining gift shop is run by her daughter, who does custom building. (The store may be closed May through October.) **Paraíso Pacífico Tours** (© **3/355-5122**), located in the lobby of the Hotel Barra de Navidad (see below) and operated by Mari Blanca Pérez, offers up-to-date maps of both Barra and Melaque; a good lineup of nearby boat excursions for snorkeling, diving, and sunning at beaches north near Tenacatita; horseback riding near Melaque; an interesting trip to Bird Island near Chamela to see nesting boobies; shopping tours to Manzanillo; a daylong trip to Colima City to see the town's volcanoes and shop; a day-trip to a village devoted to marble mining and making huaraches (leather sandals); a very long day-trip to Guadalajara and Tlaquepaque; sunset cruises; and fishing (a half day for $128 in a *panga* or $300 in a yacht).

For **golf,** the Grand Bay Hotel's beautiful and challenging 27-hole, 7,053-yard, par-72 course is open to the public. Hotel guests pay greens fees of $95 for 18 holes, or $115 for 27 holes, while nonguests pay $115 and $140, respectively; the prices include a motorized cart. Caddies are available, as are rental clubs. The Crazy Cactus (mentioned above) can also arrange golf at El Tamarindo's gorgeous, mountaintop, 18-hole course about 20 miles north of Barra.

Beer Bob's Books, avenida Mazatlán 61, between Sinaloa and Guanajuato, is a book-lover's institution in Barra and sort of a community service that the rather grouchy Bob does for fun. His policy of "leave a book if you take one" allows vacationers to select from hundreds of neatly shelved paperbacks, as long as they leave a book in exchange. It's open Monday through Friday from 1 to 4pm and occasionally in the evenings. "Beer Bob" got his name because in earlier days when beer was cheap, he kept a cooler stocked, and book browsers could sip and read. When beer prices went up, Bob put the cooler away, but he's still called Beer Bob.

WHERE TO STAY

Low season is considered any time except Christmas and Easter weeks in Barra. Except for those 2 weeks, it doesn't hurt to ask for a discount at the inexpensive hotels.

VERY EXPENSIVE

Grand Bay Hotel ⭐ *Overrated*   Across the yacht channel from Barra de Navidad, this luxurious hotel opened in 1997 on 1,200 acres next to the hotel's 27-hole golf course. It overlooks the village, bay, Pacific Ocean, and Navidad lagoon. The hotel's beach is narrow and on the lagoon. A better beach is opposite the hotel on the bay in Barra de Navidad. The spacious rooms are sumptuously outfitted with marble floors, large bathrooms, and hand-carved wood furnishings. Prices vary according to view and size of room, but even the more modest rooms are large. Each comes with a king-size or two double beds, a glass-top desk, ceiling fans plus air-conditioning, and a balcony. Executive suites are enormous and include a separate glass shower and bathtub, living room, dining room table, bar with butler's kitchen and separate entry, and enormous bedroom. Junior suites lack the dining area. All suites have a steam sauna and telephones in the bathroom as well as a sound system. The hotel is a short water-taxi ride across the inlet from Barra de Navidad; it can also be reached by paved road from Highway 200. Although the hotel bills itself as being on the Island of Navidad at Port Navidad, the port is the marina, and the hotel is on a peninsula, not an island.

Isla Navidad, Col. 45110. © **888/GRANBAY** in the U.S., or 3/355-5050 or 3/331-0500. Fax 3/355-6070. www.grandbay.com. 199 units. High season $381–$460 double, $550–$680 parlor and executive suites; low season $263–$321 double, $468–$614 parlor and executive suites. Ask about tennis, golf, fishing, and honeymoon packages. AE, DC, DISC, MC, V. **Amenities:** Two restaurants, two bars, golf club with food and bar service; swimming pool with a series of water slides and swim-up bar; 27-hole, par-72 golf course designed by Robert Von Hagge; golf club with pro shop and driving range; three lighted grass tennis courts with stadium seating; small workout room with treadmills and free weights; fishing, boat, and other excursions can be arranged; Kid's Club with activity program; 24-hour concierge; complimentary round-trip transportation between the Manzanillo airport and hotel; business center; salon; room service; laundry; dry cleaning. *In room:* A/C, cable TV, dataport, minibar, hair dryer, iron, security box, bathrobes, magnified makeup mirrors.

MODERATE

Hotel Cabo Blanco ⭐⭐   Located on the point where you cross over to Isla Navidad, the Cabo Blanco reigns as an outstanding option for family vacations or longer term stays. Rooms are pleasantly rustic, with tile floors, large tile tubs, separate dressing area, and stucco walls. Views overlook the bay, but it's a mere 5-minute walk to the beach. The beamed-ceiling lobby is housed in its own building; rooms are in hacienda-style buildings surrounded by gardens. The atmosphere is generally tranquil, except for weekends and

Mexican holidays, when this hotel tends to fill up. Because the Cabo Blanco doesn't front the beach, it's opened an affiliated beach club and restaurant, Mar y Tierra (see "Where to Dine," below).

Armada y Bahía de la Navidad s/n, 48987 Barra de Navidad, Jal. ✆ 3/355-5103 or 3/355-5136. Fax 3/355-6494. 101 units. $75 double; $144 suites with kitchenette. All-inclusive option, add $72 per person. AE, MC, V. **Amenities:** Two restaurants; four pools, two reserved for adults only; two tennis courts; concierge; tour desk; car-rental desk; laundry service; tobacco shop. *In room:* A/C, TV.

INEXPENSIVE

Hotel Barra de Navidad ⋦ At the northern end of Legazpi, this popular and comfortable beachfront hotel has friendly management and some rooms with balconies overlooking the beach and bay. Other, less-expensive rooms afford only a street view. A nice swimming pool is on the street level to the right of the lobby.

Legazpi 250, 48987 Barra de Navidad, Jal. ✆ **3/355-5122.** Fax 3/355-5303. 59 units. $53–$60 double. MC, V. *In room amenities:* A/C (only oceanview rooms).

Hotel Delfín One of Barra's better-maintained hotels, the four-story (no elevator) Delfín is on the landward side of the lagoon. It offers pleasant, basic, well-maintained, and well-lit rooms. Each has red-tile floors and a double, two double, or two single beds. The tiny courtyard, with a small pool and lounge chairs, is shaded by an enormous rubber tree. From the fourth floor there's a view of the lagoon. A breakfast buffet is served from 8:30 to 10:30am (see "Where to Dine," below).

Morelos 23, 48987 Barra de Navidad, Jal. ✆ 3/355-5068. Fax 3/355-6020. 24 units. $36–$45 double. Ask about low-season discounts. MC, V. Free parking in the front. **Amenities:** Restaurant; pool.

Hotel Sands The colonial-style Sands, across from the Hotel Delfín (see above) on the lagoon side at Jalisco, offers small but homey rooms with red-tile floors and windows with both screens and glass. Bathrooms have recently been remodeled with new tiles and fixtures. Lower rooms look onto a public walkway and wide courtyard filled with greenery and singing birds; upstairs rooms are brighter. Twelve rooms (suites or bungalows) have air-conditioning and kitchenette facilities. The hotel is known for its warm hospitality and high-season happy hour from 2 to 6pm at the pool terrace bar beside the lagoon. On weekends from 9pm to 4am, an adjacent patio "disco" has recorded music for dancing. Breakfast is served from 7:30am to noon. Fishing trips can be arranged, and tours are available to nearby beaches.

Morelos 24, 48987 Barra de Navidad, Jal. ℭ/fax **3/355-5018,** or ℭ 36/16-2859. 42 units. High season $61 double; low season $42 double. Rates include breakfast and parking. Discounts for stays of 1 week or more. MC, V (6% surcharge). **Amenities:** Restaurant/bar; pool with whirlpool overlooking the lagoon beach; children's play area; tour desk.

WHERE TO DINE

El Manglito 🏵 SEAFOOD/INTERNATIONAL   Located on the placid lagoon, with a view of the palatial Grand Bay Hotel, El Manglito serves home-style Mexican food to a growing number of repeat diners. The whole fried fish accompanied by drawn garlic butter, boiled vegetables, rice, and french fries, is a crowd-pleaser. Other enticements include boiled shrimp, chicken in orange sauce, and shrimp salad.

Veracruz, near the Fishing Cooperative. No phone. Main courses $4–$8. No credit cards. Daily 9am–11pm.

Hotel Delfín INTERNATIONAL   The second-story terrace of this small hotel is a pleasant place to begin the day in Barra. The self-serve buffet offers an assortment of fresh fruit, juices, granola, yogurt, milk, pastries, and unlimited coffee. Eggs and the delicious banana pancakes—for which the restaurant is known—are made to order and included in the buffet price.

Morelos 23. ℭ **3/355-5068.** Breakfast buffet $3. No credit cards. Daily 8:30am–noon.

Mar y Tierra INTERNATIONAL   Cabo Blanco's Beach Club is also a popular restaurant and bar, and a great place to spend a day at the beach. On the beach, there are shade *palapas* and beach chairs and a game of beach volleyball seems constantly in progress. The restaurant itself is very colorful, decorated with murals of mermaids. Shrimp fajitas come in plentiful portions and are perfectly seasoned.

Legazpi s/n (corner of Jalisco). ℭ **3/355-5028.** Main courses $3–$12. AE, MC, V. Wed–Sun 2–10pm (opens at 10am for guests of Cabo Blanco Hotel).

Restaurant Bar Ambar CRÊPES/SPANISH/FRENCH   At the corner of Veracruz and Jalisco, you'll find this cozy thatched-roof, upstairs restaurant open to the breezes. The crêpes are named after towns in France; the delicious crêpe Paris, for example, is filled with chicken, potatoes, spinach, and green sauce. Sweet dessert crêpes are also available. International main dishes include imported rib-eye steak in a Dijon mustard sauce, mixed brochettes, quiche, and Caesar salad. Ambar serves Spanish-style tapas from noon until 6pm, with French specialties added for dinner service.

Av. Veracruz 101-A. No phone. Crêpes $4–$12; main courses $4–$12. No credit cards. Daily noon–midnight (happy hour 1pm–midnight). Closed July–Oct.

Restaurant Bar Ramón 🦀 SEAFOOD/MEXICAN   It seems like everybody eats at Ramón's, where the chips and fresh salsa arrive unbidden, service is prompt and friendly, and the food is especially good—however, most options are fried. Try the fresh fried shrimp with french fries or any of the daily specials that might feature vegetable soup or chicken fried steak. Great value!

Legazpi 260. ℂ 3/355-6435. Main courses $4–$8. MC, V. Daily 7am–11pm.

Seamaster SEAFOOD/INTERNATIONAL   This cheery and colorful restaurant on the beach facing the ocean is a great place for sunsets and margaritas or a meal any time. Specialties include steamed shrimp (peeled or unpeeled), fried calamari, barbecue chicken, ribs and steak, plus chicken wings, hamburgers, and other sandwiches. During high season, it turns into a popular disco at night.

Legazpi at Yucatán. No phone. Main courses $4–$12. No credit cards. Daily noon–midnight.

BARRA DE NAVIDAD AFTER DARK

When dusk arrives, visitors and locals alike find a cool spot to sit outside, sip cocktails, and chat. Many outdoor restaurants and stores in Barra fill the bill for this relaxing way to end the day, adding extra tables and chairs to accommodate drop-ins. It's very friendly.

During high season, there is always happy hour from 2 to 6pm at the **Hotel Sands** poolside/lagoon-side bar. The colorful **Sunset Bar and Restaurant,** facing the bay at the corner of Legazpi and Jalisco, is a favorite for sunset watching, and afterward for playing a game of oceanside pool or dancing to live or taped music. It's most popular with travelers ages 20 to 30. In the same vein, **Chips Restaurant,** on the second floor facing the ocean at the corner of Yucatán and Legazpi near the southern end of the *malecón,* has an excellent sunset vista. Live music follows the last rays of light, and patrons stay for hours. **Piper's Lover Bar & Restaurant,** on Legazpi, is done in the style of the Anderson's chain—but it's not one of them. Still, it is lively, with pool tables and occasional live music.

At the **Disco El Galeón,** in the Hotel Sands on calle Morelos, cushioned benches and cement tables encircle the round dance floor. It's all open-air, and about as stylish as you'll find in Barra. It serves drinks only. Admission is $5, and it's open Friday and Saturday from 9pm to 4am.

A VISIT TO MELAQUE (SAN PATRICIO)

For a change of scenery, you may want to wander over to Melaque (also known as San Patricio), 3 miles from Barra on the same bay. You can walk on the beach from Barra or take one of the frequent local buses from the bus station near the main square in Barra. The bus is marked MELAQUE. To return to Barra, take the bus marked CIHUATLÁN.

Melaque's pace is even more laid-back than Barra's, and though it's a larger village, it seems smaller. It has fewer restaurants and less to do. Although there are more hotels or "bungalows," as they are usually called here, few manage the charm of those in Barra. If Barra hotels are full on a holiday weekend, then Melaque would be a second choice for accommodations. The paved road ends where the town begins. A few yachts bob in the harbor, and the palm-lined beach is gorgeous.

If you come by bus from Barra, you can exit the bus anywhere in town or stay on until the last stop, which is the bus station in the middle of town a block from the beach. Restaurants and hotels line the beach; it's impossible to get lost, but some orientation will help. Coming into town from the main road, you'll be on the town's main street, **avenida López Matéos.** You'll pass the main square on the way to the waterfront, where there's a trailer park. The street going left (southeast) along the bay is **avenida Gómez Farías;** the one going right (northwest) is avenida Miguel Ochoa López.

WHERE TO DINE   At the north end of Melaque beach is **Los Pelicanos,** open daily from 9am to 10pm (©**3/355-5415**), serving the usual seafood specialties; the tender fried squid is delectable. In addition, you can find burritos, nachos, and hamburgers. Many Barra guests come here to stake a place on the beach and use the restaurant as headquarters for sipping and nipping. It's peaceful to watch the pelicans bobbing. The restaurant is at the far end of the bay before the **Hotel Legazpi** (© **3/355-5397**), which, by the way, is a pleasant place to stay. It has 20 rooms, costing $32 for a double, and no credit cards are accepted.

In addition to the Los Pelicanos, there are many rustic *palapa* **restaurants** both in town on the beach and farther along the bay at the end of the beach. You can settle in on the beach and use one of the restaurants as your base for drinking and dining.

5

Manzanillo

Manzanillo has long been known as a resort town of wide, curving beaches with legendary sportfishing and a highly praised diversity of dive sites. Now, however, it is emerging as a contender as a key golf destination in Mexico, with two of Manzanillo's courses listed in the top ten of *Golf Digest*'s 2000 Mexico Golf rankings.

One reason could be Manzanillo's enticingly tropical geography—comprising vast groves of tall palms, abundant mango trees, and successive coves graced with smooth sand beaches. To the north, mountains blanketed with palms rise alongside the shoreline. And over it all lies the veneer of perfect weather—balmy temperatures and year-round sea breezes. Even the approach by plane into Manzanillo showcases the promise—you fly in over the beach and golf course. Once on the ground, you exit the airport through a palm grove to reach the main highway into town.

Manzanillo is a dichotomous place—it is both Mexico's busiest commercial seaport and a tranquil, traditional town of multicolor houses cascading down the hillsides to meet the central commercial area of simple seafood restaurants, shell shops, and a few salsa clubs. The activity in Manzanillo can be neatly divided into two zones: the downtown commercial port and the luxury Santiago Peninsula resort zone to the north. The downtown zone is dominated by its busy harbor and rail connections to Mexico's interior. A visit to the town's waterfront *zócalo* provides a glimpse into local life, with its shady plaza teeming with birds and anchored by twin gazebos. The exclusive Santiago Peninsula, home to the resorts and golf course, separates Manzanillo's two golden sand bays.

1 Manzanillo Essentials

160 miles (256km) SE of Puerto Vallarta; 167 miles (267km) SW of Guadalajara; 40 miles (64km) SE of Barra de Navidad

GETTING THERE & DEPARTING   By Plane   Aeromexico and its sister airline, **Aerolitoral** (© 800/237-6639 in the U.S., 3/ 334-1226 at the airport), as well as **Mexicana** (© 800/531-7921 in

---

Tips   **Watch for Area Code Changes**

As this book went to press, Mexico announced a country-wide change in its long-distance area codes. The new plan will affect every phone number in this book; for details, please consult the box "Changes to Mexico's Phone Numbers Announced," in chapter 1.

---

the U.S., 3/333-2323 at the airport) offer flights to and from Mexico City, Durango, Chihuahua, and Mazatlán and to connecting cities in the United States and Canada. **Alaska Airlines** (© 800/426-0333 in Mexico, or 3/334-2211) offers service from Los Angeles; **America West** (© 800/235-9292) flies from Phoenix; and **Aero California** (© 800/685-5500 or 3/334-1414) has flights from Los Angeles. Ask a travel agent about the numerous charters that operate in winter from the States.

The **Playa de Oro International Airport** is 25 miles (45 min.) northwest of town. The *colectivo* (van) airport service is available from the airport, with returns arranged by your hotel. Reservations for return trips should be arranged one day in advance. The *colectivo* fare is based on zones and ranges from $6 to $8 to most hotels. Private taxi service between the airport and downtown area is around $20. **Budget** (© 800/527-0700 or 3/333-1445) and **AutoRentas** (© 3/333-2580) have counters in the airport open during flight arrivals; they will also deliver a car to your hotel. Daily rates run $45 to $75, desirable only if you plan on exploring surrounding cities and the Costa Alegre beaches.

By Car   **Coastal Highway 200** leads from Acapulco (south) and Puerto Vallarta (north). From Guadalajara, take Highway 54 through Colima (outside Colima you can switch to a toll road, which is faster but less scenic) into Manzanillo.

By Bus   Buses run to Barra de Navidad (1½ hr. north), Puerto Vallarta (5 hr. north), Colima (1½ hr. east), and Guadalajara (4½ hr. north), with deluxe service and numerous daily departures. Manzanillo's **Central Camionera** (bus station) is about 12 long blocks east of town. If you follow Hidalgo east, the Camionera will be on your right.

VISITOR INFORMATION   The tourism office (© 3/333-2277 or 3/333-2264; fax 3/333-1426) in Manzanillo is on the Costera

Manzanillo Area

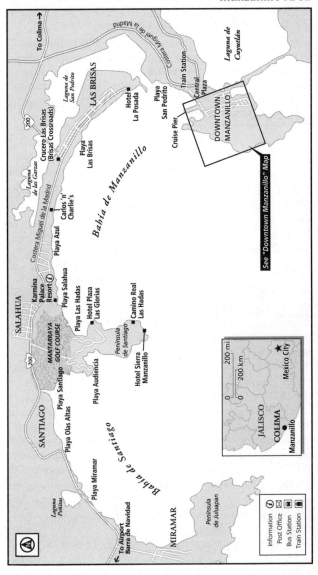

Tips Motorist Advisory: Carjackings

Motorists planning to follow Highway 200 south from Manzanillo toward Lázaro Cárdenas and Ixtapa should be aware of reports of random bus and motorist hijackings on that route, especially around Playa Azul. Before heading in that direction, ask locals and the tourism office about the current state of affairs.

Miguel de la Madrid 4960, km 8.5. It's open Monday through Friday from 9am to 3:30pm.

CITY LAYOUT   The town lies at one end of a 7-mile-long beach facing Manzanillo Bay and its commercial harbor. The beach has four sections—**Playa Las Brisas, Playa Azul, Playa Salahua,** and **Playa Las Hadas.** The northern terminus of the beaches is the high, rocky **Santiago Peninsula.** Santiago is 7 miles from downtown; it's the site of many beautiful homes and the best hotel in the area, Las Hadas, as well as the Mantarraya Golf Course owned by Las Hadas. The peninsula juts out into the bay separating Manzanillo Bay from Santiago Bay. The beach, Playa Las Hadas, is on the south side of the peninsula facing Manzanillo Bay, and **Playa Audiencia** is on the north side facing Santiago Bay. There's also the inland town of **Santiago,** which is opposite the turnoff to Las Hadas.

Activity in downtown Manzanillo centers on the **central plaza,** officially known as the Jardín Álvaro Obregón, which is separated from the waterfront by a railroad, shipyards, and a basketball court where pick-up games are played in constant succession. The plaza has flowering trees, a fountain, twin kiosks, and a view of the bay. It is a staple of local life, where people congregate on park benches to swap gossip and throw handfuls of rice to the ever-present *palomas* (doves—although they're really just pigeons). Large ships dock at the pier nearby. **Avenida México,** the street leading out from the plaza's central gazebo, is the town's principal commercial thoroughfare. Walking along here, you will find a few shops, small restaurants, and juice stands.

Once you leave downtown, the highway (the **Costera Miguel de la Madrid,** or the Costera Madrid, for short) runs through the neighborhoods of Las Brisas, Salahua, and Santiago to the **hotel zones** on the Santiago Peninsula and at Miramar. Shell shops, minimalls, and several restaurants are located along the way.

There are two main lagoons: One, **Laguna de Cuyutlán,** almost behind the city, stretches for miles south paralleling the coast. The other, **Laguna de San Pedrito,** north of the city, parallels the Costera Miguel de la Madrid; it's behind Playa Las Brisas beach. Both are good sites for bird-watching. There are also two bays: **Manzanillo Bay** encompasses the harbor, town, and beaches, and the Santiago Peninsula separates it from the second bay—**Santiago.** Between downtown and the Santiago Peninsula is **Las Brisas,** a flat peninsula with a long stretch of sandy golden beach, a lineup of inexpensive but run-down hotels, and a few good restaurants.

GETTING AROUND   By Taxi   Taxis in Manzanillo are plentiful. Fares are fixed by zones; rates for trips within town, as well as to more distant points, should be posted at your hotel. Daily rates can be negotiated for longer drives outside the Manzanillo area.

By Bus   The local buses (*camionetas*) make a circuit from downtown in front of the train station, along the Bay of Manzanillo, and to the Santiago Peninsula and the Bay of Santiago to the north; cost is 25¢. The ones marked LAS BRISAS go to the Las Brisas crossroads, then to the Las Brisas Peninsula, and back to town; MIRAMAR, SANTIAGO, and SALAHUA buses go to outlying settlements along the bays and to most restaurants mentioned below. Buses marked LAS HADAS go to Santiago Peninsula and make a circuit past the Las Hadas resort and the Sierra Manzanillo and Plaza Las Glorias hotels. This is an inexpensive way to see the coast as far as Santiago and to tour the Santiago Peninsula.

 Fast Facts: **Manzanillo**

American Express   The local representative is **Bahías Gemelas Travel Agency,** km 10, Costera Miguel de la Madrid (📞 3/333-1000 or 3/333-1053; fax 3/333-0649). Hours Monday through Friday from 10am to 2pm and 4pm to 6pm; Saturday from 10am to 2pm.

Area Code   The telephone area code is **3.**

Bank   Banamex downtown is just off the plaza on avenida México; it's open Monday through Friday from 9:30am to 5pm, but changes foreign currency only until 12:30pm.

Internet Access   The air-conditioned **Net Café** (📞 3/332-2660; mayocomp@bay.net.mx) is ½ block from the central plaza at calle Benito Juárez 115, Int. 7-B. It charges $3 per hour, and is open Monday through Friday from 10am to 2pm and 4:30 to 8:30pm. Saturday, it's open from 10am to 2pm; closed Sundays.

2 Activities On & Off the Beach

Activities in Manzanillo revolve around its golden sand beaches, which frequently accumulate a film of black mineral residue from nearby rivers. Most of the resort hotels here are completely self-contained, with restaurants and sports on the premises. Manzanillo's public beaches provide an opportunity to see more local color and scenery and are the daytime playground for those staying off the beach or without pools.

BEACHES   Playa Audiencia, on the Santiago Peninsula, offers the best swimming as well as snorkeling, but **Playa San Pedrito,** shallow for a long way out, is the most popular beach for its proximity to the downtown area. **Playa Las Brisas** is an optimal combination of location and good swimming. **Playa Miramar,** on the Bahía de Santiago past the Santiago Peninsula, is popular with bodysurfers, windsurfers, and boogie boarders and is accessible by local bus from town. The major part of **Playa Azul** drops off sharply, but is noted for its wide stretch of golden sand.

BIRD-WATCHING   There are several lagoons along the coast good for bird-watching. As you go from Manzanillo up past Las Brisas to Santiago, you'll pass **Laguna de Las Garzas** (Lagoon of the Herons), also known as Laguna de San Pedrito, where you can see many white pelicans and huge herons fishing in the water. They nest here in December and January. Directly behind downtown is the **Laguna de Cuyutlán** (follow the signs to Cuyutlán), where birds can usually be found in abundance; species vary between summer and winter.

DIVING   **Underworld Scuba,** owned by longtime resident and local diving expert Susan Dearing, conducts highly professional diving expeditions and classes. Many locations are so close to shore that there's no need for a boat. Close-in dives include the jetty with coral growing on the rocks at 45 feet, and a nearby sunken frigate downed in 1959 at 28 feet. Divers can see abundant sea life, including coral reefs, seahorses, giant puffer fish, and moray eels. A one-tank dive requiring a boat costs $50 per person with a three-person minimum,

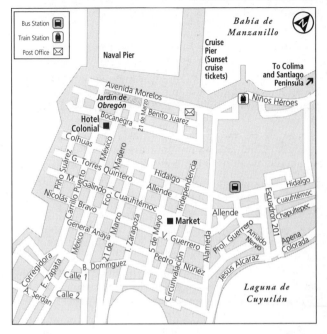

Bus Station
Train Station
Post Office

Naval Pier

Bahía de Manzanillo

Cruise Pier (Sunset cruise tickets)

To Colima and Santiago Peninsula ↗

Niños Héroes

Avenida Morelos

Jardin de Obregón

Hotel Colonial
Bocanegra
Benito Juarez
21 de Marzo

Colhuas

G. Torres Quintero
Piño Suárez
M. Puerto
Galindo
Carrillo Puerto
México
Madero
Fco. Cuauhtémoc

Hidalgo
Allende

Independencia

Nicolás Bravo
General Anaya
México
21 de Marzo
I. Zaragoza

Market
5 de Mayo
V. Guerrero

Allende

Hidalgo
Escuadrón 201
Cuauhtémoc
Chapultepec

Prol. Guerrero
Amado Nervo
Apena Colorada

Corregidora
E. Zapata
B. Dominguez
Alameda
Jesús Alcaraz

A. Serdan
Calle 1
Calle 2
Circunvalación
Pedro Núñez

Laguna de Cuyutlán

or two tanks for $80 ($10 discount if you have your own equipment); and a three-stop snorkel trip costs $35. All guides at this shop are certified divemasters, and they also offer diver certification classes (PADI, YMCA, and CMAS) in very intensive courses of various durations. The owner offers a 10% discount on your certification when you mention you read about her in a Frommer's guide. For reservations, contact Underworld Scuba at ℭ/fax **3/333-0642** (cellular 3/358-0327; www.gomanzanillo.com). MasterCard and Visa are accepted.

ESCORTED TOURS Because Manzanillo is so spread out, you might consider a city tour. Reputable local tour companies include **Hectours** (ℭ 3/333-1707) and **Bahías Gemelas Travel Agency** (American Express representative ℭ 3/333-1000; fax 3/333-0649). Tours can be scheduled at flexible times, with a half-day city tour costing around $15. Other tours include the day-long Colima Colonial Tour ($55), which includes a stop at a sugar cane plantation, Colima's Archeological Museum, principle colonial buildings, and past the active volcano. There are regularly updated tour offerings, so ask about new tours.

FISHING   Manzanillo is famous for its fishing, particularly sailfish. Marlin and sailfish are abundant year-round. Winter is best for dolphin fish and dorado (mahimahi), and in summer, wahoo and rooster fish are in greater supply. The international sailfish competition is held around the November 20 Revolution Day holiday, and the national sailfish competition is in February. Fishing can be arranged through travel agencies or directly at the fishermen's cooperative (© **3/332-1031**), located downtown where the fishing boats are moored. You can call from 7am to 7pm. A fishing boat is approximately $35 to $45 per hour, with most trips lasting about 5 hours.

GOLF   The 18-hole **La Mantarraya Golf Course** is now also open to nonguests as well as guests of Las Hadas. At one time, La Mantarraya was considered among the top 100 courses in the world, but it's been passed by newer entries. Still, this compact, challenging 18-hole course designed by Roy and Pete Dye is a beauty, endearingly tropical with banana trees, blooming bougainvillea, and coconut palms at every turn. A lush and verdant place (12 of the 18 holes are played over water), it remains in the top ten of Mexico's 115 courses.

When the course was under construction, pre-Hispanic ceramic figurines, idols, and beads were dug up at the site where the 14th hole now lies. It is believed to have been an important ancient burial site. The course culminates with its signature 18th hole, with a drive to the island green off El Tesoro (the treasure) beach and directly in front of the new Karminda Palace Resort. Local lore says this beach still may hold buried treasure from Spanish galleons, whose crews were the first to recognize the perfection of this natural harbor, and who used it during the 16th century as their starting point for voyages to the Pacific Rim. Greens fees at Las Hadas are $50 for 18 holes, cart and gear extra. Reserve in advance.

The fabulous 27-hole golf course associated with the **Grand Bay Hotel** in Barra de Navidad is also open to the public, an easy distance from Manzanillo. This Robert Von Hagge–designed course is long and lovely, with each hole placed along rolling, tropical landscapes. It is wide open, with big fairways and big greens, and features plenty of water (2 lagoon holes, 13 lakeside holes, and 8 holes alongside the Pacific Ocean). The greens fees are $95/$115 for 18/27 holes for guests of Grand Bay, $140 for nonguests, including a motorized cart. Barra is about a 1- to 1½-hour drive north of

Manzanillo on Highway 200. (Grand Bay Hotel is reviewed in chapter 4.)

MUSEUM In 1996, the **Museum of Archeology and History** opened, a small but impressive structure that houses exhibits depicting the region's history, plus rotating exhibitions of contemporary Mexican art. It's located on avenida Niños Heroes where it intersects with avenida Teniente Azueta, on the road leading between the downtown and Las Brisas areas. Every Friday evening, the museum hosts free cultural events, which might be in the form of a trio playing romantic ballads or a chamber music ensemble. Performances begin at 8pm. Open hours are Tuesday through Saturday from 10am to 2pm and 5pm to 8pm; Sunday from 10am to 1pm (© 3/ 332-2256).

SHOPPING There is a selection of shops carrying Mexican crafts and clothing, mainly from nearby Guadalajara, one of Mexico's artisan centers. Almost all are downtown on the streets near the central plaza. Shopping in downtown Manzanillo is an experience—for example, you won't want to miss the shop bordering the plaza that sells a combination of shells, religious items (including shell-framed Virgin of Guadalupe nightlights), and orthopedic supplies. The Plaza Manzanillo is an American-style mall on the road to Santiago, and there's a traditional *tianguis* market in front of the entrance to Club Maeva with touristy items from around Mexico. Most resort hotels also have boutiques or shopping arcades.

SUNSET CRUISES For one of the popular sunset cruises, buy tickets from a travel agent or downtown at La Perlita Dock (across from the train station) fronting the harbor. Tickets are on sale at La Perlita daily from 8:30am to 2pm and cost around $19. The trips vary in their combinations of drinks, music, and entertainment and last 1½ to 2 hours.

3 Where To Stay

The strip of coastline on which Manzanillo is located can be divided into three areas: downtown, with its shops, markets, and commercial activity; Las Brisas, the hotel-lined beach area immediately to the north of the city; and Santiago, the town and peninsula, now virtually a suburb to the north at the end of Playa Azul. Transportation by bus or taxi makes all three areas fairly convenient to each other. Reservations are recommended for hotels during the Easter, Christmas, and New Year's holidays.

DOWNTOWN

Hotel Colonial ⚸   An old favorite, this three-story colonial-style hotel located in the central downtown district added five new units in 2000. Enjoyed for its consistent quality, ambience, and service, it still offers the same beautiful blue-and-yellow tile, colonial-style carved doors, and windows in the lobby and restaurant. Rooms are decorated with minimal furniture, red-tile floors, and basic comforts. The hotel is 1 block inland from the main plaza at the corner of Juárez and Galindo.

Av. México 100 and González Bocanegra, 28200 Manzanillo, Col. ⓒ 3/332-1080, or 3/332-0668, 3/332-1230, or 3/332-1134. 42 units. $20 single; $27 double. AE, MC, V. **Amenities:** Restaurant/bar in the central courtyard; tour desk. *In room:* A/C, TV.

LAS BRISAS

The Las Brisas area has yet to be repaired from earthquake damage suffered in 1995 and is looking run-down, with numerous buildings in various states of disrepair. However, it still lays claim to one of the best beaches in the area and is known for its constant gentle sea breezes—a true pleasure in summer months.

Hotel La Posada   This small inn has a bright-pink stucco facade with a large arch that leads to a broad tiled patio right on the beach. The rooms have exposed brick walls and simple furnishings with Mexican decorative accents. Mattresses are beginning to sag and the place could use a general round of upkeep, but it still remains popular with longtime travelers to Manzanillo. The atmosphere here is casual and informal—you can help yourself to beer and soft drinks all day long and at the end of your stay, owner Bart Varelmann (a native of Ohio) counts the bottle caps you deposited in a bowl labeled with your room number. If a nonguest wants to come for a meal, breakfast is served between 8 and 11am and costs around $7; lunch and dinner (sandwiches) are served between 1:30 and 8pm and cost about the same. During low season, the restaurant is open only from 8am to 3pm. Stop by for a drink at sunset; the bar's open until 9pm all year. It's located at the end of Las Brisas Peninsula, closest to downtown, and is on the local Las Brisas bus route.

Av. Lázaro Cárdenas 201, Las Brisas (Apdo. Postal 135), 28200 Manzanillo, Col. ⓒ/fax 3/333-1899. www.mexonline/laposada.htm. 24 units. High season $72 double; low season $48 double. Rates include breakfast. AE, MC, V. **Amenities:** Restaurant/bar; laundry service; money exchange; safe-deposit boxes.

SANTIAGO

Three miles north of Las Brisas is the wide Santiago Peninsula. The settlement of Salahua is on the highway where you enter the peninsula to reach the hotels Las Hadas, Plaza Las Glorias, and Sierra Manzanillo, as well as the Mantarraya Golf Course. Buses from town marked LAS HADAS pass by these hotels every 20 minutes. Past the Salahua turnoff and at the end of the settlement of Santiago, an obscure road on the left is marked ZONA DE PLAYAS and leads to the hotels on the other side of the peninsula and Playa de Santiago.

Camino Real Las Hadas ⋆⋆⋆   For me, Las Hadas is the most compelling reason to visit Manzanillo. The town's signature property, Las Hadas was, along with Bo Derek, featured in the movie *10*. This elegant white beachfront resort, a member of the "Leading Hotels of the World" group, is built in a Moorish style into the side of the rocky peninsula. The service at Las Hadas is gracious, warm, and unobtrusive. Rooms overlook the bay and are connected by cobbled lanes lined with colorful flowers and palms. The resort is large but maintains an air of seclusion; rooms are spread out over meticulously landscaped grounds. (Motorized carts are on call for transportation within the property.)

Views, room size, and extra amenities differentiate the six types of accommodations, which can vary greatly. If you're not satisfied with the room you've been assigned, ask to be moved. Understated and spacious, the better units have white-marble floors, sitting areas, and large, comfortably furnished balconies. Camino Real Club rooms on the upper tier have great bay views; nine Club rooms have private pools. The lobby is a popular place for curling up for a good read in one of the overstuffed seating areas or, at night, for enjoying a drink and live music. Club Las Hadas includes La Mantarraya, the hotel's 18-hole, par-71 golf course designed by Pete and Roy Dye.

Av. de los Riscos s/n, Santiago Peninsula, 28200 Manzanillo, Col. ℂ **800/722-6466** in the U.S. and Canada, or 3/334-0000. 233 units, including 30 Fantasy Suites, 5 Magic Suites, and 1 Presidential Suite. High season $250–$300 double, $385–$440 Fantasy Suite, $350–$400 Camino Real Club; low season $190–$232 double, $309–$400 Fantasy Suite, $278–$319 Camino Real Club. AE, DC, MC, V. Free guarded parking. **Amenities:** Four restaurants, including the elegant **Legazpi** (see "Where to Dine," below), Arab, Mexican, and White Gala theme nights, featuring patio dining, available at a cost of $45 per person, four lounges and bars; two pools; shade tents on the beach; 10 tennis courts (eight hard-surface, two clay); small workout room; marina for 70 vessels; scuba diving, snorkeling, sailing, and trimaran cruises; concierge; tour desk; travel agency; car rental; shopping arcade; salon; room service, in-room massage; baby-sitting; laundry and dry cleaning services. Camino Real Club guests have an exclusive pool, reserved lounge chairs, rapid check-in, continental breakfast, cocktails, concierge, preferred restaurant reservations, late checkout. *In room:* A/C, TV, dataport, minibar, hair dryer, safe-deposit boxes, robes.

Hotel Plaza Las Glorias 🏩🏩 The sunset-colored walls of this pueblo-like hotel ramble over a hillside on Santiago Peninsula. From the restaurant on top and from most rooms is a broad vista of other red-tiled rooftops and either the palm-filled golf course or the bay. It's one of Manzanillo's undiscovered resorts, known more to wealthy Mexicans than to Americans. Originally conceived as private condominiums, the quarters were designed for living; each accommodation is spacious, stylishly furnished, and very comfortable. Each unit has a huge living room; a small kitchen/bar; one, two, or three large bedrooms with tile or brick floors; large Mexican-tiled bathrooms; huge closets; and large furnished private patios with views. Some units have en-suite whirlpool tubs and a few rooms can be partitioned off and rented by the bedroom only. Rooms can be a long walk from the main entrance, through a succession of stairways and paths. If stair climbing bothers you, try to get a room by the restaurant and pool—you'll have a great view, and a hillside rail elevator goes from top to bottom, but doesn't stop in between. Package rates are available.

Av. de Tesoro s/n, Santiago Peninsula, 28200 Manzanillo, Col. ✆ **3/334-1098.** Fax 3/333-1395. lasglorias@delfin.colimanet.com. 103 units. $96 double. AE, MC, V. **Amenities:** Restaurant, with occasional live music; pool on the restaurant level and game area; beach club on Las Brisas beach, with a pool and small restaurant; transportation to the beach club from the main hotel in the morning with return transportation in the afternoon. Boutique, elevator from bottom of property to top, room service; baby-sitters arranged with advance notice; laundry service. *In room:* A/C, TV, key-locked security box.

Hotel Sierra Manzanillo 🏩 Opened in 1990, this all-inclusive hotel has 21 floors overlooking La Audiencia beach and a full program of activities, dining, and entertainment. Its excellent kids program makes it a top choice for families. Architecturally, it mimics the white Moorish style of Las Hadas that has become so popular in Manzanillo. Inside, it's palatial in scale and covered in a sea of pale-gray marble. Room decor picks up the pale-gray theme with washed gray armoires that conceal the TV and minibar. Most standard rooms have two double beds or a king-size bed, plus a small table, chairs, and desk. Several rooms at the end of most floors are small, with one double bed, small porthole-size windows, no balcony, and no view. Most rooms, however, have balconies and either ocean or hillside views. The 10 honeymoon suites are carpeted and have sculpted shell-shaped headboards, king-size beds, and chaise lounges. Junior suites have a sitting area with couch and large bathrooms.

Av. La Audiencia 1, Los Riscos, 28200 Manzanillo, Col. © **800/448-5028** in the U.S., or 3/333-2000. Fax 3/333-2611. 332 units. High season $292 double, $342–$362 suite; low season $128–$218 double, $218–$268 suite. Rates are all-inclusive. AE, MC, V. **Amenities:** Three restaurants, four bars; grand pool on the beach plus children's pool; four lit tennis courts; health club with exercise equipment, scheduled aerobics, hot tub, and separate sauna and steam rooms for men and women; scuba-diving lessons given in the pool and excellent scuba-diving sites within swimming distance of the shore; salon with massage service; travel agency; room service; laundry service; 24-hour currency exchange. *In room:* A/C, TV, dataport, minibar, hair dryers.

Karmina Palace 𝒜𝒜𝒜 𝒱alue   The newest of Manzanillo's hotels, this all-inclusive resort has quality rooms and services that make it one of the area's—and Mexico's—very best values. The buildings resemble Mayan pyramids, and even though the architecture at first might seem a little overdone, somehow it works. Rooms are all suites, very large in size, and high quality, with rich wood accents, comfortable recessed seating areas with pull-out couches, and not one, but two, 27-inch TVs in each room. The extra-large bathrooms have marble floors, twin black marble sinks, separate tub, and glassed-in shower. Most rooms have terraces or balconies with views of the ocean, overlooking the tropical gardens and swimming pools. The master suites all have spacious sun terraces with private splash pools, plus a full wet bar, full refrigerator, and a large living room area with 42-inch TV. Two full-size bedrooms close off from the living/dining area.

   Children can enjoy a host of activities at the Kids Club, while adults can choose from a host of their own choices for fun—all included in the price of your stay. There's also an exceptionally well-equipped gym and European-style spa. In-room safe-deposit boxes are available for an extra charge of $2, or you can use the safe-deposit box in the reception for free. It's the best choice for families in Manzanillo.

Blvd. Miguel de la Madrid s/n, Peninsula de Santiago, Manzanillo, Col. © **3/334-1313.** Fax 3/334-1108. www.karminapalace.com. 324 units. $190 per person, Jr. suite; $1,000 for 4 people, master suite. Rates are all-inclusive. Ask for seasonal specials. AE, MC, V. **Amenities:** Two restaurants, snack bar, five bars; eight interconnecting swimming pools; tennis courts; health club with treadmills and Cybex exercise equipment; full spa facilities, including separate sauna and steam rooms for men and women; beach volleyball; windsurfing; kid's activity program; 24-hour concierge service; car rental; gift shop; 24-hour room service; money exchange. *In room:* A/C, TV, dataport, minibar, hair dryer, iron.

4 Where To Dine

DOWNTOWN

Roca del Mar MEXICAN/INTERNATIONAL   Join locals at this informal cafe facing the plaza. The large menu includes club sandwiches, hamburgers, *carne asada a la tampiqueña* (thin grilled steak served with rice, poblano pepper, an enchilada, and refried beans), fajitas, fish, shrimp, and vegetable salads. A specialty is its *paella*—served on Sundays and Tuesdays—and the economical *pibil* tacos are outstanding. This spot is very clean, with sidewalk dining available.

21 de Marzo 204 (across from the plaza). ℂ 3/332-0302. Main courses $2–$5. No credit cards. Daily 7am–10:30pm.

LAS BRISAS

In addition to Willy's, below, the Hotel La Posada (see "Where to Stay," above) offers breakfast to nonguests at its beachside restaurant; it's also a great place to mingle with other tourists and enjoy the sunset and cocktails.

Willy's 🏵🏵🏵 *Finds* SEAFOOD/INTERNATIONAL   You're in for a treat at Willy's, one of Manzanillo's most popular restaurants. It's homey, casual, and small, with perhaps 13 tables inside and 10 more on the narrow balcony over the bay. The exquisite cuisine belies the atmosphere, with starters that include escargot and salmon carpaccio. Among the grilled specialties are shrimp imperial wrapped in bacon, red-snapper tarragon, dorado basil, sea bass with mango and ginger, and fresh lobsters that come four to a serving and arrive tender. Live guitar jazz plays after 8pm.

If you double back left at the Las Brisas crossroads, you'll find Willy's on the right, down a short side street that leads to the ocean.

Las Brisas crossroads. ℂ 3/333-1794. Reservations required. Main courses $8–$17. MC, V. Daily 7pm–midnight.

SANTIAGO ROAD

The restaurants below are on the Costera Madrid between downtown and the Santiago Peninsula, and include the Salahua area.

Benedetti's Pizza PIZZA   Since there are several branches in town, you'll probably find a Benedetti's not far from where you are staying. The variety isn't extensive, but the pies are quite good; add some *chimichurri* sauce to enhance the flavor. They specialize in seafood pizzas such as smoked oyster and anchovy pizza. In addition to pizza, you can select from pastas, sandwiches, burgers, fajitas, salads, Mexican soups, cheesecake, and apple pie. This branch is on the Costera Madrid, on the left, just after the Las Brisas turn across from the Coca-Cola plant.

Av. del Mar 1, Crucero Las Brisas. ✆ **3/334-0141**. Pizza $9–$12; main courses $2–$5.55. AE, MC, V. Daily 1–11:30pm.

Bigotes III *(Finds* SEAFOOD   Locals flock to this large, breezy restaurant (the name translates as "Mustaches") by the water for the good food and festive atmosphere. Strolling singers serenade diners, who are rewarded with large portions of grilled seafood. To find Bigotes, follow the Costera de la Madrid from downtown past the Las Brisas turnoff. It's behind the Penas Coloradas Social Club across from the beach.

Puesta del Sol 3. ✆ **3/333-1236**. Main courses $6–$18. MC, V. Daily noon–10pm.

Manolo's Norteño Campestre INTERNATIONAL/STEAK/ SEAFOOD   Owners Manuel and Juanita López and family offer excellent dining in a tropical garden setting. They cater to American tastes with a "safe" salad that is included with dinner. Among the popular entrees are filet of fish Manolo on a bed of spinach with melted cheese, Florentine-style, and frog legs in brandy batter. Most people can't leave without first being tempted by the fresh coconut or homemade pecan pie. Coming from downtown, Manolo's is on the right, about 3 blocks before the turn to Las Hadas.

Km 11.5, Costera Miguel de la Madrid. ✆ **3/333-0475**. Main courses $5–$20. AE, MC, V. Mon–Sat 5pm–midnight.

SANTIAGO PENINSULA

Legazpi ✸✸ INTERNATIONAL   This is a top choice in Manzanillo for sheer elegance, gracious service, and outstanding food. The candlelit tables, covered in pale-pink and white, are set with silver and flowers. Enormous bell-shaped windows on two sides show off the sparkling bay below. The sophisticated menu includes prosciutto with melon marinated in port wine, crayfish bisque, broiled salmon, roast duck, lobster, veal, and flaming desserts from crêpes to Irish coffee.

Camino Real Las Hadas Hotel, Santiago Peninsula. ✆ **3/334-0000**. Main courses $8–$15. AE, MC, V. High season only daily 7–11:30pm.

5 Manzanillo After Dark

Nightlife in Manzanillo is much more exuberant than you might expect, but then Manzanillo is not only a resort town—it's a thriving commercial center. Clubs and bars tend to change from year to year, so check with your concierge for current hot spots. Perennial favorites include **Carlos 'n' Charlie's,** av. Audiencia Cocoteros s/n (© 3/334-1272), always a good choice for both food and fun. In the evening during high season, there may be a required minimum order/cover if you come just to drink and dance, but the cover includes three drinks. **El Bar de Felix** (© 3/334-1444), between Salahua and Las Brisas by the Avis rental-car office, is open Tuesday through Sunday from 9pm to 2am and doesn't charge a cover. **Vog Disco** (© 3/333-1875), km 9.2, Blvd. Costero Miguel de la Madrid, features alternative music in a cavernous setting; it's Manzanillo's current late-night hot spot, open until 5am. It features an early happy hour, from 9pm to 11pm, and waives the $4 cover for ladies on Friday nights. Also very popular—with a built-in crowd— is the nightclub at the **Club Maeva Hotel & Resort** (© 3/335-0079), located on the inland side of the main highway, north of the Santiago Peninsula. Open Tuesdays, Thursdays, and Saturdays from 10pm to 3am. Couples are given preferential entrance. Non-guests are welcome, but must pay a $10 to $15 entrance fee, after which all drinks are included. The fee varies depending on the night of the week, and the time of year. Some area clubs have a dress code prohibiting shorts or sandals, principally applying to men.

6

Settling into Guadalajara

Guadalajara is the second largest city in Mexico (with 3½ million people, it's a very distant second to Mexico City), but as the homeland of *mariachi* music, the *jarabe tapatío* (the Mexican hat dance), and *tequila*, it is considered by many to be the most Mexican of cities. Despite its size, Guadalajara is easy to navigate, and the people are friendly and helpful. And unlike in Mexico City, visitors here can enjoy big-city pleasures without big-city hassles.

Guadalajara is the capital of the state of Jalisco and, on occasion in Mexico's stormy history, has functioned as the nation's capital. The historic center of Guadalajara, especially the area around the cathedral, is a wonderful place to wander about among colonial plazas, fountains, churches, and convents. And, thanks to the relatively new Plaza Tapatía, you can enjoy a pleasant walk from the cathedral all the way to the impressive Hospicio Cabañas. With its shopping, restaurants, cultural life, history, architecture, and mild climate, Guadalajara is a great side trip into the interior from Puerto Vallarta or Manzanillo.

The handcrafts and decorative arts here are perhaps the best in Mexico. Shoppers can browse through the sophisticated shops of Tlaquepaque, which offer an immense variety of merchandise. Or they can pay a visit to Tonalá, which has hundreds of workshops and is a bargain-hunter's paradise.

While in Guadalajara, you will undoubtedly come across the word *tapatío* (or *tapatía*). In the early days, people from the area were known to trade in threes, called *tapatíos*. Gradually, the locals

---

Tips Watch for Area Code Changes

As this book went to press, Mexico announced a country-wide change in its long-distance area codes. The new plan will affect every phone number in this book; for details, please consult the box "Changes to Mexico's Phone Numbers Announced," in chapter 1.

---

came to be called *tapatíos* too, and the word now signifies "Guadalajaran" when referring to a thing, a person, or a manner of doing something.

1 Guadalajara Essentials

GETTING THERE

BY PLANE Guadalajara's international airport is a 25- to 45-minute ride from the city. Taxi tickets to Guadalajara or Chapala are sold in front of the airport and are priced by zone. Taxis are the only transport from town to the airport (around $11 to the center of town; $9 going the other way).

If you're flying out of Guadalajara, you'll be required to check in at least 1½ hours before takeoff for international flights, and at least 1 hour before takeoff for domestic flights.

Major Airlines See chapter 1 for a list of the toll-free numbers of international airlines serving Mexico. Numbers to call in Guadalajara for international airlines are: **Aeromar** (© 3/615-8509), **Aeromexico** (© 3/669-0202), **American Airlines** (© 01-800/904-6000), **Continental Airlines** (© 01-800/900-5000), **Delta** (© 3/630-3530), **Mexicana** (© 01-800-502-2000), and **United** (© 3/616-9489).

Aero California (© 3/616-2525) serves Guadalajara from Tijuana, Mexico City, Los Mochis, La Paz, and Puebla; **Aeromexico** and **Mexicana** have flights and connections throughout Mexico, as does **Aviacsa** (© 3/616-9706).

BY CAR Guadalajara is at the hub of several four-lane toll roads (called *cuotas* or *autopistas*) that can cut travel time considerably, but are expensive. From Nogales on the **U.S. border,** follow Highway 15 south (21 hr.). From **Tepic,** you can decrease this time by taking toll road 15D to Guadalajara (5 hr., $30). From **Puerto Vallarta,** go north on Highway 200 to Compostela and the toll road 68D that heads east to join the Tepic toll road. Total time is 5½ hours and the tolls add up to $25. From **Barra de Navidad,** on the coast southeast of Puerto Vallarta, take Highway 80 northeast (4½ hr.). From **Manzanillo,** you might also take this road, but it would be faster to take the toll road 54D through Colima to Guadalajara (3½ hr., $22). From **Mexico City,** take toll road 15D (7 hr., $43).

BY BUS Two bus stations serve Guadalajara: The old one near downtown has buses to Lake Chapala and other nearby areas; and

Greater Guadalajara

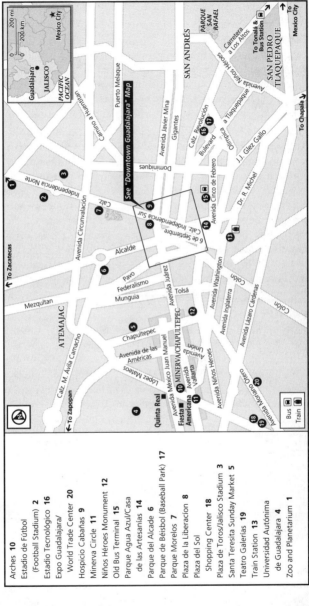

the new one 6 miles southeast of the city's center has buses to more distant destinations.

The Old Bus Station For bus trips within a 60-mile radius of Guadalajara, including to Lake Chapala, Ajijic, Jocotepec, Mazamitla, and San Juan Cosalá, go to the old bus terminal on Niños Héroes off Calzada Independencia Sur. To go to any towns in the Lake Chapala region, try **Transportes Guadalajara-Chapala,** which has frequent bus and *combi* (minivan) service beginning at 6am to Chapala (see also "Side Trips from Guadalajara," in chapter 7).

The New Bus Station The **Central Camionera** is a 35-minute ride from downtown. Taxi fare for the trip is about $6. This bus station resembles an international airport, with seven separate terminals connected by a covered walkway. Each building contains different lines, offering first- and second-class service for different destinations, so it can be a little confusing. The best place to get bus information, make reservations, or buy tickets is downtown at the **Agencia Plaza Tapatía,** Calzada Independencia 254, a "bus-ticket agency" located under Plaza Tapatía. They work with all six main bus lines that connect Guadalajara to the rest of Mexico. Also, many travel agencies will sell bus tickets to the most important destinations.

VISITOR INFORMATION

The **State of Jalisco Tourist Information Office** is at calle Morelos 102 (© **3/668-1600** or 3/668-1601) in the Plaza Tapatía, at the crossroads of Paseo Degollado and Paraje del Rincón del Diablo. It's open Monday through Friday from 9am to 8pm and Saturday, Sunday, and festival days from 9am to 1pm. They have a supply of maps as well as a monthly calendar of cultural events in the city.

CITY LAYOUT

The **downtown area (Centro Histórico),** with all its attractions, will be of great interest to the visitor. Aside from this, there are three other popular areas to visit: West of downtown is the fashionable hotel and restaurant district, with boutiques, shopping centers, and the like; to the northwest is Zapopan, home of Guadalajara's patron saint; and to the southeast are the crafts towns of Tlaquepaque and Tonalá, famous among shoppers.

The main artery for traffic going from downtown to the hotel and restaurant district is **avenida Vallarta.** It starts out from downtown as **Juárez.** The main arteries for returning to downtown are **Mexico** and **Hidalgo,** both of which are north of Vallarta. Vallarta heads due west where it intersects another major artery, **Av. Adolfo**

López Mateos, at **Minerva Circle** (*Fuente Minerva* or simply *La Minerva*). Minerva Circle, only a 15-minute drive from downtown, is the central point of reference for the west side. To go to Zapopan from downtown, take Av. Ávila Camacho, which you can pick up on Alcalde; it takes 20 minutes by car. To Tlaquepaque and Tonalá, take Calzada Revolución. Tlaquepaque is 5 miles from downtown and takes 15 to 20 minutes by car, Tonalá is 5 minutes farther. Another major thoroughfare, Calzada Lázaro Cárdenas, connects the west-side hotel district to Tlaquepaque and Tonalá bypassing downtown; it cuts travel time considerably.

GUADALAJARA NEIGHBORHOODS IN BRIEF

Centro Histórico The heart of the city contains the five main plazas, the cathedral, and several museums and public buildings. Two of those buildings hold several spectacular murals by Orozco, in my opinion the best of the Mexican muralists. Theaters, restaurants, shops, and clubs dot the area, which also holds the largest covered market in Latin America. All of this is located in a space that is roughly 12 blocks by 12 blocks, an easy area for a good walker to explore on foot. Amid the plazas and pedestrian-only streets, walking can be quite pleasant.

Parque Agua Azul This is a large inner-city green space 20 blocks south of the Centro Histórico. It has a children's area and miniature train. Nearby you'll find the state-run crafts shop (worth the short trip), performing-arts theaters, and the anthropology museum.

Chapultepec/Minerva Circle/Plaza del Sol These areas constitute the west side of the city. Chapultepec is the neighborhood between downtown and Minerva Circle. Surrounding Minerva are several malls. Southwest from Minerva Circle along Av. López Mateos is the Plaza del Sol area. The west side holds most of the fine dining spots, luxury hotels, boutiques, and galleries as well as the American, British, and Canadian consulates.

Zapopan Founded in 1542 as a separate village, Zapopan is now a suburb of Guadalajara. It's noted for its 18th-century basilica, the home of Guadalajara's patron saint, the revered 16th-century image of the Virgin of Zapopan. She is honored by enormous throngs of people every October 12. Zapopan's main square and basilica are worth seeing, and next to the basilica is a small museum about the life and customs of the Huichol Indians, who live in a remote region of the state. It has a museum shop whose proceeds go to aid these Indians.

Tlaquepaque　This was a village of artisans (especially potters) that grew into a market center. In the last 30 years, it has attracted designers from all over Mexico. Now, every major form of art and craft is for sale here: furniture, pottery, glass, jewelry, woodcarvings, leather goods, sculpture, painting. The shops are sophisticated, yet the town's center has retained a small-town feel that makes door-to-door browsing enjoyable and relaxing.

Tonalá　This has remained a town of artisans. There are plenty of stores selling mostly local products from the town's more than 400 workshops. The crafts worked in this town are wrought iron, ceramics, blown glass, and papier-mâché. A busy street market is held each Thursday and Sunday.

GETTING AROUND

BY TAXI　Taxis are the best and easiest way to get around town. Almost all of them have meters, and though drivers are reluctant to use them, you can insist that they do. Cab fares for most of town run between $4 and $7. There are three fare structures: one is for day, the second is for night, and the third is for suburbia.

BY CAR　Keep in mind there are several main arteries (see "City Layout," above). The **Periférico** is a loop around the city that connects with most other highways entering the city. Traffic on the Periférico is slow, filled with trucks, and has only two lanes. Several important freeway-style thoroughfares crisscross the city. **González Gallo** leads south from the town center and connects with the road to Lake Chapala. **Avenida Vallarta** continues past La Minerva and eventually feeds onto **Highway 15,** bound for Tequila and on to Puerto Vallarta.

BY BUS & COLECTIVO　The electric bus known as the *Par Vial* is quite handy for going from downtown to the west side and back again. It bears the sign PAR VIAL and runs east along Hidalgo and west along the next street to the north, calle Independencia (not calzada Independencia). Hidalgo passes along the north side of the cathedral. The Par Vial goes as far east as Mercado Libertad and as far west as Minerva Circle.

There are six varieties of city buses that run along many of the same routes but offer different grades of service. The best are **Línea Turquesa buses,** which have the distinguishing letters "TUR" on the side. These are air-conditioned, have comfortable seats, and carry only as many passengers as there are seats; they are worth the additional price (about 60¢ for most destinations). The handiest route is the **706 TUR,** which runs from the Centro Histórico southeast to Tlaquepaque, the Central Camionera (new bus station), and Tonalá. For more information on Tlaquepaque and Tonalá, see "Shopping," in chapter 7. The same bus also runs in the reverse direction, northwest to Zapopan. You can catch this bus on Av. 16 de Septiembre.

Many buses run north-south along the Calzada Independencia (not to be confused with calle Independencia), but the **"San Juan de Dios–Estación"** bus goes between the points you are likely to want—San Juan de Dios church, next to the Mercado Libertad, and the railroad station (*estación*) past Parque Agua Azul. Fares are generally 40¢; exact change is not necessary. The city also has a rapid-transit system called *Tren Ligero,* but it doesn't serve areas that are of interest to visitors.

 Fast Facts: Guadalajara

American Express The local office is at Av. Vallarta 2440, Plaza los Arcos (© **3/615-8910**); it's open Monday through Friday from 9am to 6pm and Saturday from 9am to noon.

Area Code The telephone area code is **3.**

Books/Newspapers/Magazines **Gonvil,** a popular chain of bookstores, but with few English selections, has a branch across from Plaza de los Hombres Ilustres on avenida Hidalgo and another a few blocks south at Av. 16 de Septiembre 118 (Alcalde becomes 16 de Septiembre south of the cathedral). **Sanborn's,** at the corner of Juárez and 16 de Septiembre, does a good job of keeping English-language periodicals in stock, but most of these are specialty magazines. Many newsstands sell the two English local papers: the *Guadalajara Reporter* and the *Guadalajara Weekly.* For the widest selection of English-language books, try **Sandi Bookstore** (© **3/121-0863**) at Av. Tepeyac 178 in the Chapalita neighborhood (on the west side).

Business Hours Store hours are generally Monday through Saturday from 10am to 2pm and 4 to 8pm.

Climate & Dress Guadalajara is mild year-round, with the occasional freak cold spell. Generally, November through March, you'll need a sweater in the evening. The warmest months, April and May, are hot and dry. June through September, the city gets afternoon and evening showers that keep the temperature a bit cooler. Dress in Guadalajara is conservative; attention-getting sportswear (short shorts, halters, and the like) is out of place here.

Consulates The largest **American consular offices** in the world are here, at Progreso 175 (✆ 3/825-2998 or 3/825-2700). Other consulates include the **Canadian consulate,** Hotel Fiesta Americana, Local 31 (✆ 3/615-6215); the **British consulate,** Eulogio Parra 2539, Oficina 12 (✆ 3/616-0629); and the **Australian consulate,** López Cotilla 2030 (✆ 3/ 615-7418). These offices all keep roughly the same hours: Monday through Friday from 8am to 4pm.

Currency Exchange The best rates are found 3 blocks south of the cathedral on López Cotilla street, between the streets Corona and Degollado. There are more than 20 *casas de cambio* on these two blocks. Almost all have their rates posted, which are better than what the banks offer and without the long lines.

Emergencies The emergency phone number for Guadalajara is ✆ 080.

Hospitals For medical emergencies, there's the **Hospital México-Americano,** Cólomos 2110 (✆ 3/642-7152).

Internet Access Most of the big hotels have business centers that you can use. If you're downtown, there's an Internet cafe just north of the Cathedral at avenida Alcalde 159-34, in a small shopping center called Plaza Alegria. Its name is **C.C.C.P.,** and the hours are Monday through Saturday from 9am to 9pm.

Luggage Storage/Lockers You can store luggage in the main bus station, the Central Camionera, and at the Guadalajara airport.

Police Tourists should first try to contact the Jalisco tourist information office in Plaza Tapatía, listed under Visitor Information (✆ 3/658-1600). If they can't reach this office, they should call the municipal police at ✆ 3/617-6060.

Post Office The main post office (*correo*) is at the corner of Carranza and calle Independencia, about 4 blocks northeast of the cathedral. Standing in the plaza behind the cathedral and facing the Degollado Theater, walk to the left and turn left on Carranza; walk past the Hotel Mendoza, cross calle Independencia, and look for the post office on the left side.

Safety Guadalajara doesn't have the violent crime that exists in Mexico City. Crimes against tourists and foreign students are infrequent and most often take the form of pickpocketing and purse-snatching. Criminals usually work in teams and target travelers in busy places, such as outdoor restaurants: One will create a distraction while the other slips off with whatever the tourist may have set down. There have been reports of purse-snatching, usually against unaccompanied women at night, and rarely in places with crowds. The same can be said of necklace-snatching, where the assailant will grab hold of a necklace, especially if it has a gold chain, and pull hard, hoping it will break.

Spanish Classes Foreigners can study Spanish at the **Foreign Student Study Center,** University of Guadalajara, calle Tomás V. Gómez #125, 44100 Guadalajara, Jalisco (© **3/616-4399**). **IMAC** is a private Spanish school at Donato Guerra #180 in the Centro Histórico (© **3/613-1080**).

Telephones Guadalajara now has 8-digit dialing, which means that you must dial the area code, which is 3, when making a local call.

2 Where to Stay

Life has been good to Guadalajara's *hoteleros*, and prices this year have risen accordingly. Rates shown are the standard rack rates and include the 17% tax. In slow periods, you should look for discounts; the big hotels are also in the habit of giving business discounts.

Almost all of the luxury hotels in Guadalajara are on the west side, which has the majority of the shopping malls, boutiques, fashionable restaurants and clubs. There is also a lot to do in the Centro Histórico, making it a good place to stay, too. Finally, Tlaquepaque is a comfortable suburb and is perfect for shoppers; the only drawback is that almost everything but the Parián shuts down very early. Chain hotels not included below are the Hilton, Camino Real, Howard Johnson, Holiday Inn, and Crowne Plaza.

VERY EXPENSIVE

Fiesta Americana ⨁⨁   A dramatic 22-story luxury hotel similar to the Presidente Intercontinental but less expensive and with fewer amenities, the Fiesta Americana caters mainly to business travelers. Location is excellent—in front of the Minerva Circle, in western

Guadalajara—and service is great. Floors 4 through 10 have been remodeled and should be requested. Rooms are large and come with two doubles or one king, carpeting, and a soundproof door. Bathrooms are large and well-equipped and come with shower/tub combinations. The furniture is modern and understated. The Fiesta Club, which is the executive level, is on limited-access floors. One room is equipped for guests with disabilities.

Aurelio Aceves 225, Glorieta Minerva, 44100 Guadalajara, Jal. ⓒ **800/FIESTA1** in the U.S. and Canada, or 3/825-3434. Fax 3/630-3671. www.fiestaamericana.com.mx. 391 units. $218–$239 double; $260 Fiesta Club; $271–$614 suites. AE, DC, MC, V. Free secured parking. **Amenities:** Restaurant, lobby bar; heated medium-size pool; golf privileges at local club; 2 tennis courts (lighted); gym' children's activities (fiesta kids' program on Sundays); concierge; tour desk; car rental; business center; executive business services; 24-hour room service; baby-sitting; same-day laundry/dry cleaning; no-smoking rooms, executive levels. *In room:* A/C, TV w/ pay movies, dataport, minibar, coffeemaker, hair dryer.

Hotel Presidente Inter-Continental ★★★ Housed in a 14-story glass building with atrium-lobby, this hotel offers top quality services and amenities. There is little turnover in staff, and the concierge has proven more capable and knowledgeable than any other in the city. Rooms are comfortable and quiet, with modern furnishings that include a desk with a modem/phone outlet, and a small table with two chairs. Club rooms have a discreet check-in and elevator entrance, are on limited-access hallways, and include a free continental breakfast, newspaper, and evening cocktails. The extra privacy and services are good for Mexican soap opera stars or repeat guests who like having their preferences known in advance. If you're neither of these, opt for one of the other rooms. The hotel is at present remodeling its rooms; 136 have been finished. The lobby bar is popular, and during the season, bullfighters relax here after the *corrida*. Across from the Plaza del Sol shopping center in western Guadalajara.

Av. López Mateos Sur y Moctezuma, 45050 Guadalajara, Jal. ⓒ **800/327-0200** in the U.S. and Canada, or 3/678-1234. Fax 3/678-1222. www.interconti.com. 409 units. $224–290 double, $299 club rooms, $368 club suite. Weekend packages available. AE, DC, MC, V. Free sheltered parking. **Amenities:** Two restaurants, lobby bar; outdoor heated pool; golfing at nearby clubs; health club with saunas, steam rooms, and whirlpools; concierge; tour desk; car rental; large business center; executive services; salon; 24-hour room service; massage; baby-sitting; same-day laundry/dry cleaning; no-smoking rooms, executive-levels. *In room:* A/C, TV w/ pay movies, dataport, minibar, coffeemaker, hair dryer, iron, safe.

Quinta Real ★★★ This chain of hotels specializes in building properties that are suggestive of Mexico's heritage, in contrast to the

comfortable-but-generic luxury hotel. No glass skyscraper here, instead there are two four-story buildings made of stone, wood beam, plaster, and tile, situated amidst lush grounds. Rooms vary quite a bit: Eight have brick cupolas, some have balconies, several have scallop-shaped headboards, and four are equipped with whirlpool tubs in the bathroom. All the rooms are large, split-level, and have antique decorative touches. And all rooms come with large, fully equipped bathrooms with tub/shower combinations and excellent water pressure. You can choose between two doubles or one king-size bed. The hotel is 2 blocks from the Minerva Circle on avenida Mexico at López Mateos in western Guadalajara. Ask for a room that doesn't face López Mateos.

Av. Mexico 2727, 44680 Guadalajara, Jal. ℂ **800/445-4565** in the U.S. and Canada, or 3/615-0000. Fax 3/630-1797. www.quintareal.com. 78 suites. $280 master suite, $290–$300 grand-class suite. AE, DC, MC, V. Free secured parking. **Amenities:** Restaurant, bar; small outdoor heated pool; golfing at local club; access to nearby health club; concierge; tour desk; car rental; business center; executive business services; room service until midnight; baby-sitting; same-day laundry/dry cleaning; no-smoking rooms. *In room:* A/C, TV, dataport, minibar, hair dryer, iron, safe.

EXPENSIVE

Holiday Inn Hotel and Suites Centro Histórico ℛ
This hotel has the most comfortable lodging in the downtown area. Its location, a few blocks from the main square, is good, too. Standard rooms are carpeted and decorated in Mexican architectural colors. The furniture is modern Mexican with a few wrought iron pieces—the overall effect is quite cheerful. The size and lighting are both good; bathrooms are medium-size, well equipped and with ample counter space. The suites are larger, but perhaps not worth the extra cost.

Av. Juárez no. 211, 44100 Guadalajara. Jal. ℂ **800/HOLIDAY** in the U.S. or Canada, or 3/612-1763. www.holidayinn.com. 90 units. $150 double; $180 suite. AE, MC, V. Free secure parking. **Amenities:** Restaurant/bar; fitness room; business center; limited room service; same-day laundry/dry cleaning; no-smoking rooms. *In room:* A/C, TV, dataport, minibar, coffeemaker, hair dryer, iron.

Hotel de Mendoza ℛ
On a quiet street next to the Degollado Theater and Plaza Tapatía, and only 2 blocks from the cathedral, the Mendoza has the best location of any downtown hotel. The decor would best be described as an attempt at old Spanish with wood paneling and old-world accents. Standard rooms are medium-size and are comfortable. Bed choices are one queen-size, two full, or two queen-size. Bathrooms are small, but have enough counter space. Suites have an additional sitting area and larger bathrooms.

Rooms face the street, an interior courtyard, or the pool. One note: The bath towels are the narrowest I've ever seen—obviously the brainchild of a demented cost-cutting expert. If the hotel hasn't changed these, ask for a couple extra when you get your room.

Carranza 16, 44100 Guadalajara, Jal. ℂ **800/221-6509** in the U.S., or 3/613-4646. Fax 3/613-7310. www.demendoza.com.mx. 106 units. $116 double; $121 suite. AE, DC, MC, V. Secured parking $2.50 daily. **Amenities:** Restaurant, bar; small pool; tour desk; room service until 10:30pm; same-day laundry/dry cleaning; no-smoking rooms. *In room:* A/C, TV, dataport, hair dryer and iron on request.

Hotel Misión Carlton ℛ   The Misión Carlton is a 20-story hotel by Agua Azul Park, a short cab ride or good walk from the historic center. Remodeled this year, it offers spacious, well-furnished rooms (large writing table, good closet area) that have large bathrooms with make-up mirrors and plenty of counter space. Despite the remodeling, the rooms seem dated, but comfortable. Rooms come with two full beds or one king. Mattresses are a little springier than the standard. Ask for a room with a view of the park.

Av. Niños Héroes 125, 44100 Guadalajara, Jal. ℂ **800/448-8355** in the U.S. and Canada, or 3/614-7272. Fax 3/613-5539. www.hotelesmision.com.mx. 193 units. $140 double. Weekend discounts. AE, DC, MC, V. Free valet parking. **Amenities:** Restaurant, 2 bars; medium pool; children's activities on weekends; concierge; tour desk; car rental; business center; executive business services; salon; limited room service; baby-sitting; same-day laundry/dry cleaning; no-smoking rooms. *In room:* A/C, TV, dataport, minibar, coffeemaker, hair dryer, irons on request.

MODERATE

Calinda Roma   This is a comfortable, modestly priced hotel in the Centro Histórico. It's located on busy Ave. Juárez, close to the main plazas. It seems to be perpetually under renovation; most rooms are decent but a few are truly dismal, yet go for the same price. So ask for a remodeled room that doesn't face Juárez. These are medium in size, well lit, with simple furniture, and good mattresses. Bathrooms are medium to small, but they have good lighting and counter space. There's a small pool and sunning area on the roof.

Juárez 170, 44100 Guadalajara, Jal. ℂ **800/228-5151** in the U.S., 01-800/ 900-0000 in Mexico, or 3/614-8650. Fax 3/614-2629. 120 units. $72 double. AE, DC, MC, V. Free secured parking. **Amenities:** Restaurant, lobby bar; small pool; room service until 11pm; same-day laundry/dry cleaning; no-smoking rooms. *In room:* A/C, TV, dataport, iron.

Hotel Cervantes   This six-story downtown hotel offers modern amenities at a good price. The rooms are attractive and medium in size. They have wall-to-wall carpeting and tile bathrooms with ample sink areas and shower/tub combinations. The lower price is with one double bed; the higher price is with a king or two doubles. This is not a particularly noisy hotel, but if you require absolute quiet, get an interior room. The Cervantes is 6 blocks south and 3 blocks west of the cathedral.

Prisciliano Sánchez 442, Col. Centro Histórico, 44100 Guadalajara, Jal. ⓒ/fax 3/613-6686. 100 units. $60–$70 double. AE, MC, V. Free secured parking. **Amenities:** Restaurant, lobby bar; small outdoor heated pool; tour desk; room service until 10pm; baby-sitting; same-day laundry/dry cleaning. *In room:* A/C, TV.

La Villa del Ensueño 🦀🦀 *(finds)* This B&B in central Tlaquepaque is a lovely alternative to big-city hotels. Built in a modern rendition of traditional Mexican architecture, it is a delight to the eye—small courtyards and beautiful gardens bordered by old stucco walls, which have been painted in muted shades of orange oxide or covered in carefully trimmed ivy, with an occasional wrought-iron balcony or stone staircase. The rooms are individually decorated and have more character than most hotel rooms. All come with ceiling fans. Doubles have either two twin or two double beds. Guests receive a complimentary cocktail on arrival.

Florida 305, 45500 Tlaquepaque, Jal. ⓒ 800/220-8689 in the U.S., or 3/635-8792. Fax 818/597-0637 in the U.S. www.mexonline.com/ensueno.htm. 18 units. $88 double; $99 deluxe double; $117 2-bedroom deluxe; $140 suite. Rates include continental breakfast, light laundry service. AE, MC, V. Free secured parking. **Amenities:** Bar; small outdoor pool.

INEXPENSIVE

Hotel San Francisco Plaza 🦀 *(Value)* This colonial-style, downtown hotel is both pleasant to stay in and a bargain. What you get is a big, clean, comfortable room with attractive furnishings. All rooms have rugs or carpeting, and most have tall ceilings except for the remodeled area behind the reception desk. The hotel is built in colonial style around four courtyards, which are decorated with fountains and potted plants. Rooms along the Sánchez Street side are much quieter now that the management has installed double windows, and these rooms look quite good. Some of the rooms along the back wall of the rear patio have small bathrooms. A small plaza out front gives the hotel its name. The San Francisco Plaza is 6 blocks south of the cathedral and 2 blocks east.

Degollado 267, 44100 Guadalajara, Jal. ⓒ 3/613-8954 or 3/613-8971. Fax 3/613-3257. 76 units. $50 double. AE, MC, V. Free parking. **Amenities:** Restaurant; limited room service; baby-sitting; same-day laundry/dry cleaning; ironing service. *In room:* A/C, TV.

3 Where to Dine

Guadalajara has many excellent restaurants either for fine dining or for eating the typical local fare. Most of the fine-dining spots are on the west side. Those in the Centro Histórico are uniformly bad, with two exceptions: La Fonda de San Miguel, and Siglo XV. Tlaquepaque has some good choices, but these all close around 8pm. Popular eateries serving good local fare are abundant, especially in the Centro Histórico. Local dishes worth trying include *birria,* which is meat (goat, lamb, or pork) that has been covered in maguey leaves and roasted. It can be served either in a tomato-based broth or with the broth on the side. To get it properly prepared, go to one of the many *birrierías* (in the downtown area, go to Las Nueve Esquinas neighborhood, where there are about a half dozen; in Tlaquepaque try **Birriería El Sope**). Another local favorite is the *torta ahogada,* something similar to a sub sandwich with a spicy pork filling. Also, there is the Jalisco-style *pozole,* a chicken-and-hominy soup to which you add lime juice, onion, Mexican oregano, and *chiles.*

If invited out by locals, you will probably be taken to the city's most popular restaurant: **El Santo Coyote.** Although it's a pretty place (in imitation of Coyote Café), I don't care much for the food. If you're in need of a quick meal, there are several **Sanborn's** in the city. This is a popular national chain of restaurants and coffee shops where the traditional dish to order is *enchiladas suizas.*

It's a good idea to keep your guidebook handy when taking a taxi; I've found that many drivers are unfamiliar with even the most popular places and require an address to get you there. Also, it's a good idea to make reservations in the evening, especially for restaurants on the west side.

EXPENSIVE

"Restaurant with No Name" ALTA COCINA   Dine in a cool, shaded patio that has the informal feel of a Mexican country house. Vegetation is allowed to grow pretty much at will and has been coaxed to form green canopies; peacocks strut around unruffled by the goings-on. This place could also be called Restaurant with No Menu; the waiters will recite the full list of dishes in English or Spanish and you can interrupt with questions at any time. I am one of those who doesn't feel comfortable without text on a page, but I was comforted by the waiter's ability to answer my questions and by how he rewound and fast-forwarded through his presentation.

Many dishes here are a bit under-spiced. I did like the strong-flavored pork in a three-*chile* sauce (rich-flavored *chiles*, not hot ones). I also liked the seafood dishes. Located 1½ blocks north of Tlaquepaque's Parián.

Madero 80 (Tlaquepaque). *©* 3/635-4520 or 3/635-9677. Breakfast $4–$7; main courses $11–$20. AE, DISC, MC, V. Daily 8:30am–10pm.

MODERATE

Adobe Fonda *⋆⋆* NUEVA COCINA   This charming restaurant shares space with a large and attractive *artesanía* store on the pedestrian-only Independencia. The menu is highly inventive and thoughtfully designed. Homemade bread and *tostadas* are brought to the table with an olive oil-based *chile* sauce, *pico de gallo*, and *requezón de epazote* (herb-flavored fresh cheese). Among the choice of soups is a delicious *crema de cilantro*, and an interesting mushroom soup with a dark beer broth. The main courses present some difficult decisions with intriguing combinations of Mexican, Italian, and Argentine ingredients: shrimp quesadillas accompanied by *chimichurri* with *nopal;* filet in a creamy ancho sauce, chicken breast in a cashew and poblano *chile* sauce. The margaritas are noteworthy, too.

Francisco de Miranda #27, corner of Independencia, Tlaquepaque. *©* 3/657-2792. Reservations accepted. Main courses $8–$17. AE, MC, V. Daily 12:30–6:30pm.

Casa Fuerte MEXICAN/INTERNATIONAL   Clothing designer Irene Pulos has turned her former showroom into this popular and charming patio restaurant. The setting is colorfully Mexicano: pastel walls and waiters sporting bold Pulos-designed vests. Imaginatively prepared dishes include shrimp in tamarind, stuffed chicken in *guajillo* sauce, fresh vegetable salads, steaks, and fajitas.

224-A Independencia (Tlaquepaque). *©* 3/639-6481. Reservations recommended. Main courses $7–$14. AE, DISC, MC, V. Daily noon–8pm.

El Sacromonte *⋆⋆⋆* ALTA COCINA   The food here is so exquisite that I try to dine here every time I'm in Guadalajara. Great emphasis is placed on presentation and artful design, from the menu in verse (haikus in Spanish that lose a lot in translation to English) to "Queen Isabel's crown," a dish of shrimp woven together in the shape of a crown and covered in a divine lobster and orange sauce. The appetizers are also things of beauty, such as quesadillas with rose petals. My favorite soup, *el viejo progreso,* is a cream soup of Roquefort and chipotle. The dining area is a pleasant, shaded, open-air patio. This place is popular so make reservations, or show up between meal times.

Pedro Moreno 1398 (west side). ℰ **3/825-5447** or 827-0663. Reservations recommended. Main courses $7–$12. MC, V. Mon–Sat 1:30pm–midnight.

Hostería del Ángel ℛ TAPAS/SPANISH-ITALIAN DELI   This
is a difficult restaurant to categorize. The owner/chef cooked for
years in Spain and Italy, where he became fascinated with the making of cheeses and deli meats such as prosciutto and the Spanish
jamón serrano. Now he has returned and opened a restaurant where
he can combine his specialties with Mexican ingredients. He serves
different tapas every day and a large variety of wines. This is a wonderful place to go in the evening for a glass of wine and some tapas,
a sandwich, or a *rotalata* of cheese, meats, and vegetables. The
restaurant is 4 blocks from the basilica of the Virgin of Zapopan,
half a block off the *calzada* or promenade.

5 de Mayo 295 (Zapopan, west side). ℰ/fax **3/656-9516.** Reservations not
accepted. *Comida corrida* $4–$5; Deli specialties and tapas $4–$6. AE, MC, V.
Tues–Sat 9am–midnight.

La Destilería ℛℛ MEXICAN   You know that with a name like
"The Distillery," tequila will somehow be involved. Although this
museum-restaurant is filled with artifacts, photos, and curios depicting every stage of the tequila-making process, it's the food that really
pulls in the Tapatíos. Specialties include *molcajete de la casa*—
steaming fajitas, *rajas* (*chile* strips), cheese, onion, and avocado in a
large, sizzling *molcajete* (three-legged stone mortar). The spicy steak
dish, *medallones Tenochtitlán,* is memorable, as is the delicately flavored fish in parsley sauce. This is one of those places almost sure to
please everyone. You can order salads here without hesitation (all
greens are washed in an antimicrobial solution), and the dessert
menu has such favorites as *pastel de tres leches.* And, with its vast
selection of tequilas, it's the perfect place to do a little tasting. It's 5
blocks northwest of the Fuente Minerva.

Av. México 2916, corner of Nelson; Fracc. Terranova (west side). ℰ **3/640-3440** or
3/640-3110. Main courses $7–$15. AE, DISC, MC, V. Mon–Sat 1pm–midnight; Sun
1–6pm.

La Fonda de San Miguel ℛℛ *Moments* MEXICAN   My favorite
way to enjoy a good meal in Mexico is to have it in an elegant colonial courtyard. I love the contrast between the bright, noisy street
outside and the cool, serene courtyard inside. This particular restaurant is in a beautiful courtyard belonging to a former convent. (You
can check out the shops and galleries as you enter.) While enjoying
the stone arches and gurgling fountain, you are served little crisp

tacos, pumpkin bread, and mildly spiced butter to awaken the appetite. For main courses, try *chiles en nogada* if it's in season (a combination of spicy and sweet), or perhaps a traditional *mole poblano.* The restaurant is 4 blocks west and 1 block south of the cathedral in the former convent of Santa Teresa de Jesús.

Donato Guerra 25 (downtown). ✆ 3/613-0809. Reservations recommended. Breakfast $5; main courses $8–$14. AE, MC, V. Sun–Mon 9am–6pm; Tues–Sat 8am–midnight.

La Trattoría Pomodoro Ristorante ITALIAN   Good food, a comfortable dining area, and fast and friendly service make this place popular. Natural wood chairs, cushioned seats, linen table-cloths, and a large span of windows look out onto Niños Héroes. There's separate seating for smokers and nonsmokers. For starters, you might want to sample the antipasto bar or the shrimp in white-wine cream sauce with *chiles.* As a main course, the fettuccine Alfredo is excellent. The superb salad bar and garlic bread are included in the price of the main course.

Niños Héroes 3051 (west side). ✆ 3/122-1817. Reservations recommended. Pasta $7–$10; chicken, beef, and seafood $10–$15. AE, MC, V. Daily 1pm–midnight. Free parking.

Mariscos Progreso ⍟ SEAFOOD/MEXICAN   In a large, open patio shaded by trees and tile roofs, waiters navigate among the tables carrying large platters of delicious seafood. Mexicans do a wonderful job with seafood, and this popular restaurant does the tradition proud. Charcoal-grilled, Mexican-style is the specialty here (for a sampling of grilled favorites, try the *parrillada* for two), but they'll cook it in a variety of ways. Sometimes, there can be quite a bit of *ambiente,* with *mariachis* adding to the commotion. At other times, the crowd thins and one can rest peacefully from the exertions of shopping with a cold drink. It's ½ block from the Parián, in Tlaquepaque.

Progreso 80 (Tlaquepaque). ✆ 3/657-4995. Reservations not accepted. Main courses $7–$14. AE, MC, V. Daily 11am–7pm.

Siglo XV SPANISH   This restaurant goes to great lengths to cre-ate a dining hall suggestive of 15th-century Spain—stone walls, tables and benches made of thick wooden planks, torches, and the like. The end result is impressive, and the food is excellent, too. Popular favorites include his scallops *cayos a la madrileña, paella,* and roasted pig *cochinillo asado a la segoviana.* Wednesday through Saturday, there are flamenco performances, and every night there is

live acoustic music. If you want to go on a weekend, make reservations. The restaurant is in the downtown neighborhood known as *las nueve esquinas.*

Colón 383 (downtown). ℂ **3/614-4278.** Reservations recommended on weekends. Main courses $7–$15. AE, MC, V. Tues–Sat 2pm–1am. Valet parking.

INEXPENSIVE

Café Madrid MEXICAN   This little coffee shop is like many coffee shops used to be—a kind of social institution where people come in, greet each other and the staff by name, and chat over breakfast or coffee and cigarettes. Change comes slowly here. For example, despite the fact that it's an informal place, the waiters wear white jackets with black bow ties, as they did 20 years ago. The coffee and Mexican breakfasts are good, as is the standard Mexican fare served in the afternoon. There's a room open to the street in front with a small lunch counter and another in the back. From the Plaza de Armas, walk 1 block on Corona to Juárez and turn right; the cafe is on the right.

Juárez 264 (downtown). ℂ **3/614-9504.** Breakfast $2–$4; main courses $3–$6. No credit cards. Daily 7:30am–10:30pm.

La Chata Restaurant REGIONAL/MEXICAN   At this popular downtown spot, tasty Mexican standards are offered at reasonable prices. Aromas waft into the street from the kitchen in front, where women with their heads wrapped in bandanas busily stir, chop, and fry. Past this is a large dining area. Local dishes include *pozole* (chicken, pork, and hominy in a broth to which you add onions, radishes, *chile*, and oregano) or a *torta ahogada* (a spicy pork sandwich), or if you're very hungry, the sampler platter of *antojitos* for four people will fit the bill. To find La Chata from the Plaza de Armas, walk 1½ blocks south on Corona; it's on the right between Juárez and López Cotilla.

Corona 126 (downtown). ℂ **3/613-0588.** Reservations not accepted. Breakfast $2:50–$5; main courses $4–$7. AE, DC, MC, V. Daily 8am–11:30pm.

Los Itacates Restaurant 🌟🌟 *Value* MEXICAN   This is the Mexican equivalent to down-home cooking—nothing exotic or unheard-of, just well-prepared traditional food. This place, very popular with office workers, is packed during the afternoon dinner hour (2–4pm), but at other times it's easy to find a table. The atmosphere is festive, with colorfully painted chairs and table coverings. You can choose to dine outdoors at sidewalk tables or in one of the three interior rooms. Specialties include *pozole, lomo adobado* (baked pork in dark *chile* sauce), and *chiles rellenos.* The *pollo Itacates* is a quarter of a chicken, two cheese enchiladas, potatoes, and rice. Los Itacates is on Av. Chapultepec, 5 blocks north of Av. Vallarta.

Chapultepec Nte. 110 (near west side). ℂ **3/825-1106** or 3/825-9551. Breakfast buffet $4; tacos 50¢; main courses $3–$6. MC, V. Mon–Sat 8am–11pm; Sun 8am–7pm.

7

Exploring Guadalajara & Beyond

Guadalajara is one of the most Mexican of Mexico's cities. Spend a few days exploring its historic downtown area, with all its cultural and architectural highlights, parks, and attractions, and even the most hard-core resort tourist will realize there is much more to Mexico than sandy beaches and souvenir shops. Several outlying towns also merit a visit, including Tequila (for those who like to imbibe), and the villages surrounding Lake Chapala, a popular vacation spot.

1 What to See & Do in Guadalajara

SPECIAL EVENTS IN GUADALAJARA

In September, when Mexicans celebrate independence from Spain, Guadalajara goes all out with a full month of festivities. The celebrations kick off with the **Encuentro Internacional del Mariachi,** in which *mariachi* bands from around the world come to their mecca to play before knowledgeable audiences and rehearse with other mariachis. Bands come from as far as Japan and Russia, and the event takes on a curious postmodern hue. There are concerts in several venues. In the Degollado Theater, you can hear orchestral arrangements of classic *mariachi* songs with solos by famous *mariachis*. You might be acquainted with many of the classics without even knowing it. The culmination of this *Encuentro* is a parade of thousands of *mariachis* and *charros* through downtown Guadalajara. Catch it if you're there during the first 10 days of September.

On **September 15,** a massive crowd assembles in front of the Governor's Palace to await the shouting of the traditional *grito* (shout for independence) at 11pm. The grito commemorates Fr. Miguel Hidalgo de Costilla's cry for independence in 1810. The celebration features live music on a street stage, spontaneous dancing, fireworks, of course, and shouts of *"¡Viva México!"* and *"¡Viva Hidalgo!"* The next day is the official Independence Day with a traditional parade; the plazas downtown resemble a country fair and Mexican market,

Downtown Guadalajara

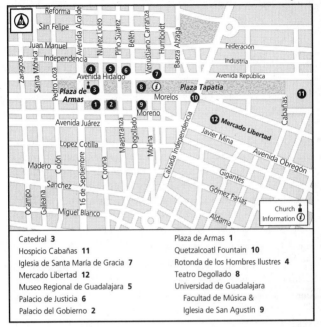

Catedral **3**	Plaza de Armas **1**
Hospicio Cabañas **11**	Quetzalcoatl Fountain **10**
Iglesia de Santa María de Gracia **7**	Rotonda de los Hombres Ilustres **4**
Mercado Libertad **12**	Teatro Degollado **8**
Museo Regional de Guadalajara **5**	Universidad de Guadalajara
Palacio de Justicia **6**	Facultad de Música &
Palacio del Gobierno **2**	Iglesia de San Agustín **9**

with booths, games of chance, stuffed-animal prizes, cotton candy, and candied apples. Live entertainment stretches well into the night.

On **October 12**, the feast day of the Virgin of Zapopan is celebrated with a **procession** 🎭🎭 honoring Our Lady of Zapopan. Around dawn, her small, dark figure begins the 5-hour ride from the Cathedral of Guadalajara to the suburban Basilica of Zapopan (see "Other Attractions," below). The original icon dates from the mid-1500s; the procession began 200 years later. Today, crowds spend the night along the route and vie for position as the Virgin approaches. She travels in a gleaming new car, virginal in the sense that it must never have had the ignition turned on, and this car is pulled through the streets by the Virgin's caretakers. During the previous months, the figure visits churches all over the city. You will likely see neighborhoods decorated with paper streamers and banners honoring the passing of the figure to the next church.

The celebration has grown into a month-long event, **Fiestas de Octubre,** which kicks off with an enormous parade, usually on the first Sunday (or possibly Saturday) of the month. Festivities include

> *Tips* **Watch for Area Code Changes**
>
> As this book went to press, Mexico announced a country-wide change in its long-distance area codes. The new plan will affect every phone number in this book; for details, please consult the box "Changes to Mexico's Phone Numbers Announced," in chapter 1.

performing arts, rodeos (*charreadas*), bullfights, art exhibits, regional dancing, a food fair, and a Day of Nations incorporating all the consulates in Guadalajara. By the time this is over, you enter the holiday season of November and December with the Revolution Day (November 20th) and saint's day for the Virgin of Guadalupe (December 12) and several other celebrations. There's always something going on September through December.

DOWNTOWN GUADALAJARA

The most easily recognized building downtown is the **cathedral** *⋒*, around which four open plazas make the shape of a Latin cross. Later, a long swath of land was cleared to extend the open area from the cathedral east to the Hospicio Cabañas, creating **Plaza Tapatía.** Most of the downtown attractions are adjacent to this area.

Construction on the cathedral started in 1561 and was an ongoing project into the 18th century. With such a long time span, it was inevitable that remodeling would take place before the building was ever completed. The result is an unusual facade that is actually an amalgam of several architectural styles, including baroque, neoclassical, and Gothic. An 1818 earthquake destroyed the original large towers; their replacements were built in the 1850s, inspired by designs on the bishop's dinner china. The colors on the towers—blue and yellow—are the symbolic colors of Guadalajara and match the city's coat of arms. Inside, the cathedral is open, airy, and majestic. Items of interest include a painting in the sacristy ascribed to the renowned 17th-century Spanish artist Bartolomé Estaban Murillo (1617–82).

To the cathedral's left is the **Plaza de Armas,** the oldest of the plazas and the loveliest. It's recognizable by the Art Nouveau bandstand in its center. This bandstand, made in France, was a gift to the city from the dictator Porfirio Díaz in the 1890s. The female figures on the bandstand exhibited too little clothing for conservative Guadalajarans, who then dressed the figures in cloth apparel. The dictator, recognizing when it's best to let the people have their way, said nothing.

Facing the plaza is the **Palacio del Gobierno** ✿✿. This handsome palace, built in 1774, blends Spanish and Moorish elements. Inside the central courtyard, above the staircase to the right, is a spectacular mural of Hidalgo by the modern Mexican master José Clemente Orozco (1883–1949). The Father of Independence appears high overhead, bearing directly down on the viewer and looking as implacable as a force of nature. Guadalajara's native son achieved this effect through the dramatic use of proportion and perspective that are the hallmarks of his work. On one of the adjacent walls is another mural, *The Carnival of Ideologies*, a dark satire on the prevailing fanaticisms of Orozco's day. There is another mural by Orozco inside the second-floor chamber of representatives. It shows Hidalgo again, but this time in a more conventional posture, writing the proclamation to end slavery in Mexico. The palacio is open from 10am to 8pm.

On the opposite side of the cathedral from the Plaza de Armas is the **Rotonda de los Hombres Ilustres.** Sixteen white columns, each supporting a bronze statue, stand as monuments to Guadalajara's, and the state of Jalisco's, distinguished sons.

Facing the east side of the rotunda is the **Museo Regional de Guadalajara,** Liceo 60 (✆ **3/614-9957**). Originally a convent, it was built in 1701 in the *churrigueresque* style (Mexican baroque) and contains some of the region's important archaeological finds, fossils, historic objects, and art. Among the highlights are a giant reconstructed mammoth's skeleton and a meteorite weighing 1,715 pounds, discovered in Zacatecas in 1792. On the first floor, there's also a fascinating exhibit of pre-Hispanic pottery and some exquisite pottery and clay figures recently unearthed near Tequila during the construction of the toll road. On the second floor is a small but interesting ethnography exhibit of the contemporary dress of the state's indigenous peoples, including the Coras, Huicholes, Mexicaneros, Nahuas, and Tepehuanes. It's open Tuesday through Saturday from 9am to 6:45pm and Sunday from 9am to 2:45pm. Admission is $2.50 for adults; $1 for children (children enter free Sunday); on Tuesday admission is free for all.

Behind the Cathedral is the Plaza de la Liberación, with the **Teatro Degollado** (deh-goh-*yah*-doh) on the opposite side. This neoclassical, 19th-century opera house was named for Santos Degollado, a local patriot who fought with Juárez against Maximilian and the French. Apollo and the nine muses decorate the theater's pediment, but the best part of this theater is its interior, famous for both the acoustics and the rich decoration. It hosts a variety of performances during the year, including the Ballet Folklórico on Sunday at 10am. It's open Monday through Friday from 10am to 2pm and during performances (see "Guadalajara After Dark," below for more information).

To the theater's right, on the opposite side of the street is the sweet little **church of Santa María de Gracia,** built in 1573 as part of a convent for Dominican nuns. On the opposite side of the Teatro Degollado is the **church of San Agustín,** and occupying the former convent is the **University of Guadalajara School of Music.**

Behind the Teatro Degollado begins the Plaza Tapatía, which leads to the Instituto Cabañas. It passes between a couple of low, modern office buildings. The Tourism Information Office is in a building on the right-hand side.

Beyond these office buildings, the plaza opens into a huge pedestrian expanse, now framed by department stores and offices and dominated by the abstract modern **Quetzalcoatl Fountain.** This fluid steel structure represents the mythical plumed serpent Quetzalcoatl, who figured so prominently in pre-Hispanic religion and culture, and exerts a presence even today.

At the far end of the plaza is the Hospicio Cabañas, formerly an orphanage and known today as the **Instituto Cultural Cabañas** ⟨⟨, Cabañas 8 (© **3/617-4322**). This vast structure is impressive for both its size (more than 23 courtyards) and its grandiose architecture, especially the cupola. Created by the famous Mexican architect Manuel Tolsá, it housed homeless children from 1829 until 1980. Today, it's a thriving cultural center offering art shows and classes. The interior walls and ceiling of the main building display murals painted by Orozco in 1937, at the height of his powers. His *Man of Fire,* occupying the dome, is said to represent the spirit of humanity projecting itself toward the infinite. Other rooms hold additional Orozco works, as well as excellent contemporary art and temporary displays. The institute's own Ballet Folklórico performs here every Wednesday at 8:30pm (see "Guadalajara After Dark," later in this chapter for more info). Hours are Tuesday through Saturday from 10:30am to 6pm and Sunday from 10:30am to 3pm. Admission is $1.

Just to the south of the Hospicio Cabañas (to the left as you exit the door) is the **Mercado Libertad** ⟨, Guadalajara's gigantic covered central market, said to be the largest in Latin America. This site has been a market plaza since the 1500s; the present buildings date from the early 1950s (see "Shopping," below).

OTHER ATTRACTIONS

At the **Parque Agua Azul** (Blue Water Park), the plants, trees, shrubbery, statues, and fountains create a perfect refuge from the bustling city. Many people come here to exercise early in the morning. The park is open daily from 7am to 6pm. Admission for adults is $1; children 50¢.

Across Independencia from the park, cater-cornered from a small flower market, is the **Museo de Arqueología del Occidente de Mexico,** Calzada Independencia con Av. del Campesino. It houses a fine collection of pre-Hispanic pottery from Jalisco, Nayarit, and Colima. The museum is open Tuesday through Sunday from 10am to 2pm and 4 to 7pm. There's a small admission charge.

The state-run **Casa de las Artesanías** (② 3/619-4664) is just past the park entrance at the crossroads of Calzada Independencia and González Gallo (for details, see "Shopping," below).

The Basílica of the Virgin of Zapopan ⊛

A wide promenade several blocks long leads to a large, open plaza and the basilica. This is the true religious center of Guadalajara, with the plaza holding hundreds of thousands of people on the Virgin's feast day (see "Special Events," above). The church dates from the 18th century and is a lovely (and somewhat anachronistic) combination of baroque and plateresque styles. The cult of the virgin of Zapopan practically began with the foundation of Guadalajara itself. She is much revered and the object of many pilgrimages. In front of the church, you will find several stands selling religious figures and paraphernalia. On one side of the church is a lovely museum and store dedicated to the betterment of the Huichol Indians. It is well worth a visit.

Main Plaza, Zapopan (6 miles northwest of downtown), Jalisco. No phone. Free admission. Daily 7am–7pm; museum hours 10am–7pm.

Museo de las Artes de la Universidad de Guadalajara

This museum gets many important traveling exhibitions. An early show featured contemporary artists from all over the Americas. Several rooms house the university's permanent collection, consisting mainly of Mexican and Jaliscan artists. There are also some bold Orozco murals: On one wall of the auditorium and the cupola above are *Man, Creator and Rebel,* and *The People and Their False Leaders.* The museum is a short ride west of downtown, across from the University of Guadalajara.

Juárez 975. ② 3/625-7553. Admission $2. Tues–Sat 10am–8pm; Sun and holidays noon–8pm.

Museo de la Ciudad This fine museum, which opened in 1992 in a former convent, chronicles Guadalajara's fascinating past. The eight rooms, beginning on the right and proceeding in chronological order, cover the period from just before the city's founding to the present. Unusual artifacts, including rare Spanish armaments and equestrian paraphernalia, give a sense of what day-to-day life was like in Guadalajara's past. As you browse, dust off your Spanish and read the explanations, which give details not otherwise noted in the displays.

Independencia 684 at M. Barcena. ⓒ 3/658-2531. Admission 50¢. Wed–Sat 10am–5:30pm; Sun 10am–2:30pm.

2 Shopping

Many visitors to Guadalajara come specifically for the shopping in Tlaquepaque and Tonalá (see below). But if you have little free time to shop, try the government-run **Casa de las Artesanías** ⊛ in Agua Azul, just south of downtown. It's at González Gallo #20, where it intersects Calzada Independencia (ⓒ 3/619-4664). This place is perfect for one-stop shopping, with two floors of pottery, silver jewelry, dance masks, glassware, leather goods, and regional clothing from around the state and the country. As you enter, on the right are museum displays showing crafts and regional costumes from the state of Jalisco. The craft store is open Monday through Friday from 10am to 6pm, Saturday from 10am to 5pm, and Sunday from 10am to 3pm.

Guadalajara is known for its shoe industry, so if you're in the market for a pair, try the **Galería del Calzado**—a shopping center made up exclusively of shoe stores. It's on the west side, about 6 blocks from the Minerva Circle, at the intersection of Av. México and Yaquis.

Mariachis and *charros* come to Guadalajara from all over Mexico to buy their highly worked belts and boots, wide-brimmed *sombreros*, and embroidered shirts. There are several tailor shops and stores that specialize in these outfits, one is **El Charro,** which has a store in the Plaza del Sol shopping center, across the street from the Hotel Presidente Intercontinental, and one downtown on Juárez.

And if you're interested in viewing a good slice of what constitutes the material world for most Mexicans, try the mammoth **Mercado Libertad** ⊛ downtown. Besides food and produce, you will find some crafts, household goods, clothing, magical preparations, and much, much more. Although it opens at 7am, the market doesn't get in full swing until around 10am. Come prepared to haggle.

SHOPPING IN TLAQUEPAQUE & TONALÁ

Almost everyone who comes to Guadalajara for the shopping has Tlaquepaque and Tonalá in mind. These two suburbs are traditional handcraft centers that produce and sell a wide variety of *artesanía*.

TLAQUEPAQUE (TLAH-KEH-*PAH*-KEH)

Located about 20 minutes from downtown, **Tlaquepaque** ⭐⭐⭐ has the best shopping for handcrafts and the decorative arts in all of Mexico. Over the years, it has become a fashionable center for shopping, attracting talented designers in a variety of fields. Even though it's a suburb of a large city, there is a cozy, small-town feel to Tlaquepaque; it's a pleasure simply to stroll through the central streets from shop to shop. No one hassles you; no one does the hard sell. There are some excellent places to eat (see "Where to Dine," in chapter 6), or you can grab some simple fare at El Parián, a building in the middle of town housing a number of small eateries.

A taxi from downtown Guadalajara will cost you $5, or you can take one of the deluxe **Turquesa buses** that make a fairly quick run from downtown to Tlaquepaque and Tonalá (see "Getting Around," in chapter 6).

The **Tlaquepaque Tourism Office** has a helpful, English-speaking staff. It's located at Morelos 288 (© **3/635-5756** or 3/657- 3846) and is open Monday through Friday from 9am to 3pm and Saturday from 9am to 1pm. Most stores in Tlaquepaque close in the afternoon between 2 and 4pm and stay open in the evening until 7 or 8pm. Most are either closed or have reduced hours on Sunday.

If you are interested in pottery and ceramics, there are two museums worth a visit. The **Regional Ceramics Museum,** Independencia 237 (© **3/635-5404**), displays several aspects of traditional Jalisco pottery as produced in Tlaquepaque and Tonalá. There are high-quality examples dating back several generations. Note the cross-hatch design known as *petatillo* on some of the pieces; it's one of the region's oldest traditional motifs and is, as so many other motifs, a real pain to do. Look for the wonderful old kitchen and dining room, complete with pots, utensils, and dishes. The museum is open Tuesday through Saturday from 10am to 4pm and Sunday from 10am to 1pm; free admission. The **Museo Pantaleón Panduro** 𝕽𝕽 (named after a famous local artisan of the 19th century) at P. Sánchez 191 (© **3/635-1089,** ext. 17), displays prize-winning pieces from the national ceramics contest held each year in Tlaquepaque. There are several categories including miniatures, traditional designs, and original designs. Many of these display a virtuosity that is astounding. It's open Tuesday through Sunday from 10am to 6pm; admission is free. If you still haven't had your fill, there is also the Museo Nacional de Cerámica in Tonalá (see below).

There are also a number of workshops where you are permitted to watch the creative process unfold. A popular workshop is **La Rosa de Cristal,** a glassblowing factory at Contreras Medillín 173. It's open from 10am to 7pm Monday through Saturday. If there is a

---

Tips Packing It In

If you need your purchases packed safely for the ride home, or if you buy so much that you want it shipped back (which can be expensive), talk to **Margaret del Rio.** She is an American who runs a large packing and shipping company in Tlaquepaque at Juárez 347 (© **3/657-5652**). The cheapest way to get merchandise home is to check it as baggage and pay the extra fee; however, with large items this isn't possible.

particular craft that you're interested in, talk to the city tourism office; they can help locate workshops open to the public.

The following list of Tlaquepaque shops will give you an idea of what to expect. But this is just a small fraction of what you'll find here; the best thing might be to just follow your nose. The main shopping is along **Independencia,** a pedestrian-only street that starts at El Parián. You can go door to door visiting the shops until the street ends and then work your way back toward El Parián on calle **Juárez,** the next street over, north of Independencia.

Agustín Parra   So you bought an old hacienda and are trying to restore its chapel—where do you go to find traditional baroque sculpture, religious art, gold-leafed objects, and even entire *retablos*? Parra is famous for exactly this kind of work, and the store is lovely. Open Monday through Saturday from 10am to 7pm. Independencia 158. ℂ 3/657-8530.

Bazar Hecht   One of the village's longtime favorites, here you'll find wood objects, handmade furniture, and a few antiques. Open Monday through Saturday from 10am to 2:30pm and 3:30 to 7pm. Juárez 162. ℂ 3/657-0316.

Casa Canela   One of the most elegant stores in Tlaquepaque, this is a feast for the eyes. Browse through rooms full of furniture and decorative objects. Open Monday through Friday from 10am to 2pm and 3 to 7pm, Saturday from 10am to 6pm, and Sunday from 11am to 3pm. Independencia 258, near Calle Cruz Verde. ℂ 3/635-3717.

Ken Edwards   Ken Edwards was among the first artisans to produce high-fired, lead-free stoneware in Tonalá, and his blue-on-blue pottery is now sold all over Mexico. This showroom has a large selection of his work. There's a section of seconds for bargain hunters. The shop is next door to the "Restaurant With No Name." Open Monday through Saturday from 10:30am to 7pm. His factory is in Tonalá. Madero 70. ℂ 3/635-5456.

Sergio Bustamante   Sergio Bustamante's imaginative and original bronze, ceramic, and papier-mâché sculptures are among the most sought after in Mexico—as well as the most copied. He also designs silver jewelry. This is an exquisite gallery showcasing his work. Open Monday through Saturday from 10am to 7pm and Sunday from 11am to 4pm. Independencia 236 at Cruz Verde. ℂ 3/639-5519.

Tete Arte y Diseño   Architectural decorative objects are mixed in with pottery, antiques, glassware, and paintings at this shop. Open

Monday through Saturday from 10am to 7pm. Juárez 173. ℂ 3/
635-7347.

Tierra Tlaquepaque   Here, you'll find unusual, rustic, and finely
finished pottery, as well as wood sculptures, table textiles, and decorative objects. Open Monday through Saturday from 10am to 7pm
and Sunday from 11am to 5pm. Independencia 156. ℂ 3/635-9770.

TONALÁ: A TRADITION OF POTTERY MAKING

Tonalá 𝒢𝒢 is a pleasant, modest town not far from Tlaquepaque.
The streets were paved only recently, and there aren't any fancy
shops. You will find Tonalá easier on the wallet than Tlaquepaque.
The village has been a center of pottery making since pre-Hispanic
times; half of the more than 400 workshops here produce a wide
variety of high- and low-temperature pottery. Other local artists
work with forged iron, cantera stone, brass and copper, marble,
miniatures, papier-mâché, textiles, blown glass, and gesso. This is a
good place to look for custom work in any of these materials; a large
pool of craftspeople can be located by just asking around a little.

Market days are Thursday and Sunday: You can expect large
crowds and blocks and blocks of stalls displaying locally made pottery and glassware, as well as cheap manufactured goods, food, and
all kinds of bric-a-brac. "Herb-men" sell a rainbow selection of dried
medicinal herbs from wheelbarrows; magicians entertain crowds
with sleight-of-hand; and craftspeople spread their colorful wares on
the plaza's sidewalks. I really prefer to visit Tonalá on non-market
days, when it's much easier to get around and see the glass and pottery stores. This is the place for buying sets of margarita glasses, or
the widely seen rustic glassware with the blue rim, or some of the
pottery typically associated with Mexico, as well as some finely
painted *petatillo* ware.

The **Tonalá Tourism Office** (ℂ **3/683-1740;** fax 3/683-0590) is
in the Artesanos building set back from the road at Atonaltecas 140
Sur (the main street leading into Tonalá) at Matamoros. Hours are
Monday through Friday from 9am to 3pm and Saturday from 9am to
1pm. It offers free walking tours Monday, Tuesday, Wednesday, and
Friday at 9am and 2pm and Saturday at 9am and 1pm. These include
visits to artisans' workshops (where you'll see ceramics, stoneware,
blown glass, papier-mâché, and the like). Tours last between 3 and 4
hours and require a minimum of five people. Visitors can request an
English-speaking guide. Also in Tonalá, cater-cornered from the
church, you'll see a small tourism information kiosk that's staffed on
market days and provides maps and useful information.

Tonalá is also the home of the **Museo Nacional de Cerámica,** Constitución 104, between Hidalgo and Morelos (© **3/683-0494**). The museum occupies a huge two-story mansion and displays work from Jalisco and pottery from all over the country. There's a large shop in the front on the right as you enter. The museum is open Tuesday through Friday from 10am to 5pm and Saturday and Sunday from 10am to 2pm. Admission is free, but a fee of $8.50 per camera will be charged for use of any video or still cameras.

3 Guadalajara After Dark

FOLKLORIC BALLET

Ballet Folclórico de la Universidad de Guadalajara ✪✪ This dance company, acclaimed as the finest of its kind in Mexico, performs traditional dances not only from Jalisco, but other parts of Mexico as well. For more than a decade, it has been performing at the Degollado Theater. Performances are on Sunday at 10am. Degollado Theater, Plaza Tapatía. © **3/614-4773** or 3/613-1115. Tickets $3–$17. Ticket office open daily 10am–1pm and 4–7pm.

Ballet Folklórico Nacional del Instituto Cultural Cabañas
Performances are every Wednesday at 8:30pm at the theater of the
Instituto Cultural Cabañas (see "Downtown Guadalajara," above).
At the far end of the Plaza Tapatía. ℂ **3/618-6003**. Tickets $6–$8.

MARIACHIS

You can't go far in Guadalajara without coming across some *mari-achis*, but to see really talented performances takes some effort (see
"La Feria," below). If what you're really interested in is the flavor
and atmosphere of the music, try **El Parián** in Tlaquepaque, where
mariachis serenade diners under the archways.

THE CLUB & MUSIC SCENE

Tapatíos are notoriously fickle about clubs and discos. One moment
a particular club is the place to be, the next moment, it's passé. At
present, the disco of choice is **El Mito** (℃ **3/615-7246**) in the popular shopping center Centro Magno on Av. Vallarta. Entrance is
restricted to people over 25; most of what you here is pop music
from the '80s, and the cover is $7.

Bar Copenhagen 77 ℛ   This dark, snug little den with uphol-
stered walls and wood trim is the perfect setting for listening to jazz.
The house band is led by the pianist Carlos de la Torre, whose elegant and economic style infuses his interpretations of bebop, modern, and Latin jazz. This is the real stuff, a fact demonstrated by the
number of jazz heavyweights who come to sit in with the band or
just listen. The club faces the Parque de la Revolución (along Juárez,
9 blocks west of the Plaza de Armas), on your left as you walk down
López Cotilla. You can just have drinks, or you can order from the
small, but well-thought-out menu; the specialty is paella. Marcos
Castellanos 140-Z. ℃ **3/826-7306**. No cover. Restaurant Mon–Sat 2pm–1am; jazz
8:30pm–1am.

El Cubilete ℛℛ   El Cubilete ("the dice cup") is a small club
tucked away in an old downtown neighborhood called Las Nueve
Esquinas (the nine corners). This is an up-and-coming neighborhood that has a couple of other clubs worth checking out, as well as
the Siglo XV restaurant (see chapter 6). The house band at El
Cubilete is very tight, and the club gets some excellent traveling
Cuban bands; but on weekends the place really gets cooking when
Rosalía takes the stage. This talented Cuban diva has an easy and
natural stage presence, and an ability to ad-lib that makes her a joy
to watch. When Rosalía is singing, the club can get very crowded.
El Cubilete serves drinks and Cuban and regional foods including

birria, tortas ahogadas, and *carne asada.* Gral. Río Seco 9. © **3/658-0406** or 3/613-2096. Mon–Sat 2pm–1am; Tues–Sat live salsa 10pm–1am. $5 cover on weekends; reservations recommended.

La Feria 🏵️🏵️   To get a good sampling of local color, try this multilevel restaurant-bar with a center stage. The afternoon and nighttime shows feature a variety of acts including a great mariachi band, some very impressive (and expressive) singers, a *charro* who performs rope tricks, some *ballet folklórico* dancers, and a few games involving the audience. The owner promised a free drink to anyone who shows a Frommer's book—so hold him to it. You might want to try a *paloma,* the most popular *tequila* drink in Guadalajara. The menu is standard Mexican with emphasis on grilled meats. La Feria is downtown, 5 blocks south of the Plaza de Armas. Corona 291. © **3/ 613- 7150** or 3/613-1812. Daily noon–3am. Variety show at 3:30 and 10pm. Call for reservations. No cover.

4 Side Trips from Guadalajara
RIO CALIENTE: A NEARBY SPA
Río Caliente Spa 🏵️ *Finds*   About 20 miles out of town in the same direction as Tequila, you'll find this spa, beautifully located in a hilly pine forest with a river of steaming hot water cutting right through the place. Temperatures here average 80°F year-round, and the elevation is 5,550 feet. This is the perfect place to regain simplicity, enjoy relaxing massages and other spa treatments, and dedicate some time to yourself. All rooms have one double and one single bed, fireplace, full-length mirror, desk, chest, and bedside reading lamps. The simply furnished rooms near the activity area are smaller and cost less than the newer rooms with patios near the river and pool. Jars of fresh purified water are supplied daily in each room.

Guests have a choice of two outdoor thermal pools, as well as two private pools and sunning areas (separate for men and women). There is also an outdoor whirlpool. Self-serve vegetarian meals are taken in a cozy dining room. Aside from the normal spa treatments listed below, there is a variety of programs or treatments offered throughout the year for an extra cost; such offerings might include instruction in Spanish or nutrition, or electro-acupuncture. Huichol Indians sell crafts on Sundays.

Pickup from the airport can be arranged upon request for around $40 one-way, or you can take a taxi for around $50 one-way. If you're driving, follow avenida Vallarta west, which becomes Highway 15. Go straight for almost 10½ miles and pass the village of La Venta del Astillero. Take the next left after La Venta and follow the rough road through the village of La Primavera for almost 5 miles. Keep bearing left through the forest until you see the hotel's sign on the left. There's no phone at the spa; reservations must be made through the United States.

Primavera Forest, La Primavera, Jal. (Reservations: Spa Vacations Limited, P.O. Box 897, Millbrae, CA 94030. *©* **650/615-9543.** Fax 650/615-0601. www.riocaliente. com. 48 units. Patio area $240 double; Pool area $276 double. Rates include all meals and exercise classes. Discounts Apr 15–Dec 15; 7- and 10-night packages available. No credit cards. **Amenities:** Restaurant; 4 pools; whirlpool; complete spa services at an additional cost; activities desk; laundry. *In room:* safe.

AJIJIC: A PICTURE-PERFECT LAKESIDE TOWN
26 miles (42km) S of Guadalajara

For a long time, the area surrounding Lake Chapala, Mexico's largest lake, has drawn foreigners with its near-perfect climate, gorgeous scenery, and several distinct and charming lakeshore towns, including Ajijic (ah-hee-*heek*), inhabited mostly by artists and Canadian and American retirees. As you approach Ajijic, the highway becomes a tree-lined boulevard through La Floresta, an expensive residential district. The village is about a mile past the LA FLORESTA sign. There will be a traffic light, a small corner grocery called SIX and a business called Montaña Center. Turn left. This will put you on Colón/Morelos, Ajijic's main street, which leads you past the main plaza and ends at the lake. The cobblestone streets and arts-and-crafts stores give the town its charm.

Note: The year-round climate is so pleasant that few hotels offer air-conditioning and only a handful have fans; neither is usually necessary.

ESSENTIALS
GETTING THERE & DEPARTING   By Car   Having a car is a definite advantage when exploring the Lake Chapala area. From Guadalajara, drive to Lake Chapala via the new four-lane Highway 15/80. Leave Guadalajara via avenida González Gallo and follow it all the way out of town past the airport, where it becomes Highway 15/80 (signs may also call it Highway 44). This is the main road to Chapala. The first view of the lake isn't until just outside of the town of Chapala. Turn right at the one traffic light in town (a block before the pier) to go toward Ajijic.

By Bus   Buses to the lakeside towns leave from Guadalajara's old Central Camionera. **Transportes Guadalajara-Chapala** serves the

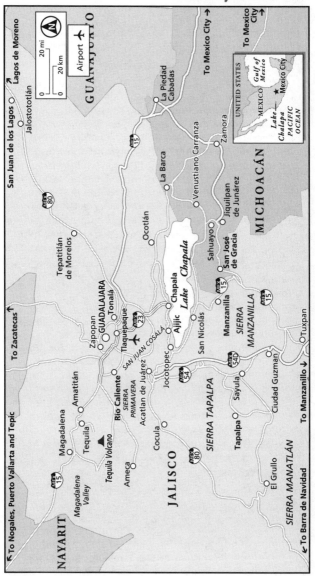

Tequila: The Name Says It All

Tequila is an entertaining (and intoxicating) town, well worth a day trip from Guadalajara. There are several taxi drivers (a few of whom speak English) who charge about $55 to take you to the town, get you into a tour of a distillery, take you to a restaurant, and then haul you back to Guadalajara. One such driver is José Gabriel Gómez, who has a new car and drives carefully. Call him in the evenings at his home (*②* **3/649-0791**). Tour companies also arrange bus trips to Tequila; see a travel agency in Guadalajara.

Tequila has many distilleries, including the famous brands **Sauza** and **José Cuervo.** All the distilleries—the big, modern ones and the smaller, more traditional factories— offer tours. If you're on your own, a good place to get hooked up with a tour is at the little booth outside the city hall on the main square. Two young women who speak English run tours to any of the local factories. The tour costs only $3 and lasts about 2 hours. All tours show how tequila is made, what traditions are followed, and what differences exist between tequilas; they end, of course, with a tequila tasting. The same highway that heads toward Rio Caliente (see "Rio Caliente: A Nearby Spa," above) will take you straight into the town of Tequila, which is about an hour outside of Guadalajara.

Another way to learn about tequila is to take the **Tequila Express,** which leaves from the train station every Saturday at about 10am and goes to the town of Amatitán, home of the Herradura distillery. This trip is organized by the Guadalajara Chamber of Commerce (Cámara de Comercio), located at the intersection of Vallarta and Niño Obrero (*②* **3/122-7920**). You can buy tickets there or at an office in the centro histórico at Morelos 395, at the intersection of Colón (*②* **3/614-3145**). Office hours are Monday through Friday from 9am to 2 pm and 4 to 6pm. Tickets cost $58 for adults and $32 for children 6 to 12. The fare includes an open bar and tequila tasting that begins while still on the train, a variety show, a tour of a distillery and a maguey plantation, and dinner, before returning to Guadalajara at about 7:30pm.

route. A bus ticket to Ajijic is $3. Buses and minibuses run every half hour to Chapala and many continue on to Ajijic and San Juan Cosalá. From Chapala there are frequent buses to the neighboring towns.

FAST FACTS   The **area code** for the whole northern lakeshore area is **3**. The **Clínica Ajijic** (© **3/766-0662;** for emergencies 3/766-0875, fax 3/766-0500), on the main highway at the corner of Javier Mina, has a two-bed emergency section with oxygen and electrocardiogram, ambulance, and five doctors with different specialties. **Línea Profesional** (© **3/766-2555;** fax 3/766-0066) is a locally owned car-rental agency in Ajijic. There is one cash machine and two currency exchange businesses.

EXPLORING AJIJIC

In La Floresta, immediately after the modern sculpture on the left, you'll see a cluster of buildings, one of which is marked ARTESANÍAS. The **state-owned crafts shop** (© 3/766-0548) has a good selection of pottery from all over Mexico and local crafts such as pottery, glassware, rugs, and wall tapestries. The shop is open Monday through Friday from 10am to 6pm, Saturday from 10am to 4pm, and Sunday from 10am to 2pm.

Ajijic has long been a center for weavers, though now there are few left. There are a number of stores selling handcrafts, most on Colón and the streets leading immediately off of it for a block or so. You'll find designer clothing and decorative accessories such as hand-loomed fabrics made into pillows and bedspreads, furniture, and pottery.

As for performing arts in the region, productions of the Lakeside Little Theater are usually announced in the local paper or on the bulletin board at La Nueva Posada (see "Where to Stay," below).

Meeting local foreign residents is easy; just go to the popular hangouts: the Restaurant La Posada Ajijic, La Nueva Posada Ajijic, the Rose Café, and Los Veleros Restaurant and Sports Bar.

WHERE TO STAY

La Laguna Bed and Brunch   The rooms in this small inn are handsomely furnished: king-size beds or two twins with bright loomed bedspreads, thick tile floors, and fireplaces. Breakfast/brunch is served Monday through Saturday from 8:30am to noon, Sunday from 9am to noon; it is quite substantial and well prepared. The glassed-in dining area faces the back patio. Nonguests can also have brunch ($4 to $5). To find La Laguna from the main highway, look for the Laguna Ajijic Real Estate Office (which faces the main highway); the B&B is behind it, fronting the next street over. The lower rates are for the summer season April through September.

Zaragoza 29, 45920 Ajijic, Jal. © 3/766-1174 or 3/766-1186. Fax 3/766-1188. laguna@laguna.com.mx. 4 units. $25–$30 double (including brunch). No credit cards.

La Nueva Posada ⋒ Modeled after a Mexican-style country house, La Nueva Posada appears much more expensive than it really is. Rooms are large, well furnished, and come with large bathrooms with showers. Some rooms overlook the lake, others the patios, and all come with small outdoor sitting areas. The rooms off the patio are quieter. You have a choice of one king or two double beds. Three rooms are equipped for people with disabilities. In addition, there are four villas that rent for a minimum of two weeks (and lower rates for longer stays). These come with a full kitchen and one or two bedrooms, some with a view of the lake. The hotel's restaurant, La Rusa, and casual bar (see "Where to Dine" below) are among the most popular meeting places in the village. La Nueva Posada is often booked up way in advance for holidays. The hotel is east of the Plaza at the lakeshore corner of Independencia/Constitución and Donato Guerra.

Donato Guerra no. 9 (Apdo. Postal 30), 45920 Ajijic, Jal. © 3/766-1444 or 3/766-1460. Fax 3/766-1344. www.nuevaposada.com. 23 units. $60–$75 double; $67–$75 villa (2-week minimum). Rates include full breakfast except with villas. MC, V. Free secured parking. **Amenities:** Restaurant; bar; small pool; room service; same-day laundry. *In room:* TV, (villas also come with full kitchen and iron).

Los Artistas B&B ⋒ One of Ajijic's loveliest homes also offers one of the best, most relaxing lodging values in Mexico. Rooms are for the most part quite large and most come with their own outdoor sitting area, from which one can enjoy the peaceful, beautiful garden, and the view of the mountains in the distance. The choice of beds includes one king, one queen, or two twins. Guests have the run of the pool and the garden, and the downstairs, which includes a comfortable living room with stereo. Breakfasts provide plenty of incentive for getting out of bed and can be served out by the pool and patio. The inn is 5½ blocks east of the main square between Aldama and J. Álvarez, which is a particularly quiet part of the village. You'll see the name on a small tile plaque on the brick wall beside the iron gate.

Constitución 105, 45900 Ajijic, Jal. © 3/766-1027. Fax 3/766-1762. www.losartistas. com. 7 units. $53–$76 double. Rates include full breakfast. No credit cards. Free secured parking. **Amenities:** Small pool.

Ajijic

Church

To Chapala-Guadalajara

Paseo de la Loma
Paseo de la Colina
Paseo del Lago
Paseo de las Canoas
Paseo de los Veleros
del Prado
Paseo de las Brisas

El Camino Real
Paseo de la Huerta

Rinconada Tapatía
A. Revolución
San Nicolás
J. Manuel

Los Artistas Bed & Breakfast
J. Álvarez
Aldama
F.I. Madero
J.E. Rosas
D. Guerra
16 de Septiembre
Constitución

La Nueva Posada/La Rusa

La Laguna Bed & Brunch
Galeana
Nicolás Bravo
Ramón Corona

To Highway
General A. Flores
Marcos Castellanos
Ajijic Grill
Colón
Morelos

Plaza

Manix Restaurant
Juárez
Hidalgo
Ocampo
5 de Mayo
Aguiles Serdán
Independencia
P. Moreno

Zaragoza
A. Torres
Ángel Flores
5 de Febrero
N. Héroes
Libertad
A. Obregón
E. Villa

Lake Chapala

200 mi
200 km

Mexico City
JALISCO
Ajijic
PACIFIC OCEAN

183

WHERE TO DINE

The restaurant scene here changes quite a bit, but at any given time there are about 10 acceptable eateries in town offering anything from Italian to Japanese, even Mexican.

Ajijic Grill GRILL/JAPANESE   This pleasant open-air patio, with tile roofs and adobe walls, is furnished with *equipal* chairs and tables. Such modest surroundings in such an out of the way town as Ajijic give no hint that you will find some of the best Japanese food in Mexico here. The chef lives in Guadalajara and does the daily shopping there for the restaurant. The food is very fresh, and the specialties are mesquite-grilled salmon and several varieties of tepanyaki and tempura.

Morelos 5. ✆ 3/766-2458. Reservations recommended. Main courses $8–$15. MC, V. Sun noon–8pm; Mon–Thurs noon–9pm; Fri–Sat noon–10pm.

La Rusa ✿ INTERNATIONAL   La Rusa, the restaurant and bar of La Nueva Posada, is an attractive setting for dining or cocktails. You can dine inside under brick and stone arches and a vaulted ceiling where you have a view out to the lake or you can dine outside in the garden. Popular with locals and *tapatíos* alike, it usually gets a good crowd. The lunch menu is simple: crêpes, sandwiches, and salads. Dinner choices are elaborate with selections such as the *filete chipotle* (beef tenderloin with *tomatillo* and *chipotle* sauces and manchego cheese), rigatoni with creamy vodka-tomato sauce, or chicken breast breaded in corn meal and bathed in a lemon sauce with sesame seeds. There's live music on Friday and Saturday. To reach the restaurant from the Ajijic plaza, walk toward the lake on Colón, turn left on Independencia/16 de Septiembre, and look for Donato Guerra. Turn right.

Donato Guerra no. 9. ✆ 3/766-1444 or 3/766-1344. Reservations recommended Dec–Apr. Breakfast $3–$5; lunch $7– $10; main courses $8–$15; Sun brunch $7. MC, V. Sun–Thur 8am–9pm; Fri–Sat 8am–11pm (Sun brunch served until 1pm).

Manix Restaurant INTERNATIONAL   This is a dependable restaurant where you can count on a delicious meal served in a pleasant, serene setting. Usually four different main dishes are offered— seafood, beef, or poultry. Typical dishes include chicken cordon bleu, osso buco, or chicken Parmesan. Portions are generous and each meal comes with soup or salad and dessert. To get here from the plaza, turn your back to the church, walk straight ahead on Colón for 2 blocks, and turn right on Ocampo; the restaurant is down the street on the right, but the sign is obscured by the lone tree on the street.

Ocampo 57. ✆ 3/766-0061. *Comida corrida* $8–$10. MC, V. Mon–Sat noon–9pm.

Index

See also Accommodations and Restaurant indexes below.

ACCOMMODATIONS INDEX

RESTAURANT INDEX

Frommer's® Memorable Walks

Chicago
London
New York
Paris
San Francisco
Washington, D.C.

Frommer's® Great Outdoor Guides

Arizona & New Mexico
New England
Northern California
Southern California & Baja
Southern New England
Vermont & New Hampshire

Frommer's® Born to Shop Guides

Born to Shop: France
Born to Shop: Hong Kong,
Shanghai & Beijing
Born to Shop: Italy
Born to Shop: London
Born to Shop: New York
Born to Shop: Paris

Frommer's® Irreverent Guides

Amsterdam
Boston
Chicago
Las Vegas
London
Los Angeles
Manhattan
New Orleans
Paris
San Francisco
Seattle & Portland
Vancouver
Walt Disney World
Washington, D.C.

Frommer's® Best-Loved Driving Tours

America
Britain
California
Florida
France
Germany
Ireland
Italy
New England
Scotland
Spain
Western Europe

The Unofficial Guides®

Bed & Breakfasts in California
Bed & Breakfasts in
New England
Bed & Breakfasts in the
Northwest
Bed & Breakfasts in Southeast
Beyond Disney
Branson, Missouri
California with Kids
Chicago
Cruises
Disneyland
Florida with Kids
Golf Vacations in the
Eastern U.S.
The Great Smokey &
Blue Ridge Mountains
Inside Disney
Hawaii
Las Vegas
London
Mid-Atlantic with Kids
Mini Las Vegas
Mini-Mickey
New England with Kids
New Orleans
New York City
Paris
San Francisco
Skiing in the West
Southeast with Kids
Walt Disney World
Walt Disney World for
Grown-ups
Walt Disney World for Kids
Washington, D.C.
World's Best Diving Vacations

Special-Interest Titles

Frommer's Britain's Best Bed & Breakfasts and
Country Inns
Frommer's France's Best Bed & Breakfasts and
Country Inns
Frommer's Italy's Best Bed & Breakfasts and
Country Inns
Frommer's Caribbean Hideaways
Frommer's Adventure Guide to Australia &
New Zealand
Frommer's Adventure Guide to Central America
Frommer's Adventure Guide to India & Pakistan
Frommer's Adventure Guide to South America
Frommer's Adventure Guide to Southeast Asia
Frommer's Adventure Guide to Southern Africa
Frommer's Gay & Lesbian Europe
Frommer's Exploring America by RV
Hanging Out in England

Hanging Out in Europe
Hanging Out in France
Hanging Out in Ireland
Hanging Out in Italy
Hanging Out in Spain
Israel Past & Present
Frommer's The Moon
Frommer's New York City with Kids
The New York Times' Guide to Unforgettable
Weekends
Places Rated Almanac
Retirement Places Rated
Frommer's Road Atlas Britain
Frommer's Road Atlas Europe
Frommer's Washington, D.C., with Kids
Frommer's What the Airlines Never Tell You